MARY ANN COTTON

BRITAIN'S FIRST FEMALE SERIAL KILLER

DAVID WILSON

Mary Ann Cotton
Britain's First Female Serial Killer
David Wilson

ISBN 978-1-904380-91-7 (Paperback)
ISBN 978-1-908162-30-4 (Adobe E-book)
ISBN 978-1-908162-29-8 (Kindle /Epub E-book)

Cover design © 2013 Waterside Press. Design by Verity Gibson/www.gibgob.com

Cataloguing-In-Publication Data A catalogue record for this book can be obtained from the British Library.

e-book *Mary Ann Cotton* is available as an ebook and also to subscribers of Myilibrary and Dawsonera.

Main UK distributor Gardners Books, 1 Whittle Drive, Eastbourne, East Sussex, BN23 6QH. Tel: +44 (0)1323 521777; sales@gardners.com; www.gardners.com

USA and Canada distributor Ingram Book Company, One Ingram Blvd, La Vergne, TN 37086, USA. (800) 937-8000 / +01 615 213-5000, orders@ingrambook.com ipage.ingrambook.com

Published 2012 by
Waterside Press Ltd.
Sherfield Gables
Sherfield on Loddon
Hook, Hampshire
United Kingdom RG27 0JG

Telephone +44(0)1256 882250
E-mail enquiries@watersidepress.co.uk
Online catalogue WatersidePress.co.uk

Mary Ann Cotton

Britain's First Female Serial Killer

David Wilson

❧ WATERSIDE PRESS

Contents

Acknowledgements

There are a number of people that I would like to thank who have helped immeasurably with the completion of this book. At Birmingham City University Barbara McCalla and Charlotte Wasilewski have continued to answer the calls of and written letters to many members of the public who want to discuss public criminology with me, and so too I would like to thank my colleagues at the Centre for Applied Criminology—especially Michael Brookes, Laura Caulfield, Lyndsey Harris, Sarah Pemberton, Craig Jackson, Donal MacIntyre, Edward Johnson, Adam Lynes, John Lamb and Di Kemp. Before leaving acknowledgements at the University I would also like to thank my undergraduate, masters and PhD students, who continue to inspire me to think about Criminology in different and diverse ways.

The librarians and staff of a number of universities showed me a great deal of kindness—particularly at Birmingham City University, Cambridge University, The Radzinowicz Library in Cambridge, the Brotherton Library of Leeds University and Newcastle City Library. I am also grateful to various staff of Beamish Museum who very generously gave up their time to help me with my research; and The Byron Centre for the Study of Literature and Social Change, University of Nottingham.

I am indebted to two health care professionals—Jacintha Godden and Sue Foster—who helped me to think through the various Victorian ailments that are encountered within the book, and who advised me more generally about the culture of nursing.

I would also like to thank Nick Pyke of the *Mail on Sunday Magazine* for encouraging me to write about Mary Ann in a more popular form, and especially to Brian Taylor who accompanied me on a research trip to the north east to walk in the footsteps of this Victorian serial killer. That trip was memorable for a number of reasons, and I would like to thank the various people in West Auckland, Seaham Harbour, Sunderland and Durham who welcomed me into their homes or businesses to describe what they remembered or knew about Mary Ann.

Bryan Gibson at Waterside Press has long championed my work and I am very grateful to him for his continued support and encouragement.

I am also very grateful to Judith Flanders and somewhat humbled by her warm words of support that appear on page ix of this book.

Finally, no book of mine would ever be completed but for the encouragement of Anne, Hugo and Fleur.

About the author

David Wilson is professor of criminology at Birmingham City University where he is Director of the Centre for Applied Criminology. A former prison governor, he is the editor of the *Howard Journal* and well-known as an author, broadcaster and presenter for TV and radio, including the BBC, Channel 4 and Sky. He has written a number of books for Waterside Press, including: *The Longest Injustice: The Strange Story of Alex Alexandrowicz* (with the latter) (1999), *Prison(er) Education: Stories of Change and Transformation* (with Ann Reuss) (2000), *Images of Incarceration: Representations of Prison in Film and Television Drama* (with Sean O'Sullivan) (2004), *Serial Killers: Hunting Britons and Their Victims 1960-2006* (2007), and *Looking for Laura: Public Criminology and Hot News* (2011).

This book is an enthralling read. I started off firmly believing that Mary Ann Cotton was innocent—that, indeed, there had been no murders. David Wilson's meticulous research, his eye for detail, his forensic ability to reconstruct the material that survives, and assess the probabilities where gaps remain in the record, opened my eyes. David Wilson does not write generic "true crime", but history of the highest order.

Judith Flanders, Best-selling author, journalist and historian.

Introduction: Searching for Mary Ann Cotton

What you are about to read is a detective story—a true detective story. It's about a "serial killer"—perhaps our first ever serial killer, as we now define someone who kills three or more people in a period of greater than 30 days—who was once relatively well known, but who has over time been allowed to disappear. It's about the victims who were murdered (some have suggested as many as 21), the person who killed them, and the various Victorians who brought this serial killer to justice. And so it's also concerned with the science of criminal investigation, and the way that crime makes its way into the writing of History—or doesn't. It's about looking for the clues, and the evidence that will bring this person, and all the others who are part of this story, back to "life". So it is about false trails, dusty documents, and the towns and villages of the north east of England where this murderer lived, and killed. It's about policing, the Victorian forensic science of the Leeds based toxicologist Dr Thomas Scattergood, and it's about a woman. Yes, that's right, a woman. However, chances are that you've never heard of Mary Ann Cotton.[1]

There has only ever been one biography of Cotton, Britain's first female serial killer, written by Arthur Appleton, which was published on the centenary of her execution in 1973. It is simply entitled *Mary Ann Cotton*. Then, in 2000, Tony Whitehead personally published a "Supplement to the Appleton Masterpiece", based on his research using registers of births, baptisms, and marriage, and death and burial certificates, and in doing so was able to correct a number of factual errors in Appleton's text.[2] Apart from this, there are a few notes, and an occasional mention of Cotton in

---

1. The sense that no one had heard of Mary Ann was the basis of an article which I wrote for the *Mail on Sunday Magazine* published on 5 February 2012: See *Appendix 1*.
2. Appleton, A (1973), *Mary Ann Cotton*, London: Michael Joseph Ltd.; Whitehead, T (2000), *Mary Ann Cotton Dead, But Not Forgotten: A Supplement to the Appleton Masterpiece*, np. I am grateful to Tony Whitehead for sending me a copy of his book.

other—mostly local—histories of the north east of England,[3] and one chapter about her in Richard Lambert's rather quaint book, published in 1935 about "Nine Peculiar Trials", and called *When Justice Faltered*.[4] Lambert's chapter is riddled with factual errors, and is rather tartly called "Mrs Cotton's Profession". This is an obvious nod towards the playwright George Bernard Shaw's "Mrs Warren's Profession"—that of a high class prostitute—which is frankly rather fanciful, as far as Cotton is concerned, even if there were rumours after her arrest that she had sold sexual services.

But, with the exception of an occasional documentary, that's it. No other books; no films, no plays; and not much academic interest either. To all intents and purposes, Mary Ann Cotton has disappeared from public view, or, to use a more academic description, she has become "unseen".[5] Why should this be so?

Cotton's disappearance is all the more difficult to explain given that she may have killed up to 21 people, and, more than this, she was killing some 16 years before the serial killer known as "Jack the Ripper" was murdering in Whitechapel, London. Jack the Ripper is generally, and incorrectly, regarded as Britain's "first" serial killer, even if he is usually attributed with

3.   This is not to deny that Mary Ann Cotton's case does feature in a number of books about poisoning, such as Whorton, J (2011), *The Arsenic Century: How Victorian Britain was Poisoned at Home, Work & Play*, Oxford: Oxford University Press; and, Emsley, J (2005), *The Elements of Murder: A History of Poison*, Oxford: Oxford University Press. However, quite clearly the focus of these books is poison, rather than Cotton. Even so, Burney, I (2006), *Poison, Detection, and the Victorian Imagination*, Manchester: Manchester University Press, makes no mention of Cotton at all, and concentrates instead on the case of William Palmer who was executed in 1856. There is no question, especially in relation to the activities of Jack the Ripper, that Mary Ann's crimes remain relatively obscure, and that discussion about her as a serial killer is virtually non existent. To take but one recent example, Adrian Gray's (2011), *Crime and Criminals of Victorian England*, Stroud: The History Press, which states that it will cover crimes "that have been forgotten for 150 years but also some examples of very well-known major Victorian cases," (p.7) devotes just five lines to Mary Ann Cotton in its 224 pages. To be fair Gray also only discusses the case of Jack the Ripper in a few paragraphs, but as he points out, "there is already a whole library of books about this one series of crimes and little point in adding further to it", p. 21.

4.   Lambert, R S, (1935), *When Justice Faltered: A Study of Nine Peculiar Trials*. London: Methuen, pps.108-137.

5.   The idea of a serial killer being "unseen" is taken from my work about the English serial killer Trevor Hardy in Wilson, D, Tolputt, H., Howe, N, and Kemp, D (2010) 'When Serial Killers Go Unseen: The Case of Trevor Joseph Hardy," *Crime Media Culture*, Volume 6 Number 2: 153-167. Hardy murdered three young women in Manchester in the mid-1970s, but is—like Cotton before him—"unseen".

only a third of the tally of Cotton's victims. He has also remained a source of inspiration for film makers, authors and academics alike. There is even a walking tour that retraces his steps across modern-day Whitechapel. Cotton, on the other hand, is barely remembered at all, and when she is it is difficult to separate fact from fantasy.

In trying to track her down, a couple of research visits to Beamish Museum — "the living museum of the north" — for example, ostensibly to help me to understand more about the importance of mining to the north east, unexpectedly allowed me to further reflect on Mary Ann's disappearance.[6] The museum states that it holds a tea pot and a stool that are reputed to have once belonged to Cotton, and one local author called Harry Thompson also describes how he virtually "tripped over" an exhibit in 1976 — a "painted wooden board containing a moralising stanza in contemporary script about Mary Ann Cotton, the Victorian multiple murderer from West Auckland".[7] I was eager to find this painted wooden board, which contained the following verses, as quoted by Thompson:

> She murdered her husbands and lodger as well,
> The numbers she poisoned no one can tell,
> So anxious she was for money 'tis said,
> That she ordered their coffins before they were dead.
> The strong hand of justice compelled her to stay,
> And her crimes have been proved as clear as the day,
> Now in Durham Prison condemned she does lie,
> And soon on the scaffold she will have to die.

This tells us a little about the notoriety that Cotton must have had at the time of her trial — there were also other nursery rhymes about her which are

---

6. Beamish's guidebook not only describes the museum as "the living museum of the north", but also "the experience of a lifetime". The museum is set over 300 acres and has some pit cottages, a colliery, a school, and a Methodist chapel which can be viewed. To add to the period detail, staff at the museum dress in appropriate historical costumes. The museum also has a number of collections, including books, photographs, and their Regional Resource Centre also holds more fragile artefacts, which are not on display. Their website is www.beamish.org.uk

7. Thompson, H (1976), *Durham Villages*. London: Robert Hale, pps.99-100.

quoted later in the text—and which also gives us a flavour of the story as it was understood by her Victorian contemporaries. In short, they viewed Cotton as having killed for money, and within the current research literature about female serial killers she would therefore be described as "purpose-orientated".

But how accurate is this view of Cotton's motivation, and what else did the "painted wooden board" contain? Unfortunately I couldn't answer this last question, as the board has literally disappeared from Beamish. Staff working at the museum have suggested to me that Thompson might have been mistaken, and that a copy of the poem had simply been pinned to a notice board, so as to allow it to have been exhibited. Indeed, some very helpful staff allowed me access to their museum's collections, and I was able to track down the whole poem that they hold about Cotton. This is called "Trial, Sentence & Condemnation of Mary Ann Cotton, the West Auckland Secret Poisoner", which was published in London by H P Such, prior to Cotton's execution. The poem is much longer than that quoted by Thompson, and runs to six verses, plus a chorus that had to be sung to the tune "Driven from Home", which states: "No one can pity, no one can bless, Mary Ann Cotton for her wickedness; The West Auckland poisoner condemned doth lie, she murdered her children, and soon she must die".

Nonetheless, Thompson clearly states that the painted wooden board "contained" the poem, rather than had something pinned to it, and I'm left with the impression that if it had simply been—in effect—a notice board, why would he have mentioned it at all? Nor is the poem which the museum holds in "contemporary script". Instead, it is typed. So it is tempting to see this disappearing painted board as a metaphor for the disappearing Cotton. She is remembered—sort of—but not quite clearly, or with any precision. She has become a half-remembered memory (if any memory at all); a character that no one can quite place with any precision; she is a photograph taken out of focus. Paradoxically, this lack of clarity has allowed her to pop up potentially everywhere, but therefore, in one of the recurring ironies about her story, in reality, nowhere at all.

And what about the teapot and the stool on display at Beamish? The teapot—from which it is presumed that she served her poisoned tea—is more than likely not Mary Ann's. Reading a letter that was sent to describe the history of the teapot after it was acquired by the museum in the 1970s suggests that its provenance has taken too many twists and turns for it to be genuine.[8] The stool, almost certainly, did not belong to Cotton.

That leaves the poem, about which we can have greater confidence. Its verses also remind us that Cotton was executed. Her execution—by the state hangman, William Calcraft—was a rather sad affair, and came only a few years after public executions had ended. The manner of her death, which generated considerable public sympathy at the time—as did the fact that she had given birth to a daughter in prison while awaiting trial—might also have contributed to her disappearance from history. After all, the state was executing a woman and a mother, and at a time when the state's authority and right to take a life was being widely debated—a debate not eased by moving executions behind prison walls. There is even some contemporary evidence to suggest that Cotton was "reclaimed" by the Victorians given that she was a woman and a mother hanged by the state, and that this reclamation might have contributed to her disappearance from history.

Of course, while Cotton may have disappeared, as my reference to Jack the Ripper suggests, the same is not true for other serial killers.[9] Serial killers! They really do seem to be everywhere. One academic criminologist has even argued that serial killing is patterned in modernity's self-image, and that in particular, "a symbiotic relationship exists between the media and serial killers. In the quest for audience share the media have become addicted to portrayals of serial killers". Part of this addiction stems from the fact that serial killers offer:

---

8. The teapot had been sent to the museum by Dr W A Prowse, and the letter—which actually dates from 1989—was sent to the museum by Dr Prowse's daughter, Elizabeth Roe. Ms Roe wanted to provide some further information about the provenance of the teapot. She states that her father had never liked the teapot, and that it had come to him "from my step mother", who had in turn received it from her mother—in other words, Ms Roe's step grandmother. Ms Roe's step grandmother had been given the teapot "by an old woman in West Auckland". However, this "old woman" is not named, and nor is it explained how she might have acquired Mary Ann's teapot. Ms Roe seems to have been prompted to write to the museum, as some of her friends had visited Beamish "and the teapot was not on display with other items connected with Mary Ann Cotton".

9. See, for example, some recent critiques about the serial killer phenomenon, such as Schmidt, D (2005), *Natural Born Celebrities: Serial Killers in American Culture*. Chicago, IL.: University of Chicago Press; Gibson, D.C. (2006) Serial Murder and Media Circuses. Westport, CT.: Praeger; Jarvis, B. (2007) 'Monsters Inc.: Serial Killers and Consumer Culture', *Crime, Media, Culture* 3(3): 326–44.

... rich opportunities to capture public attention by capitalising on deeply resonate themes of innocent victims, dangerous strangers, unsolved murders, all coalescing around a narrative of evasion and given moral force through implied personal threats to audience members. Serial killers were apparently ready-made for prime time.[10]

Mary Ann Cotton was never "prime time". While her case was closely followed by the local press during her trial and execution, even this Victorian media interest in her was largely regional, and hardly matched that which would be generated nationally and internationally by Jack the Ripper only 16 years later. However, while Cotton may have rarely made it onto the front pages of Victorian newspapers, the method that she used to kill her victims was always newsworthy.

Mary Ann was a poisoner, and specifically she used arsenic—the poison of choice for almost the entire Victorian era. It has been calculated that more than a third of all cases of homicide involving poison during this period were as a result of arsenic. So prevalent was the use of arsenic more generally that one historian has described Victorian Britain as "the arsenic century", and subtitled his book "How Victorian Britain was Poisoned at Home, Work and Play."[11] A by-product of the mining industry, arsenic was everywhere—from rat poison to cosmetics, Christmas tree ornaments, candles, cookware and home furnishings, such as wallpaper and curtains. Arsenic seeped into the everyday life of the Victorians, even if its presence was rarely enough to kill. We should note this tension between arsenic as an "everyday" Victorian household item, and also as a means to commit murder—a tension that Mary Ann's barrister would attempt to harness as a defence at her trial, and catch the prosecution unawares. Of course murder required greater doses of the substance—if the perpetrator wanted the victim to die quickly—or less acute doses, which would prolong the victim's life and suffering, but allow the murderer to present any subsequent death as the result of a number of other, more innocent ailments and illnesses. "Gastric fever", "continued fever", "cholera", and

10. Haggerty, K (2009) 'Modern Serial Killers', *Crime, Media and Culture* 5(2): 168–87, p.174.
11. Whorton, J (2011). *The Arsenic Century: How Victorian Britain was Poisoned at Home, Work & Play*, Oxford: Oxford University Press.

especially that great Victorian killer "typhoid"—all mimicked the symptoms of arsenic poisoning, such as diarrhoea, vomiting, and severe stomach pains. Cotton excelled in this ability.

Thinking About Female Serial Killers

Only a very few women become serial killers, and serial murder remains an overwhelming male phenomenon. But a small group of women *have* repeatedly killed, and there have been a number of attempts to suggest why. Over a decade ago, Kelleher and Kelleher (1998) were developing a typology of female serial killers that included the "black widow", "angel of death", "sexual predator", "revenge" and "profit or crime" killer, and Holmes, Hickey and Holmes (1991), amongst others, have also tried to suggest different typologies[12] (see *Table 1*).

So too there have been a variety of true crime accounts of individual British female serial killers (see, for example, Davies, 1993; Masters, 1996), with Myra Hindley—one of the so-called "Moors Murderers"—in particular, having become iconic of the genre (see, most recently, Lee, 2010).

In all of this it is tempting to view Cotton as a "black widow" or as a "comfort killer" although, as I shall show, her nursing background may also have allowed her to escape detection and, as such, we might also call her an "angel of death", or a "power seeker". However, we might just as easily reflect that attempting to place female serial killers into one, distinct typology is problematic, and that the lines between such typologies are often blurred, as they are with male, serial killer typologies.[13] More helpfully, recent research about female serial killers has looked at their motivation based on "purpose-orientated" goals (for example, in relation to acquiring money, to support a religious or cult movement, or infanticide and medical murder to generate sympathy), as opposed to "pleasure-orientated" murder "which would include elements of sado-masochism, paedophilia or torture".[14]

---

12. Holmes, S., Hickey, E, and Holmes, R (1991). 'Female Serial Murderesses: Constructing Differentiating Typologies', *Journal of Contemporary Criminal Justice* Vol. 7 No. 4.: 245-256.
13. See, for example, Fox, J A, and Levin, J (2005) *Extreme Killing: Understanding Serial and Mass Murder.* Thousand Oaks: Sage.
14. See, for example, Gurian, E (2011), "Female Serial Murderers: Directions for Future Research on a Hidden Population," *International Journal of Offender Therapy and*

Table 1: Serial Killers (Female)

Visionary	Killer is impelled to murder because she has heard voices or seen visions demanding that she kill a particular person, or category of people. The voice or vision may be for some a demon, but for others may be perceived as coming from God.
Comfort	The killer is motivated to murder for material reasons, not for psychological gain. This tends to be the most prevalent form of female serial killer. No voices or visions, and they usually kill someone with whom they are acquainted. Material gain is usually money.
Hedonistic	Least understood and least reported type of female serial killer. Killing is motivated as a result of striving for pleasure—especially sexual gratification.
Power Seekers	Killer kills so as to gain the ultimate form of domination over another person. Sometimes associated with Munchausen Syndrome by Proxy, with the killer often inducing medical problems in children under their care.
Disciple	The killer kills because she is under the influence of a (usually) male charismatic leader, and the gain that is sought is the personal acceptance of her "idol".

Source: Adapted from Holmes, Hickey and Holmes, 1991

As this preceding discussion has perhaps just illustrated, we have come a long way in thinking about serial murder since Appleton published his biography of Cotton in 1973, and it is right to try and incorporate

---

Comparative Criminology, 55(1), 27-42. It should be noted that Gurian's article does include British examples, but only post-1900, and therefore does not consider Mary Ann Cotton. Gurian also defines serial killing as involving only two rather than three victims.

this type of theorising when considering Cotton and what might have driven her to murder. I use this opportunity to place Mary Ann into our current understanding of how and why serial killers kill, and especially why they are able to escape detection for the duration of their killing cycle. In this latter respect, Cotton's murders are particularly interesting in that her killing cycle may have lasted for as long as 20 years. Of even greater interest, when she committed these murders they did not take place furtively — hidden behind closed doors — but were instead often accomplished in full view of neighbours, and the various doctors who came and went, but who seemed unable to guess what was actually the problem that had caused their patients to become ill. In all of this I am clearly going to use my background as a criminologist and, as such, will describe, for example, issues related to serial killers having antisocial personality disorders — being "psychopaths" — whether they are "geographically stable or transient", "organized or disorganized", policing techniques and forensic developments.

As is obvious from what has just been argued, I believe Cotton to have been a serial killer — she killed three or more people in a period of greater than 30 days. But how many people did she kill? Whitehead — her most stalwart, if at times tongue in cheek, defender — suggests that she may have killed only four people, and that ten other murders attributed to her are, using the Scottish judicial verdict, "not proven". It is also true that Cotton was in fact only found guilty of one charge of murder, and that three other murder charges against her were left on file, given that the finding of guilt on the first count was a capital offence. Nor was she particularly well defended at her trial. However, there are always debates about how many murders to attribute to any single serial killer. For example, even after a formally established inquiry to investigate the numbers of murders within the killing cycle of Dr Harold Shipman — Britain's most prolific serial killer — confusion still persists about how many people he actually dispatched.[15] Whitehead, in trying to see beyond the local hysteria of the reporting of her case at the time of her trial and execution, has been too

15. For a general introduction to the Shipman case see Peters, C (2005) *Harold Shipman: Mind Set on Murder*. London: Carlton Books. The official enquiry can still be accessed via www. the-shipman-inquiry.org.uk

kind to Mary Ann, although his research into her life in Cornwall does seem to prove that she did not have several children there whom she may subsequently have murdered. Excluding these children, the total that we are left with as far as Mary Ann is concerned is likely to have been 16, perhaps 17 — although the issue of the likely number of victims is discussed further in the narrative.

What about my claim that Mary Ann was the "first" female serial killer? After all, there were indeed other women convicted of murdering several people before Mary Ann and which would qualify them as a "serial killer". Women such as Mary Milner who was executed in 1847 and Rebecca Smith who was hanged two years later, both of whom generated much more contemporary media interest than Cotton.[16] Do they not qualify as serial killers too? The simple answer would be that they do, and some might wish to lay claim to them as being the "first" female serial killers. But how far back in time can, or should, we go before this criminological label becomes meaningless and no longer able to contain our contemporary understanding of the phenomenon?

Perhaps a more nuanced reply would be that we need to draw a line somewhere in the past, so as to separate the criminological world which we now inhabit from one that is quite clearly, and distinctly historical. There is always going to be an element of interpretation here, but there is still something recognisable about the world of 1870 — something that would be difficult to claim for the criminological world of 1840, when a state police force was in its infancy, and there were still around 30 offences which could attract the death penalty. So too our social, cultural and economic realities have been built on developments from the mid and late Victorian period, so that comparisons between then and now seem comprehensible, and in ways that simply wouldn't work if we were comparing

16. There was what criminologists now call a "moral panic" about female poisoners in the 1840s — especially about female poisoners active in the Essex village of Clavering, and centred on the trials and murder(s) of Sarah Chesham (Chesham was convicted of only one murder — having been previously acquitted of several others). See Whorton *op cit*, pp. 33-51 for an account of the Essex poisoning cases. Edward Bulwer Lytton would capitalise on this moral panic in his best-selling novel *Lucretia*. This was published in 1846, and had poison as the main driver behind the narrative of the story and, of course, the name of the main character in the novel was "Lucretia Clavering" thus both evoking historic poisoning cases, and ones which would be familiar to Victorian readers.

our current circumstances with, for example, Georgian England. In other words the bridge between Cotton's "then" and our "now" is not so precarious as to make it impassable, and so, for example, Appleton was even able to interview Mary Ann's grandson when he was conducting research for his book in 1973.

So I suggest that Cotton is our first serial killer, because in Mary Ann we have someone who is clearly recognisable as connected to us and our culture, and who was behaving in a manner that we can all too easily identify and abhor.

From Criminology to History

Criminology is a rendezvous discipline. It finds inspiration — and is often at its best — when it crosses both theoretical and disciplinary boundaries. In the narrative that follows Criminology and History combine to bring a fresh insight into Mary Ann Cotton, and the circumstances that allowed her to kill again and again. These insights have been formed by re-reading many of the historical documents that Appleton used, and here it should be acknowledged that his close reading of various contemporary newspapers, and some of the official details collected about Mary Ann when she was in prison, is exemplary. Appleton regularly appears throughout the text, because his biography has almost become a *de facto* primary source for information about Cotton, as there are no "collected papers" about Mary Ann in any university or other records archive. We might see this as another small measure of her disappearance (and see *A Guide to Sources and Further Reading*). For instance, when Appleton acknowledges that the "bulk" of his research was done at Durham County Record Office, this must have been a reference to his use of Victorian newspapers which are located there, and which often published correspondence written by Cotton to various people in the community from her condemned cell. It was not possible to locate any letters from her held in private collections.

However, given that Mary Ann was a prisoner at Durham Gaol, there are a number of records about her held at the National Archives at Kew, London, although these were not particularly helpful. While these papers contained police reports, witness statements and other materials that emerged during Cotton's appearances at the magistrates' court and subsequently at the Durham Assizes, their institutional purpose meant that they had a particular story that they wanted to tell, and in doing so they rarely revealed anything that was not reported upon by contemporary newspapers. They certainly did not bring to life the voices of Mary Ann's victims, or indeed the voice of Cotton herself—something which a variety of local and regional newspapers did to much greater effect. [17] Whitehead's supplement—which also provides copies of a number of relevant birth and death certificates—has also proved to be invaluable, and it is clear that Whitehead has been able to correct a number of factual errors in Appleton's text. Some of Whitehead's conclusions seem far-fetched, but even so his supplement has also proven to be extremely useful.

As with most histories, a measure of luck has been involved in bringing Cotton back to life. Finding the collected papers of Dr Thomas Scattergood at Leeds University has been the greatest help of all, and while it was already well known that he had given evidence against Mary Ann at her trail, no one has previously connected his notes and notebooks to what he described as "The West Auckland Arsenic Cases"—by which he meant Mary Ann Cotton. Dr Scattergood—it's almost as if he had been named by Dickens—provides us with a wealth of forensic information about Mary Ann, and how poisoners were brought to justice.

All of this historical research and the textual analysis that flows from it has been undertaken so as to attempt to put Cotton into the social, economic and cultural context that dominated her life. Here, too, in the pages that follow, some more academic concerns related to gender, class

---

17. The newspapers that I used to construct the background to Cotton's case were: the *Northern Echo*, 6, 7, 8, 10, 15, 20, 21, 22, 24 , 25 and 28 March 1873; the Leeds Mercury, 24 October 1872 and 29 March 1873; the *Newcastle Courant*, 20 December 1872, and 7, 14, 28 March 1873; *Illustrated Police News*, 31 August, 16, and 30 November 1872; *The Times*, 7 October 1872, 8 March 1873; *Newcastle Journal*, 11 March 1873; *Durham County Advertiser*, 11 March 1873; and the *Sunderland Times*, 21 March 1873. Flanders, J. (2011), *The Invention of Murder: How the Victorians Revelled in Death and Detection and Created Modern Crime* also has a helpful summary about the press reporting about Mary Ann Cotton. Of note, many of the newspapers published letters written by Cotton from prison to a number of her friends and acquaintances. I also freely used extracts from newspapers quoted by Appleton and Whitehead (see above). It is also interesting to reflect that contemporary newspaper accounts usually titled their reports as "The West Auckland Poisonings". Once again it is the method that Cotton used which is important—and the place where these poisonings took place—that were the "news", rather than Cotton herself.

and power will become the necessary backdrop against which Cotton's story has to be told and understood. However, none of this is meant to excuse, or even champion Mary Ann. Indeed, to use a quote by Mrs Warren from Shaw's play, and which may have been the inspiration for Lambert's chapter about Cotton: "People are always blaming their circumstances for what they are. I don't believe in circumstances. The people who get on in the world are the people who get up and look for the circumstances they want, and, if they can't find them, make them". Cotton is not some sort of anti-heroine, overcoming the conditions of her life as a working class woman, and attempting to make something better for herself—sometimes through marriage and often through murder—and making the circumstances that she wanted when, like the fictional Mrs Warren, she couldn't find them. Without doubt women in Victorian England had little power, especially working class women—an issue discussed further in *Chapter 1*.

In looking at Cotton's history it is hard to lose sight of the crushing poverty of the Northumberland mining villages and towns that she, her husbands and lovers, and their children inhabited. As long ago as 1942, the British historian Arthur Bryant noted that for the 19th century miner and their families conditions were horrific, and that they fought a "long losing battle with poverty, undernourishment and insecurity… the risk of accident and maiming… the rot of body and soul and the dread of the workhouse at the end of that bitter road."[18] Poor relief and the workhouse were never far from the narrative of Mary Ann's life, although this should not be seen as an excuse—thousands of others in similar circumstances made something of their lives without resorting to murder—but, rather, this is simply the context within which Cotton's story unfolds.

All of this requires us to be aware of the social and economic circumstances of the Northumberland mining villages that Cotton grew up in as a child, and then lived in when she was married. Alan Metcalfe's social history of the 37 colliery villages of Victorian east Northumberland is helpful here, given that it included the village of Murton, where Cotton spent much of her childhood, and was also the place where she first lived after her marriage to William Mowbray. Even so, Metcalfe acknowledges

---

18. Bryant, A (1942) *English Saga, 1840-1940. London*: The Reprint Society, p.231.

that who is missing from his history are women, although "there was never any mistaking their place in society—they were inferior and subordinate to men".[19] As a consequence, it has sometimes been difficult to build up a complete historical picture as accurately as possible, because it was, by and large, men who left records, or who were seen as important enough to demand the attention of their contemporaries, and which, in turn, would result in their mark being left to history.

A desire to put Cotton and her crimes into a social and structural context will not chime well with current fashions and policies that seek to blame and pathologise the individual, and exonerate the society in which that individual lives. However, Mary Ann Cotton is not being let "off the hook". Nor, as Mary Midgley warns against in her philosophical essay about wickedness, is society being blamed for every sin.[20] However, to understand how serial killers operate we need to appreciate that they can only repeatedly kill when the social structure in which they operate allows them to do so, by having placed value on one group to the detriment of others. For when this happens and communities become fractured by class, gender and power; when people feel isolated and cut off from each other, and when the bonds of mutual support have been all but eradicated, it is then that those who want to kill large numbers of their fellow human beings are able to achieve their purpose. It is in societies where each individual believes that they have to struggle simply to survive that serial killers flourish. Sadly, in this way, Cotton's serial killing becomes a useful guide that reveals the limits of Victorian social arrangements, and the inadequacy of their provision for the social and economic protection of the poor, children and the vulnerable.

Her killing also suggests something more personal. It implies who Mary Ann was as an individual, the type of values that she came to hold and to which she was encouraged to aspire. Cotton was one of the first children born into an age that would increasingly become dominated by industrial capitalism—the first generation that would see their lives dominated not by agriculture but by industry; not by the countryside but by towns and

19. Metcalfe, A (2006). *Leisure and Recreation in a Victorian Mining Community: The Social Economy of Leisure in North-East England, 1820–1914.* London: Routledge, p. 18.
20. Midgley, M (1984), *Wickedness: A Philosophical Essay,* London: Routledge.

cities; not by the rhythms of the seasons but by the awful possibilities that could come from selling your labour. Mary Ann embodied capitalism, and much of her life can be read as her dirty, desperate attempt to move on both economically and socially. Cotton was as much part of Victorian culture as any factory or mine owner, even if hers was a more obviously perverted rather than eminent entrepreneurialism.

Mary Ann was much more of a "typical" Victorian in her values (and even in the method that she chose to kill), than an aberration from those values that characterised Victorian England. This analysis will be pushed further to see if, like much more traditionally successful capitalists, Mary Ann simply tried to put her mistakes behind her by killing those that she no longer needed or wanted, and having done so, start again.

There are, of course, many ways in building up an historical picture. Contemporary newspapers—local, regional and national—have been consulted, numerous university and public libraries visited,[21] and I have walked the streets of various villages, and towns in the north east of England in the hope of improving my understanding of Cotton. However, even this has proved to be challenging. Some of the areas within several of the towns that meant so much to Cotton and her contemporaries have been destroyed, or subsumed into the larger, urban areas of Durham, Newcastle or Sunderland. The houses where she once lived—such as in Durham Place in Murton—have long since been demolished to make way for housing that is more suited to current needs.[22]

Questions of Gender

Of course, throughout the book questions of gender are never far from the surface, and the reality that female murderers and serial killers such as Mary Ann Cotton simultaneously undermine, and reinforce gender

---

21. Here I would like to pay tribute to Newcastle City Library where the researcher can still consult actual Victorian newspapers, rather than read them on microfilm. Many of the newspapers that I have used and quote from can be accessed on line, but for me nothing beats the dusty, musty smell and yellowing pages of the real thing. There are other advantages too—the eye naturally scans a "real" newspaper, and in doing so can often pick up bits and pieces of information that might otherwise have been missed when you click a mouse, or turn the handle of the microfilm reader.

22. I have written about this process before in a *Mail on Sunday Magazine* supplement: see *Appendix 1*.

stereotypes. Women who murder disrupt, confuse and challenge long held cultural views about who women are, and how they should behave. As a consequence when they do kill their murders are often used to generate meanings about the particular time and society in which these murders took place; or, as it has recently been expressed, their murders become a "window" into a culture.[23]

So why did Mary Ann's murders not disrupt and confuse her mid-Victorian contemporaries in the way that Jack the Ripper's would in the late-Victorian period? Might the difference in our interest in these two serial killers stem from who it was they targeted and how they killed? These differences in method and victim selection might also tell us something about gender differences more generally within serial murder. Indeed, research by two American academics has questioned, in an American context, whether "light can be shed on the controversial issue of gender differences by considering the phenomenon of female serial murder vis-à-vis the analogous atrocities perpetrated by men".[24]

In other words, what is being argued is that female serial killers undermine the conception of women as the "gentler sex", even if they are often not judged as morally wicked as male serial killers, given that their preferred methods of murder—such as poisoning—can sometimes be interpreted as "mercy killing". Cotton was a poisoner, who murdered her husbands, lover, mother, children and step-children, but she also gave birth while in prison, prior to being hanged by the state. In the process and before she was executed, it was almost as if she was able to recreate an acceptable moral and appropriate gender role for herself which chimed with Victorian sensibilities. So too this argument that female serial killers are "commonly denied, or merely ignored, as something of a conceptual impossibility"[25] might also be another way to understand Cotton's disappearance. On the

23. Seal, L., (2010), *Women, Murder and Femininity: Gender Representations of Women Who Kill*, New York: Palgrave. Again it is interesting to note that while Seal discusses a Victorian murder case—and the bulk of her research is about more contemporary cases—she does not mention Mary Ann Cotton.

24. Schechter, E and Schechter, H (2010), 'Killing with Kindness: Nature, Nurture and the Female Serial Killer,' in S Waller (ed.) *Serial Killers: Philosophy for Everyone*, pps. 117-128, Oxford: Blackwell, p.119.

25. Schechter and Schechter, *op cit*, p. 124.

whole Mary Ann wasn't made into a "monster"[26] (although there were some contemporary attempts to do so) as most female murderers are, and perhaps by being able to avoid this process her crimes were simply ignored, then over time largely forgotten, or as I have suggested, have become "unseen". In one sense the Gothic nature of Mary Ann and her crimes were turned into a melodrama, with all the ambiguities and uncertainties that go with that genre. Are these the processes which allowed Cotton to disappear?

Trying to answer these questions forms a running thread to the narrative, although there is also a continuing tension in what is going to be described. A desire to keep Mary Ann in historical context does not sit easily with the application of current theorising about serial killing to her crimes. It is hoped that the end result gives History and Criminology their respective academic dues. However, the early chapters inevitably concentrate on simply telling Cotton's story, and with providing the historical background with which to make sense of Mary Ann as a serial killer.

Throughout these more historical chapters the phrase "Victorian" makes a regular appearance. By this what is meant is the period 1837 to 1901, which are, or course, the dates of the reign of Queen Victoria, although given the focus of the book there is a concentration on the period between 1840 and 1873, when Cotton was executed. The later chapters are more focused on Criminology when we begin to try to make sense of Cotton as a woman and as a serial killer. In doing so the concepts of antisocial personality disorder and psychopathy are discussed to try to understand—and explain—Mary Ann, and her behaviour.

What ultimately emerges from these disparate themes is the portrait of a Victorian female serial killer who was organized, persistent and showed a degree of calculation and cunning so as to achieve the ends that she wanted, no matter who stood in her way. That Cotton should be better known is without doubt—she was, after all, the first of a dreadful kind

---

26. I am using this description in a general way, but more specifically "Monster" was also the title of a 2004 Hollywood film about the American female serial killer Aileen Wournos. Wournos was convicted in 1991 of the murders of seven men between 1988 and 1989, and executed in Florida in 2002. Quite apart from "Monster", there have been at least two other cinematically released documentaries about Wournos—Aileen: "The Selling of a Serial Killer" (1992) and "Aileen: Life and Death of a Serial Killer" (2003). This interest in Wournos' case can again be contrasted with the comparative lack of interest in Cotton's.

that has become all too common.

Searching for Mary Ann — making her "seen" — has not been easy, and nor has finding her been a particularly pleasant experience. Walking in the footprints left by a serial killer has always had its dangers. However re-discovering Cotton will bring back into public view the first of a modern murdering phenomenon — cunning, ruthless, charming, seducing, and deadly. Be warned.

Chapter One

Early Days

"the time you speak of my dark eyes i was happy then, and them Wos days of joy to all of our soles"

Mary Ann Cotton, in a letter to Henry Holdforth, 11 March 1873.

Mary Ann Cotton was born Mary Ann Robson sometime in October 1832, in a small mining village called Low Moorsley in County Durham, and was baptised at Rainton Chapel, now called St Mary's, West Rainton on the 11th November of that year. Her parents were Michael and Margaret Robson (nee Lonsdale), and her father is recorded as a "pitman", which meant that he worked in the local coal mine. In the 1841 census Michael and Margaret's ages were recorded as 25 and Mary Ann's as eight, and so when she was born we can infer that her parents were still in their teens—perhaps as young as 17. However, the recording of age (as well as other details) was always a precarious business in the these early censuses and, so, in the 1851 census Margaret's age, for example, had jumped to 38, and in the 1861 census it is recorded as 47.[1]

Some time after her baptism, the Robsons moved to East Rainton, situated midway between Sunderland and Durham, where Michael worked—perhaps as a "sinker"—in the Hazard Colliery, which had been opened in 1818. A sinker was a skilled workman who was employed to sink new shafts so as to open up different seams of coal, and Appleton notes that if Robson did have this specialism it would have been more normal for him to have listed this as his profession when his children were baptised. Nonetheless, he is consistently listed as a "pitman", and so there is no way to definitively corroborate Michael's working role or responsibilities.

---

1. This account of her early years has been largely culled from the combined efforts of Appleton and Whitehead, ops cit in the *Introduction*.

Not that a sinker's work was all that attractive. A man employed in this capacity had to dig — as part of a team — from the top downwards without any mechanical help until the team hit water, at which point some rudimentary pumps would be used to clear the water from the shaft. A sinker relied on his physical prowess, and as a result his wages were correspondingly high. There is also some evidence to suggest that Margaret's father had worked at the Hazard pit as a "brakesman" — the engineman who attended to the winding wheel — and so this early move might have been as a result of some family connections.

Whether as a sinker, a brakesman, or any of the scores of other trades that men could be employed to perform, working as a miner was dangerous. The Durham Mining Museum Records, for example, which cover mines in County Durham, Northumberland, Cumberland and Westmorland, list a number of fatalities in the Hazard pit during the 1840s which give a flavour of the dangers of the job. In June 1845, for example, John Fenwick, aged 67, was crushed between two tubs of coal and a prop. He was taken home, but died the following day. The following year, 53-year-old John Pearson was crushed by a large piece of stone, and while he was able to get out of the mine alive, he died before he could get medical assistance. And, in October 1847, Thomas Dodds, aged 32:

> went down the Hazard Pit, East Rainton in the company of the "keeker" to shut a water tap about 100 yards from the bottom of the shaft. This completed, they returned to an opening in the shaft about seven fathoms higher, and on arriving there gave the usual signal and the "brakesman brought up the tub to them". Dodds was about to get in, but slipped between it and the bunting and fell into the sump at the bottom of the shaft. It took an hour to recover his body using grappling irons.[2]

It did not pay to slip or fall, or to lose your concentration in the coal mine, and fatalities were correspondingly high. Friedrich Engels, who travelled to Manchester in 1842 to work in his family's cotton factory, suggested in *The Condition of the Working Class in England*, which was

---

2.   The stories of these miners and what befell them can be accessed via www.dmm.org.uk

published in Germany in 1845, that as far as mining was concerned, "in the whole British realm there is no occupation in which a man may meet his end in so many diverse ways as in this one. The coal-mine is the scene of a multitude of the most terrifying calamities."[3] To illustrate his point, Engels then went on to describe the explosion in Haswell Colliery, situated some six miles east of Durham, which killed 96 men in September 1844.

As all of this indicates, the Robsons and their children were living through that period of history usually described as "the industrial revolution", and which would see Britain become what one historian has described as "the first industrial nation."[4] The "industrial revolution" would transform the British economy away from its agricultural roots and heritage — roots which had been dominated by the rhythms of the harvests and the seasons — and into one which was instead characterised by the more incessant rhythm of industrial capitalism. This, in turn, saw the emergence of a new working class within British society — to which the Robsons belonged — and who would sell their labour, rather than grow crops to subsist, and who lived in villages, towns or cities, rather than in the countryside. Their work was long, hard, dirty and dangerous, but this new working class expected to prosper as a result of their physical efforts. In this respect industrial capitalism was both exploitative, and, for a few, potentially liberating.

Coal mining was one of the industries which were central to the development of the "industrial revolution", and the output of coal over this period correspondingly increased tenfold.[5] However, this improved output was not the result of technological advance and innovation, but was achieved through a simple increase in the numbers of people working in the mines. In the census of 1851 some 150,000 adult men and 65,000 children under the age of 18 were listed as coal miners — the latter a feat all the more remarkable given that the employment of children (and women) had been severely curtailed by the Mines Act of 1842.[6] The north east in general and

3.　For an excellent biography of Engels see Hunt, T (2009). *The Frock-Coated Communist: The Revolutionary Life of Friedrich Engels*. London: Allen Lane. Quote taken from *The Condition of the English Working Class*, p.253.
4.　Mathias, P (1969). *The First Industrial Nation: An Economic History of Britain, 1700-1914*. London: Methuen.
5.　See Pollard, 1978, p.136.
6.　Pollard, *op cit*, p. 139.

County Durham in particular benefited from this population expansion of those working in the mines. In 1801 the total population of the county was 150,000 — most of whom were concentrated in the ancient towns of Durham, Darlington, Sunderland, Bishop Auckland, Stockton and Hartlepool. By the end of Victoria's reign just under 2,000,000 people lived in the county, and miners made up a significant proportion of that number.

Table 2
Some Working Roles in Victorian Pits

Brakesman	The engineman who attends to the winding machine.
Deputies	A set of men employed in setting timber for the safety of the workmen; also in putting in brattice and brattice stoppings. They also draw the props from places where they are not required for further use.
Foal	A little boy who was formerly employed to assist a stronger boy (called a **Headsman**) to put (below); he pulled in front of the tub by a pair of ropes or traces called soams whilst the headsman pushed behind.
Half-marrow	One of two boys "putting together" (below).
Hand-putter or Barrowman	One who puts without the assistance of a pony.
Keeker	Pit inspector.
Kenner	An expression signifying time to give up work, shouted down the shaft by the **Banksman** where practicable, and where not, signalled and conveyed into the workings from mouth to mouth or by further signalling.

Master-shifter	A person who has charge of the mine during the night.
Onsetters	Men who put the full tubs in and take the empty ones out of the cage at the shaft bottom.
Overman	The person who has the daily supervision and responsible charge of the mine, under the direction of the manager or under-manager.
Pony-putter	A lad who brings the tubs from the working places to the flat with a pony.
Putter	A person who brings the full tubs from the hewer to the flat and takes the empty ones in to him.
Putting-hewer	A young hewer who is liable to be called upon to put if necessary.
Shifters	Underground workmen employed at miscellaneous work, such as timbering trolleyways, taking up bottom stone or taking down top to make height where necessary, setting doors, building stoppings, etc.
Stone-men	Men employed in driving stone drifts, taking up bottom, or taking down top stone to make height for horses, etc.
Trapper	A little boy, whose employment consists in opening and shutting a trap-door when required for the passage of tubs.

Source: Adapted from W E Nicholson (1888), A Glossary of Terms Used in the Coal Trade of Northumberland and Durham.

In all the Robsons had three children, one of whom would follow the family tradition of working in the pits. Apart from Mary Ann they also had another daughter, who took the same name as her mother, but who seems to have died young, and a boy called Robert who was born on the 5th October 1834, and who would also become a coal miner. Evidence for the death of young Margaret Robson comes from the 1841 census, when only Mary Ann and Robert are recorded, along with their parents. By the time of this census—when Mary Ann was eight-years-old—her family was living in Murton, and the first police report about Cotton records this incorrectly as her place of birth. Indeed, it was Appleton who was to discover that, in fact, Mary Ann had been born in Low Moorsley, which perhaps reflects both the reality that people—including the Robsons—were constantly on the move at this time, and that Cotton's personal history quite quickly became the stuff of local myth and fantasy, rather than of fact.

Murton was important in the life of Cotton, and indeed in the letter that she writes to Henry Holdforth prior to her execution—part of which is quoted at the start of this chapter—she fondly remembered her childhood, and adolescence in the village. "I wos happy then and them Wos days of joy", she suggested to Holdforth, who had also been a miner at the Murton colliery. It was also at Murton that Cotton was likely to have gone to school, taught a Sunday school class at the Methodist Chapel, and first got a job as a nursemaid to the family of Edward Potter—who had supervised the founding of the Murton Colliery in 1838. It was also the place where she first fell in love, and married. This letter is worth quoting in full (and in its original form)[7] for it reveals something of what

7.   The letter was published verbatim by the *Northern Echo* on 21 March 1873, but for ease of access those who wish to consult this, and several other letters that Mary Ann wrote from her cell should use Appleton (1973) *op cit*, in the *Introduction*, pps. 102-134. It is of course interesting to speculate how her letters found their way into the hands of the newspapers, and we might see this as the beginning of the market in serial killer memorabilia. Fox and Levin, *op cit* (in the *Introduction*) discuss "the selling of multiple murder" in the USA, although this aspect of the serial killing phenomenon has been less discussed in a British context. The *Northern Echo* published a number of letters written by Mary Ann to her friends, and her last lodger—William Lowrey—also wrote to the paper on Cotton's behalf. He may have acted as an intermediary for Mary Ann in her dealings with the media, given that she was eager for her side of the story to be told. From what the newspaper described, it would appear that Henry Holdforth's letter had been given, or sold to the paper by Holdforth himself. We should also consider the question of Cotton's

Cotton thought about her time when she was growing up, and when she was still very much under the influence of her family, and friends. In fact, this letter is also the closest evidence that we have as to how Mary Ann justified her behaviour, and can be seen as the context of any defence that she might have given if she had taken the stand. It also introduces other themes which are of interest, which will be important to consider later in our story, and which will help us in our search for Mary Ann.

My der friend

i reseved your most kind And Welcome Letter this morning Whitch it hurt my feelings very mutch you say you have read my case in the papers Well my der friend I hope you Will not Juge me rong As i have been on the Awfill crime of murder of Charles Edward Cotton Whitch i am not guilty of it those to reade the evidence that come sin against me you may think i am but if ie must Tell you I am not guilty I have been miss Lead With a man thea call smith he took upon him to looke after my case He told me not to speake a worde Let the witnesses say what thaye would I had not to speake it woulde be all don at durham and my evedens was never given propley into the Counsler or I should not come to what i have for i had a first class Counsler to defend me but i should like to get a portison up to spare my Life you speake of mother, had i my mother i should not been hear, fore my father i have not seen him since mother death, that is 6 years 15ᵗʰ of this month, so he has no mor fealing now

---

poor spelling—something that her step father George Stott would rebuke her for when he visited her in her condemned cell. Cotton replied that it was little wonder that her spelling was so poor given the circumstances that she found herself in—see report in *Durham County Advertiser*, 23 March 1873. Even so, the *Northern Echo* describes her letters as "ill-spelled and badly written wailings for life", 24 March 1873. In fact her writing was not much different to the letters written by Fred West to his family from his cell at HMP Winson Green in 1994, prior to his suicide in 1995. He wrote to his daughter, for example, "Hi May it is your Dad Writeing to you. Or lette me have your telephone number… or Write to me as soon as you can, please may I have to sort out watt Mr Ogden did to me, my new solicitors are Brillaint I Read What you sead about me in News of the that was loylty you read what Scott canavan sead he had [.]" Quoted in Wilson, D, (2009), *A History of British Serial Killing*, London: Sphere. Appleton also discusses a number of letters written to Mary Ann which were retained by Margaret Robinson, the prison matron and then "held by a relation", (p.123). I have not been able to locate these letters, but given that Appleton quotes from them in his text it is obvious that he did see them and was able to use them in developing his understanding of Mary Ann.

then he had when we had mother but thanke god she is i hope in heaven, she Left evry reason to beleave she Was happy my Dearly bloved Brother, father Robson, and my husbent W. Mowbray and if my Dear Child is there so i shall hope to meet them on the other side of Jordon the time you speak of my dark eyes i wos happy then, and them Wos days of joy to all our soles but this last 6 years my Life has been miserable for i married A Man they call James Robinson he had 3 sisters i never Wos Looked on as i should be With non of them he and i not Ergree We had some Words About sum money and i Left the house fore a few days I did not wish to part from him As i had no home i went to south hetton stayed ther When i returned ther wos no home for me he had sold what he did not Want And tooke the othe things and Went to Live With his sister so i might go where i Liked so i got married to this man Cotton he dide the Month After We come to Aucland to tell you All the past i can not As it is to hartrenden to think on i should like if you could Write to gorge hall and do What you can fore me to be spared With my Life i have that faith to believe if the trouth Wos told i should be sparde so I hope you Will do What you can for me As i have no frends to Looke Afer me nothing But strangers What has only knone me A few month so i hope And trustin god you Will do All you Can And get gorge hall to do the same I do not knone Whar to write to him so i must Come to A Close give my kind love to All that know me hoping they Will do the same so far Well i must say ther will not be enny Mor Sunday schoule teaching for me now but i shall try and put my trust in god As you knone i Wons did And ther was non on Earth happier then i wos then but He says he Will not Leave us in trouble he says if We Aske in faithe it shall be given in troubles i Will not leave th All Mine enemys Whispers together against me do they imagine this evil So no mor from A frendless Woman no i may say is forsaken By the World, but I hope not by god.

M A Cotton

If we leave to one side, at least for the moment, how self-serving this letter is, it is significant that a number of people from Cotton's past are mentioned, while others are ignored. This *dramatis personae* of those that she acknowledges include: Charles Edward Cotton, whom she has just been convicted of murdering and so it would be hard to ignore him; "a man thea call smith", who was her rather ineffectual and venal lawyer; her mother, whom she murdered (not that we might gather this from her statement "had i my mother i should not been hear"); her step-father, whom she calls "my father", and about whom she complains that she has not seen since her mother's death (although he would later visit her in her condemned cell); "Dearly bloved Brother" — Robert Robson; "father Robson"; "and my husbent W. Mowbray"; "my Dear Child"; James Robinson — another of her husbands, but one who would survive her; Robinson's three sisters; "this man Cotton" — in fact, her former husband whom she killed, and Charles Edward's father; and, finally, "gorge hall".

Some of these people will come to dominate the narrative of what follows, especially the Cotton family, James Robinson and his three sisters, about whom it is clear that Cotton still harboured some resentment. After all, it was the Robinsons (and her former husband James in particular) whom she held responsible for making her last six years "miserable", and which can again be compared with the warmth with which she remembered Murton. However, there is no mention of her lover Joseph Nattrass, or of her second husband George Ward — both of whom, like several of the others that she names in this letter, she also murdered.

Of course, it might simply have been that in writing to a friend who had known her from her time in Murton that she wanted to remember these times fondly, partly as a way of rekindling a connection to Holdforth. She was, after all, asking him, with only days to go before her execution, to "get a portison up to spare my Life". However, there does seem to be more going on here than simple, if understandable, emotional blackmail. Her "dearly bloved" brother, her parents, and her first husband are all mentioned, even if the latter is reduced to an initial, rather than given his full name. Nor, it should be acknowledged, do we really know to whom she is referring when she described her "Dear Child". And who was "gorge hall"? The *Northern Echo* suggested that he was her "sweetheart" in her youth, and so perhaps he was her first love, but whoever he was, like Holdforth, she saw them both as real friends, rather than as "Strangers What has only knone me A few months".[8] As such it would be wise to take seriously her

---

8.   The *Northern Echo* discusses George Hall in its edition of 21 March 1873.

suggestion that she was happy in Murton, and that her time there really "Wos days of joy to all our soles". Why should that have been the case? What was it about life in Murton that made her so happy? And, equally, what was it about her life after Murton that would lead inexorably to the chain of events that saw her awaiting execution in Durham Gaol?

The Mining Villages of East Northumberland

The historian Alan Metcalfe can help us in our search. Metcalfe has produced a social and economic account of the 37 mining villages of Victorian East Northumberland, including the village of Murton. His history allows us to concentrate more closely on specific patterns of work and life that the earlier description of the "industrial revolution" could only sketch very broadly. Within his history Metcalfe attempts to see whether the inhabitants of these villages could make something of their lives for themselves, or whether they were instead subject to the arbitrary actions of colliery managers, overseers, and all the other new officials who would come to administer relations within the industrial revolution.

In building up his picture Metcalfe concentrates on one particular village—Seaton Delaval—as a "typical mining village", and then expands his analysis outwards to the remaining villages. What he means by "typical" is a village that had a relatively small population, slow economic growth and where coal mining dominated the life of the community. Seaton Delaval fitted that bill perfectly. It had been created in 1837 by a mining company and comprised some 360 cottages of varying quality, with a better standard of house provided for the local doctor, clergy, school teachers, colliery agent, and other mining officials. The cottages in which the miners lived would have consisted of three rooms—two downstairs—with an attic accessed by a ladder. There was no sanitation, and no running water. Metcalfe calculated that in Seaton Delaval these three rooms could accommodate between three to 19 people, but that in the mid-1850s the average was five people living in these three rooms. As he puts it:

[they] lived in crowded conditions, hardly conducive to living the family life envisaged by the Victorian middle classes. Privacy and space were at a premium. It was virtually impossible to "get away" from anyone.[9]

Metcalfe argues that the villages were characterised in the early and mid-Victorian periods by continual movement of people in and out, and the near total power of the colliery officials. The reasons as to why people would move would vary depending on broader economic or more specific and individual circumstances. Sometimes people would come and go in search of work, or for a better quality of work, or when the demand for coal would see old mines closing, and new ones opening up, with all the opportunities that this would provide. Prior to 1844, this movement was also prompted when the "bond" under which a miner was tied to a particular colliery came to an end—usually on the 31st of March of any given year. As a result, underlying the life of a mining village was "instability and movement", so that "Seaton Delaval was in a constant state of flux with people coming and going on a regular basis".[10] By 1891, for example, Metcalfe calculated that of the some 2,000 people living in the village, only 34 per cent had been born there.

Metcalfe's other finding that is of relevance is that, far from being homogeneous, these small mining villages were characterised by patterns of difference, and division. As he argues:

> There were clearly defined positions of responsibility and status within the village. At the top of the hierarchy was a small group of "outsiders", individuals born outside of the district, who were not miners. These comprised the "elite" of the village—the administrative staff of the colliery, the doctor, the school teachers, the stationmaster, and the ministers of the cloth.[11]

But there were also differences between the miners, with a basic division between those who worked underground, and those who worked above the surface. Those who worked underground tended to earn more, and to

9. Metcalfe, *op cit*, in the *Introduction*, p.13.
10. *Ibid*, p.16.
11. *Ibid*, p.17.

have greater status than those who worked above the ground. Even below the ground, there was a difference between those who worked as hewers, and those who were putters, drivers, and so forth (and see *Table 2*). All of these men were then subject to the authority of a group of overmen, and deputies. These divisions have led one commentator to suggest that the life in the pit villages was ruled by "the law of the jungle. There were many fights and a great deal of bullying and intimidation between workers."[12] Crime was also a factor, although while Steve Jones lists the numerous fights, sexual assaults and murders that took place in the various villages, towns and cities of the north east during the Victorian era, Clive Emsley suggests that mining communities were reluctant to involve the police, and instead tried to dispense their own justice.[13]

So, these mining villages were neither stable, nor homogeneous, and were instead patterned by division, and difference. They were also dominated with people coming and going; moving on, if rarely moving up. We might also speculate that unless you were from these areas that these differences would be hidden and subtle, and therefore that visitors to these villages might not necessarily appreciate these social, and professional gradations. On the other hand, if you lived in these communities you probably had a very clear view of who you were, and where you stood in this Victorian mining social hierarchy.

Of course, given the focus of his book, which is largely about sport and leisure, Metcalfe acknowledges that women are mostly absent from his history, but that in any event they had few occupational outlets. As such, he argues that "marriage [was] the fate of the majority of women", and continues:

> Married women were not allowed to work and thus were forced to remain within the confines of their homes. The "home" was the focus of their lives and in the home they frequently ruled supreme. However, it is important to

---

12. Whitehead, *op cit*, in the *Introduction*, p. ix.
13. See Jones, S (2009), *Northumberland and Durham… The Sinister Side. Nottingham: Wicked Publications;* Emsley, C (2005), Crime and Society in England, 1750-199, p. 135.

emphasise that there was never any mistaking their place in society—they were inferior and subordinate to men.[14]

Whitehead describes a miner's wife as "a child-bearing drudge whose existence was completely absorbed with the maintenance of her husband and the rearing of their usually large brood of children."[15]

Some measure of all of this from a contemporary source comes in the shape of the philosopher John Stuart Mill. Just before Mill married Harriet Taylor in 1851 he wrote to his bride-to-be protesting against the laws that would govern their marriage, which in effect amounted to a "civil death" for Harriet. As he was later to argue:

> That the principle which regulates the existing social relations between the two
> sexes—the legal subordination of one sex to the other—is wrong itself, and
> now one of the chief hindrances to human improvement, and that it ought to
> be replaced by a principle of perfect equality, admitting no power or privilege
> on the one side, nor disability on the other.[16]

Simply by marrying in the period that Cotton was born, raised and became active as a serial killer, meant that her legal existence was surrendered under the common law doctrine of "coverture"—which literally means to be hidden—so that her legal personality was subsumed by the legal personality of her husband. As such a married woman could not sue, or be sued unless her husband was also party to the suit; she could not sign a contract unless her husband joined her; nor could she make a valid will unless her husband agreed to its contents. So too a husband assumed legal rights over his wife's property on marriage, and any property that came to his wife during their marriage also legally belonged to him. Worse still, all of her personal possessions—including her clothing and any money that she might have saved, or have earned—passed entirely

14. Metcalfe, *op cit*, p. 18.
15. Whitehead, *op cit*, p. x.
16. *The Subjection of Women* by John Stuart Mill can be accessed at ebooks@adelaide. I have previously written about the impact of coverture on Victorian women in Wilson, D (2009) *op cit*, pps. 55-83. However, when I have discussed these legal arrangements in the past I was interested in how men could use coverture to kill women.

to her husband. A woman's body was also held to belong to her husband, and it was not until 1891 that a High Court ruling denied a husband the right to imprison his wife in pursuit of his conjugal rights. A husband decided where the couple should live—often taking his new bride away from her family and friends—how any children should be brought up, and dominated virtually every aspect of their relationship.

Even after reforms such as the Married Women's Property Acts of 1870 and 1882, the legal and social position of women was hardly, to use Mill's phrase, "perfect equality". Women were denied the right to vote, join most professions, had only limited access to higher education, and were left under pressure to marry at a time when the average wage for a single, working class woman was below subsistence level. Put simply, marriage became a vocation for women in a culture where legal rules, social convention and economic structures all conspired to induce a woman to marry, and then ensured that she would be dependent upon her husband thereafter. Indeed figures from 1871 show that nearly 90 per cent of women between the ages of 45 and 49 were, or had been married.[17]

Murton

There is little doubt that the situation faced by women in Murton would have been as it has been described for women in Seaton Delaval, and more generally in mid-Victorian England. From this outline provided about Seaton Delaval, and the small part that it played in the "industrial revolution", what can we say about the economy and social life of Murton, which lies just over six miles south of Sunderland?

We know that work on Murton Colliery was started in February 1838, under the supervision of Edward Potter (and for whose family Cotton would act as a nursemaid), for Colonel Bradyll and Partners, and that the pit opened in April 1843, which rather neatly dovetails with the development of Seaton Delaval. Murton Colliery was to remain a working pit until it closed on 29th November 1991. In 1841 there were around 500 people living at Murton, which was a considerable increase on the 98 who were listed as living there in the 1831 census. By 1901, Murton's population

17. Shanley, M L (1989), *Feminism, Marriage and the Law in Victorian England, 1850-1895*, Princeton: Princeton University Press, p.9.

was over 6,500. Because of the costs associated with opening the pit, coal was mined continuously throughout the day so that the pit owners could make a return on their investment. The Robsons lived in one of the new streets that were built to accommodate the incoming miners, and which was called Durham Place. The house was stone built, and in all likelihood was not dissimilar to those described at Seaton Delaval, although this would eventually be demolished in the 1950s. Appleton believes that the Robsons lived between the Welfare Hall and the Travellers' Rest public house, which in the early days of the colliery had also doubled as a company shop.

Two of the men in Mary Ann's life now become important in the trajectory of her story, although in different ways. Her father, Michael Robson, was killed in early 1842, although there is no account of his death in the Durham Mining Museum Records.[18] However, Appleton suggests that Robson was killed when he slipped and fell down a shaft when repairing a pulley wheel at the Murton Colliery, and that the age on his death certificate was 30, rather than 26, which would have been consistent with the 1841 census. In any event, he died young, and this must have put the Robson family under some financial pressure. In particular it would have put pressure on Mary Ann to find work.

Whitehead also suggests that Mary Ann saw her father's body brought home from the pit in a sack labelled "Property of South Hetton Coal Company".[19] There are echoes here with Dennis Nilsen — the Scottish serial killer, who murdered 15 young men between 1978 and 1983 — and who claimed to his biographer Brian Masters that he "killed for company".[20] Masters also suggests that Nilsen may have begun to associate love with death, after having seen his beloved grandfather laid out prior to burial when Nilsen was six-years-old. We have no way of knowing what Mary Ann thought about the death of her father, or how she reacted when she saw her dead father's body. Even if we did — and surely we can presume something about how she might have felt — would that necessarily explain why she would later repeatedly kill? After all, who amongst us has not had a parent, or grandparent die?

---

18. These can accessed via www.dmm.org.uk
19. Whitehead, *op cit*, p.iii.
20. B Masters (1986), *Killing For Company: The Case of Dennis Nilsen*, London: Coronet Books.

Two years after Michael Robson died, there was a strike at the colliery in 1844, but there is no evidence to suggest that this had an impact on the surviving Robson family, although it is worth noting that teams of Cornish miners moved into the north east at this time, and helped to break the Murton strike. This strike was part of what Engels described as the "great strike" of the "great coal district of the north of England", and he specifically and enthusiastically mentioned the Northumberland and Durham coalminers. With a touch of elaboration that suited his purpose, Engels noted that "not a hand stirred, and Newcastle, the chief coal port, was so stripped of its commodity that coal had to be brought from the Scotch coast, in spite of the proverb"[21] He was also particularly scathing about Lord Londonderry—"who owns considerable mines in Durham"—and "his town of Seaham", where he had threatened any small tradesman who extended credit to the striking miners.

It was also around this time that a Methodist Sunday School started in the village, and Mary Ann would become a teacher there. Methodism was of course the religious movement led by Charles and John Wesley in the early 18th century, and the latter in particular built up an enormous following among the labouring poor of the new industrial areas of Britain, which tended to be neglected by the established Church of England. By the early Victorian period there were hundreds of Methodist chapels in the north east of England, presided over by itinerant lay preachers, and providing a sense of community and reassurance to people living in towns and villages dominated by mining, and thus experiencing profound economic and social change. Some historians have suggested that Methodism was "tailor-made" for pit communities, where disaster and scarcity were common, and thus some greater purpose was therefore constantly needed to explain suffering and death. Methodism also specifically offered women opportunities outside of a domestic setting—an opportunity that Cotton was keen to exploit.[22]

---

21. Engels, *op cit* p.258.
22. For an account of Methodism and its impact on artisan and mining communities see Colls, R (1977), *The Collier's Rant*, London: Croom Helm; Hempton, D (1984), *Methodism and Politics in British Society, 1750–1850*; Hempton, D (1996), *The Religion of the People: Methodism and Popular Religion, 1750–1900*, London: Routledge. There is also always still value in re-reading E P Thompson's (1980) *The Making of the English Working Class*, London:

Religion had clearly once been important to Cotton. Indeed, in her letter to Henry Holdforth, she mentions sin and evil, thanks God, hopes that she had not been "forsaken" by God, remembered days that were a "joy to all our soles", and hoped to meet dead loved ones on "the other side of Jordon". And, perhaps with a flash of humour too, she noted that "ther will not be enny Mor Sunday schoule teaching for me now". All of this might simply be seen as the accumulated emotional impact of her impending execution, or indeed as yet another means of establishing a connection with Holdforth, who had also mined in Murton and worshipped at the same Methodist chapel. However, it would be wrong to dismiss this as mere contrivance, and Cotton would not be the last serial killer who would return to her faith in custody, as Myra Hindley, who rediscovered the Catholicism of her youth had done, prior to her death in November 2002. Nor should we forget that Dennis Rader, who killed ten people between 1974 and 1991, and was known as the "BTK Killer" (Bind, Torture and Kill) was a Lutheran Deacon in Wichita, Kansas.[23]

Around 1846 Cotton became a nursemaid to the family of the colliery manager Edward Potter in South Hetton, where they lived at South Hetton House, which Appleton suggested was known as "The Hall". This was without doubt a much grander house than anything that Cotton had been used to, and so too we should also remember the social prestige that colliery managers had within the north east. Some of that prestige probably rubbed off onto Cotton. Her time at "The Hall" may also have been when she first aspired to have cleaners and staff of her own. Mary Ann was to stay as a nursemaid for almost three years, but then tried her hand at dressmaking. Around this time her first husband William Mowbray arrived at Murton, and they were married on 18 July 1852, when Cotton was 19. Mowbray is widely believed to have been attracted to Murton

---

Penguin given that Thompson was himself the son of Methodist missionaries.

23. The story of Dennis Rader is told in Douglas, J (2007), *Inside the Mind of BTK: The True Story Behind the Thirty Year Hunt for the Notorious Wichita Serial Killer*. New York: Jossey-Bass. However, I have criticised this book at length in an academic article published in the journal *Amicus*, but the more general reader might like to consult instead a lively critique of Douglas' account by Gladwell, M (2009), *What The Dog Saw: And Other Adventures*. London: Allen Lane, pps. 336-356. A recent book about Myra Hindley is Lee, C A (2010), *One of Our Own: The Life and Death of Myra Hindley*, Edinburgh: Mainstream Publishing.

because of the work that was available at the colliery, and some reports after Cotton's arrest suggested that he had been a native of Peterborough. However, Appleton noted that in the 1861 census Mowbray's place of birth was Shotley in Northumberland, and that his age was recorded as 35. On his death certificate in 1865 William's age was given as 47, and Appleton suggests that "Mary Ann wanted to make it appear he was older than he was,"[24] probably to help cover-up the fact that she had murdered him.

Twelve years before, Mary Ann and Mowbray had been married in Newcastle Register Office, and they gave their address as Westgate, Newcastle. At the time of this marriage Mary Ann stated that she was 21, when in fact she was still 19. Their choice of venue for their marriage is also very significant. Not for Mary Ann a marriage in the chapel where she had worked as a Sunday School teacher, in the village where she had gone to school, grown up, and had—as her letter to Henry Holdforth suggested—real "friends". Instead a register office marriage, some 20 miles north of Murton, in the more anonymous surroundings of Newcastle, which probably implied that she was pregnant with Mowbray's child, and that she felt, or there was, some local gossip about their circumstances that she would prefer to avoid.

Perhaps for this reason Cotton and Mowbray then moved away from Murton and the north east, and settled in Cornwall, in the south west of England. However, it should be noted, that scores of Cornish miners had moved to Murton to break-up the pit strike in 1844, and it may well have been that they heard something of a better life elsewhere from this source. Cornwall was also a Methodist stronghold, and so religion may have had something to do with this move too. Very little information exists as to what life was like for Cotton and Mowbray in Cornwall, although there is some evidence to suggest that Mowbray found work for a railway construction firm, and that they settled for some time in Penzance,[25] or St Germans.[26] In total Cotton and Mowbray were away from the north east for about four years, and when they returned to the north they took with them one child—called Margaret Jane—and there are accounts that

---

24. Appleton, *op cit*, in the *Introduction*, p.51.
25. Appleton, *op cit*, claims Penzance—see pps. 51-52.
26. Whitehead, *op cit*, claims St Germans—see p.iii.

Cotton suggested that she had also had three other children, all of whom had died. Sometimes these deaths are included in the total of Cotton's victims, but there is actually no evidence to suggest that she did in fact have, or indeed kill, any of these three children. However, we can presume that she gave birth to the child that she was carrying when she left the north east, and which had caused her to quickly marry Mowbray in Newcastle. On the other hand, Margaret Jane, named after her maternal grandmother, who was to survive until June 1860, was probably murdered by Cotton—the cause of death on her death certificate was listed as "scarletina anginosa and exhaustion"—although we should also bear in mind that many formal certificates related to births, marriages, and deaths from this period were often incorrectly completed.

Northern Murders

Back in Murton from their time in Cornwall, Mowbray found work as a storekeeper at the colliery, and in April 1857 Margaret Jane was baptised at St Andrew's Church, Dalton-le-Dale, which was then the parish church for Murton. This child did not survive for long, and Cotton used the same name for another daughter born in the autumn of 1861. Mowbray and Cotton made the short move from Murton to South Hetton in September 1858, perhaps because Mowbray had found work as a stoker, and it was there that their daughter Isabella was born. Isabella was the child who was to live longest of all the children that Mary Ann gave birth to—she was nine-years-old when Cotton killed her—and it may well have been Isabella that Cotton was referring to when she wrote of her "Dear Child" in her letter to Henry Holdforth. The second Margaret Jane was born in October 1861, and a son, called John Robert was born in July 1863. By this stage the Mowbrays were living in Hendon in Sunderland. John Robert was to die in September the following year, with the cause of his death recorded as "diarrhoea".

After working as a storekeeper, Mowbray found work first as a fireman, and then as a stoker on the steamer "Newburn", which was based in Sunderland. Indeed, Sunderland was fast becoming increasingly important to the development of the economy of the north east, through shipbuilding, sea-faring, and the coal trade. In particular the opening of the new South (or Hudson) Dock, and the development of a railway network that linked the pits to the harbour, meant that coal exports from the town reached more than 1,500,000 tons by 1847.[27] As a result working people flocked to Sunderland, and the town saw its population double between 1801 and 1841, and by 1871 it had doubled again to 98,000 people. It appears that Cotton and Mowbray left South Hetton to settle in Sunderland, for it is a Sunderland address that is recorded on the death certificate for John Robert.

William Mowbray died in January 1865, and according to his death certificate, signed by Dr Gammage, he had succumbed to "typhus fever" and diarrhoea—the same cause of death as John Robert. He had actually been on leave from his ship with a sore foot, but the attack of diarrhoea had seemingly been so severe that he had died from its effects within a few hours. Diarrhoea is, of course, also a symptom of arsenic poisoning, although "typhus fever"—if this diagnosis was accurate—is not. Cotton was described as being distraught after the death of her husband of 12 years, but Appleton noted that there were later also some "fanciful tales" about Dr Gammage peering through her window after Mowbray's demise, and noticing her singing and pirouetting before a mirror.[28] There is no evidence to support these accusations, although Cotton did receive £35 insurance money from the British Prudential, as a result of her husband's death. This was a significant sum, and the money clearly facilitated her move out of Sunderland. With her two daughters—the second Margaret Jane and Isabella—Cotton then moved out of the town to Seaham Harbour, a coal port on the north east coast, where yet more deaths would follow.

Deceptive Appearances

There is one last issue which we should consider, before trying to conclude more generally about the impact of these early experiences on Cotton. That issue relates to Mary Ann's appearance. Mrs Edward Potter—for whom Cotton had worked as a nursemaid in South Hetton—was later reported as describing Mary Ann as "beautiful", and revealed that a local cleric had at some point fallen in love with her. Contemporary newspapers, such as the *Newcastle Journal* wrote of expecting Cotton to have been a "monster

27. Corfe, T (1973), *Sunderland: A Short History*, Newcastle: Frank Graham, p.82.
28. Appleton, *op cit*, pps.53 and 138.

in human shape", but in fact Mary Ann was neither "horrible nor repulsive". Rather, "Mary Ann Cotton seems to have possessed the faculty of getting a new husband whenever she wanted one" (11 March 1873), which implies something about her charms. The *Durham County Advertiser* also commented that Cotton had had "no difficulty in getting four men to marry her" (11 March 1873); *The Times* described her as "a comely-looking, gentle-eyed woman" (8 March 1873); and the *Royal Cornwall Gazette, Falmouth Packet and General Advertiser*, described her as "an English Borgia", who "had no difficulty in getting four men to marry her" (22 March 1873).[29] Richard Lambert describes Cotton as "pleasant" and "interesting", and "a woman of considerable energy, intelligence, and ability for her station in life"[30] and even her very proper biographer notes with some awe how "men had liked her! And she must have liked men".[31] What are we to make of Appleton's use of an exclamation mark?

This issue of physical appearance, and the "hold" that it might allow a serial killer to have over their victims is a recurring theme in popular writing about the phenomenon of serial murder, and also within early attempts to explain this phenomenon. The Edwardian serial killer George Joseph Smith, for example, who murdered his three wives between 1912 and 1914 by drowning them in the bath, so as to inherit their life assurance, was supposed to have "an extraordinary power over women". One author went as far as to suggest that women were attracted to him as a result of "a certain magnetism about the eyes", and that he may even have been hypnotising his victims.[32] However, Smith was in effect merely a grotesque reflection of the male-dominated, hierarchical culture of the Victorian and Edwardian periods, and this "extraordinary power" was not centred on his appearance, or even hypnotism, but was in fact enshrined in the law of the time—something that John Stuart Mill had complained about as early as 1851. Smith, for example, was in particular very aware of his legal rights

---

29. This newspaper's interest in Mary Ann—it devotes some three paragraphs to the case—might suggest that her time in Cornwall was remembered by and therefore of interest to a number of her south west contemporaries, given that it was very unusual for the paper to cover cases from the Durham Assizes.

30. Lambert, *op cit*, in the *Introduction*, 108.

31. Appleton, *op cit*, p.11.

32. Watson, E (1922), *The Trial of George Joseph Smith*. London: William Hodge & Co., p.102.

as a "husband" in relation to his wife's property, and wasted no opportunity to tell others of these rights if the occasion demanded. In short, this "extraordinary power" was not so extraordinary after all, even if what it amounted to was power based on gender and marital status.

Even so these early musings about murder, physical qualities and personal experiences — coming as they did when the discipline of criminology and psychology were becoming more popular — is the beginning of the medical-psychological tradition that has come to dominate the discussion of, and writing about, serial killers. In this tradition it is the story of the serial killer — their childhood, the relationship that they might have had with their father, mother, or siblings, how they progressed at school, and what work they chose — that has become the means by which we try to understand the phenomenon of serial killing, rather than considering who it was that the serial killers were able to kill. Yet, if we were to look more closely at those who are murdered by serial killers we would see clear patterns emerge — whether we are talking about Cotton or Smith, or the others who will be referred to later — and it is these patterns which probably best help us to understand serial murder.

There's another problem with these deceiving appearances. If we expect serial killers to be "monster(s) in human shape", then we will imagine that it will be easy to spot them, for clearly there will be obvious physical clues as to which person will be dangerous to us, and alternatively who we can trust. It's almost as if we expect serial killers to have metaphoric horns on their heads, and a long pointed tail following behind. Yet every serial killer needs to get access to their victims, so as to use the opportunity of that access to repeatedly murder. No one would give access to someone with horns on their head, but what about the trusted, respected, local doctor — the only doctor in the community to make home visits? Or a police officer? A nurse? The local businessman who dresses as a clown, and raises money for the local Democratic party? Surely we can trust them? Only problem is that the respected, local doctor was Harold Shipman who killed 215, and possibly as many as 260 of his patients; the police officer the serial killer Dennis Nilsen. The nurse? Well, take your pick between, in the British context, Beverly Allitt or Colin Norris, or the American Jane Toppan, who murdered 31 people between 1885 and 1901, and who had the dubious distinction of having murdered more people than any other American before John Wayne Gacy confessed to 33 murders. Gacy also liked to dress as a clown at local children's parties, and raise money for the local Democrats.[33] What perfect camouflage.

But what did Mary Ann Cotton actually look like? Lambert describes her as "a little over medium height; she had a swarthy complexion, thin compressed lips and dark piercing eyes"[34] and Appleton as "neat, clean, with fine dark eyes [and] above medium height".[35] He also states that those who attended her trial had expected to "gaze at a cruel appearance", and in that the public were to be disappointed. In short, we have returned to the deceiving appearance. Is this not the greatest fallacy of the popular tradition of thinking about serial killers? In other words, we have come to expect that those who are going to do damage to their fellow human beings will not be charming, handsome, beautiful, or even caring when the occasion demands, and instead we expect them to be grotesque and diabolical. Perhaps it's easier to think of them as monsters, for it makes fewer demands on our common sense judgements. Indeed, in some of the broadsides to commemorate Mary Ann's execution her face was deliberately coarsened and disfigured, so as to better conform to public expectations about what a murderer might look like. One author has even suggested that a picture being passed off as Cotton was actually Flora Macdonald, even though a genuine photograph had been taken of a clearly demure, and somewhat depressed Mary Ann when she was in Durham Gaol.[36] Appleton uses a

33. The cases of Toppan and Gacy are described and compared in Schechter and Schechter *op cit* (in the *Introduction*), and Fox and Levin, *op cit* (in the *Introduction*) discuss Gacy. For a good account of the Allitt case see Davies, N. (1993), *Murder on Ward Four: The Story of Bev Allitt, and the Most Terrifying Crime Since the Moors Murders*, London: Chatto & Windus. The report of the official enquiry into the Allitt case is Clothier, C (1994), *Allitt Inquiry: Independent Inquiry Relating to Deaths and Injuries on the Children's Ward at Grantham and Kesteven General Hospital During the Period February to April 1991*, London: The Stationery Office Books. There is no love lost between this account and that provided by Davies. For Dennis Nilsen see B Master (1986) *Killing for Company: The Case of Dennis Nilsen, London: Coronet Books*, and for Colin Norris—a nurse who worked in a number of hospitals in Leeds, see Wilson (2009), *op cit.*
34. Lambert, *op cit*, p.108.
35. Appleton, *op cit*, p.11.
36. Flanders, *op cit*, in the *Introduction*, p.393.

picture of one such broadside as the cover for his book.[37]

The Importance of Early Influences?

Having warned against paying too much attention to the tropes of the medical-psychological tradition, with its incessant desire to telescope backwards, peering ever more closely into the serial killer's background, childhood and relationships, we can still, nonetheless, acknowledge that these issues will have played some part in creating the adult who would go on to kill. Indeed, one of the oldest questions within criminology is to try and understand to what extent an individual is personally responsible for his or her criminal behaviour, or alternatively how that personal responsibility might be constrained, and limited by the reality of the social, cultural and economic circumstances that that individual finds him/herself inhabiting. This question is often posed in a number of ways. Are "criminals born or made"; is the cause of crime "nature or nurture"; and, does the offender have "free will", or are his/her actions "determined" by external forces? As befits an essentially philosophical question, there is never an easy way of answering, and perhaps the best that we might conclude is that there is always going to be a subtle, or sometimes even a messy relationship between individual motivation, and how that individual responds—in whatever way—to the circumstances that he or she faces.

In other words, this is not a question of either/or. Allowing room for free will, and also for "determinism", helps us to explain how individuals in essentially the same set of circumstances might behave differently, but also how those circumstances might more generally create, for example, more poverty in some communities than in others, or more crime. It helps us to explain why some women made the most of their world—no matter how unfair that Victorian world might have been—by keeping a home, raising a family, or campaigning for political and social change, while others resorted to murder.

So, what might we conclude about Cotton's early years, up until her

---

37. This broadside was also used as the cover for the *Illustrated Police News* on 16 November 1872. Unsurprisingly, that publication was keen to promote the activities of Sergeant Hutchinson in bringing Mary Ann to justice, whereas a less partisan view might instead have championed Thomas Riley or Dr Thomas Scattergood as Cotton's nemesis.

move to Seaham Harbour, and the impact that they might have had on creating the woman that she became? Why was her time in Murton "days of joy"? If we leave to one side the reality that as a young girl she had relatively few responsibilities while she was growing up, and that many children such as Mary Ann would have encountered death as they matured, there does seem to have been a number of issues that are worth considering further.

The first issue to consider is the geographic mobility that characterised Cotton's early years. First her family moved around the north east — often following better work opportunities as one mine closed, and new seams were opened up — and then she herself moved with Mowbray to Cornwall. Even after their return to the north east, the Mowbrays moved from Murton to South Hetton, and then on to Sunderland, prior to Cotton's move to Seaham Harbour. This "geographic transience" does seem to have been a significant and consistent behaviour throughout Cotton's life, and had the added advantage of allowing her to never put down too many roots and of never having to make too many friends with too many people, who might just notice odd behaviours that might later raise suspicion. It also allowed her to make a series of claims to the same insurance company, without raising suspicion. Even today the most successful serial killers — in other words, those who are going to kill for the longest period of time before they are caught — also display this "geographic transience", rather than "geographic stability". Here too we should remember that in the early, and mid-Victorian period someone did not need to travel too far before they could effectively disappear.

The second issue to consider is that, with so many people moving about the country in search of work, the new, industrial communities that were being created were rarely homogeneous. It was expected that people would come and go; that they would be part of a community for a few years, or perhaps even simply for a few months, and then move on in search of other, better opportunities. This was one of Metcalfe's conclusions about the 37 east Northumberland mining villages and towns that he studied. Metcalfe also observed that women in these towns and villages had an inferior social status, and were seen as being subordinate to men. The home was their provenance, and so a woman who could claim to be, or to have been a nursemaid — and later a nurse — must have been a relatively exotic, and therefore noticeable woman. We should also remember that as a result of her efforts during the Crimean War, Florence Nightingale had become a national heroine by 1856, and elevated the status of nurses onto an altogether different footing, even those nurses who had had little, or no training. Perhaps other women were envious of Cotton? Lambert certainly thought that Cotton had "energy, intelligence, and ability for her station in life", which is also clearly a reference to the fact that as a working class woman Mary Ann was not expected to have been as restless, and opportunistic. Perhaps it was these very qualities that were admired by those women in the various communities where she lived that she did converse with, and with whom she socialised.

The fact that she was a nursemaid to Edward Potter's family also seems to have been significant. Potter would have been held in high esteem in the community, and working at "The Hall" must also have brought a certain glamour into Mary Ann's life. Perhaps it also provided her with a sense of what might be possible, if she worked hard enough, and gave her a glimpse of another way to live her life. In a number of the villages where she lived, for example, Cotton would regularly employ local women to clean for her. Remember too that Murton, and the other mining villages and towns were characterised by difference and division, according to Metcalfe. A young woman — described later as "beautiful" by her employer — must have stood out as different from the crowd of her contemporaries, and this must have meant that Mary Ann thought of herself as being special. Perhaps as a consequence she also thought that great things were expected of her; perhaps she expected great things of herself. In any event, we do know that when, in all likelihood Cotton fell pregnant with Mowbray's child, she did not feel able to stay on in Murton to get married, but moved to more cosmopolitan Newcastle. It is tempting to think that she needed some distance and anonymity from the pressures that come with being seen as different and special, and that William Mowbray's charms might not have been quite as desirable to her in the cold light of day — especially when compared with the cleric who was supposed to have fallen in love with her.

There is also a more generalised influence that we should acknowledge from these early years in Murton. Mary Ann was caught up in the heady days of the development of industrial capitalism, when simply by selling your labour there was a possibility that you could become the person that you had always wanted to be. Not for her a subsistence existence; a life determined by the rhythm of the seasons—forever at the mercy of the weather, and the fate of the crops in the field. Not for her to be at the mercy of a man. Rather, she must have thought that her fate was in her own hands. A fate, moreover, that could be shaped by all that was possible in the new culture of the towns and cities that were springing up all over the north east, to support the new, exciting economic order of credit, markets, and banks; of fortunes that could be made, and lost. Mary Ann was a child of industrial capitalism, and just like any good speculator, if one plan didn't quite work out, then the important thing was not to dwell too long on that failure by looking backwards, but to continue to look to the future, where things would be better, and where she could finally achieve what it was that she wanted to achieve; to be the person that she had always wanted to be. That was Mary Ann. Always looking forward, and never dwelling too long in the past, until she thought that the past in the shapes of Henry Holdforth and George Hall might come to her aid.

Most important of all, this was the period during which Cotton became a killer. We have no way of knowing why she started to kill, or what specific trigger might have led her down this particular road. Perhaps it all started out tragically enough. After all children did die in great numbers during the Victorian period, and then slowly, time after time, death began to offer a way to cope when there were just too many mouths to feed, or when these children were seen to be holding her back. Whitehead suggests that Cotton may have started to murder after she "snapped" in the autumn of 1864, when William was away at sea, and she was left at home with three small children to look after.[38] This is perfectly possible, although difficult to prove.

However, we do know that Mary Ann had started to murder before taking up her job as a nurse in Sunderland, where she would gain access to drugs and poisons. So whatever Cotton would learn as a nurse simply made her a better killer; she became more skilled, and part of this was to learn how to keep her victims alive for long enough to allay suspicion.

---

38. Whitehead, *op cit*, in the *Introduction*, p.ii.

This skill also gave her time to call for an unsuspecting doctor to come and prescribe medication; time for her to talk to her neighbours, and prepare them for the death that was about to take place; time to allow her to present herself as a concerned wife, and mother; time for her to "perform" gender for those who surrounded her, and conform to the accepted stereotype. And time was what she needed. After all, wasn't there something odd about William Mowbray's sudden death? Home from the sea nursing a sore foot, he succumbed to a bout of diarrhoea only hours later. And while this clearly did not raise suspicions at the time, this was perhaps because people in the community simply didn't know the Mowbrays well enough to make a more informed judgement.

And what about motive? Why murder her husband of over 12 years, and eventually all of the children that they had produced together? Money is clearly an obvious candidate as far as motive is concerned, but there must be more going on here than simply the small amounts of cash that she was able to generate from William's, and their children's deaths? Perhaps she blamed William for the circumstances that she found herself in. Perhaps she saw him as the source of her gradually worsening fate. After all, it was William who had got her pregnant, and therefore had probably caused her to leave Murton—away from her friends, family, and her "days of joy". Perhaps she had simply met someone else while her husband was at sea, and just wanted William out of the way. We know that she had an affair with Joseph Nattrass in Seaham Harbour. Perhaps that affair had already started, and so William's death, and her subsequent move to the coast might actually have been engineered to put this affair on a more permanent footing. After all, think back to the revelation that we had never heard of "gorge hall" until her execution cell letter. Might there have been other lovers too that have escaped the historical record? Looking at her motivation in this way, and not simply as being based on money, also helps us to understand why William is reduced to a mere initial in her letter to Henry Holdforth. Even eight years after his death, she still cannot bear to call him "William".

Whatever her motive might have been, Mary Ann utterly obliterated the Mowbrays. If we accept that she had had three children in Cornwall by William—all of whom had died prior to her returning to the north—that would mean that she perhaps killed all eight, and at least five, plus their father. It's hard to avoid the rather depressing conclusion that she took what she needed from the Mowbrays, until there was nothing left to take. Like a miner moving on when an old seam dried up, and new shafts needed to be sunk elsewhere; when the bond to the colliery was finally over for the year, Cotton put the Mowbrays behind her, and headed off to pastures new.

Chapter Two

Seaham Harbour, Sunderland and Nursing

"Upon this dreary coast we have nothing but county meetings and shipwrecks; and I have this day dined upon fish, which probably dined upon the crews of several colliers lost in the late gales":

Lord Byron writing to his friend Thomas Moore
from Seaham Hall, 2 February 1815.

Lord Byron found himself on the "dreary" north east coast as a result of his marriage to Anne Isabella Milbanke, the daughter of Sir Ralph Milbanke, at Seaham Hall on 2nd January 1815. It was not a happy union, and by March the following year the couple had separated, although not before Anne had given birth to their daughter. More generally, the Milbankes sold their properties, including Seaham Hall and the surrounding land, to the 3rd Marquis of Londonderry, who very quickly set about developing his investment so as to generate a profit from the mines that dominated the region. In particular it was Londonderry who founded the town and port of Seaham Harbour in 1828, to export the coal that was being mined from his own and other pits, including the Hazard Colliery, where Michael Robson had worked at the time of Cotton's birth in 1832. Two railroads — the Rainton & Seaham Railway and the South Hetton Railway — were also constructed to connect the town and its harbour to the coalfields, and it can be safely presumed that Londonderry would have been keen to see a profit returned from these various developments. The "great strike" of 1844 — which earned Londonderry the censure of Engels — must have been particularly worrying. A decade later, Londonderry was dead, and his estate was being managed by his wife, Lady Frances Ann Vane Tempest, who died in January 1865, just a few days after Cotton had arrived in the town.

Why did the newly widowed Mary Ann move to Seaham Harbour, with her two surviving daughters? It is reasonable to presume that she must have known Seaham Harbour, given that there were established railway links between Murton, where she had grown up, and the town. Perhaps this was a place where her family shopped on special occasions, or where they might have made trips to the coast? In 1861 Seaham Harbour's population was over 5,000 — a not inconsiderable size in the area — with all the advantages that come when there are larger concentrations of people, although we should also remember that Mary Ann was moving from the more densely populated Sunderland. Then there is her affair with Joseph Nattrass to consider. It might well have been that this affair had started when William Mowbray had been away at sea, and that she simply followed Nattrass to Seaham Harbour — as she would later follow him to West Auckland a decade later. What Mary Ann perhaps didn't know was that Nattrass had already married Catherine Tempest in October 1860 — a fact that Whitehead has been able to establish — and which therefore casts doubt on the account provided by Appleton, who wrongly suggested that Cotton was disappointed when Nattrass married in 1865.

Cotton seems to have lodged in a ground floor room at 19 North Terrace in Seaham Harbour, next door to a pub which, at the time, was called the Lord Seaham Inn, a name that would no doubt have displeased Engels! North Terrace still exists, but Whitehead noted in 2000 that the then owner of the pub — which by that stage had become (and remains) the Harbour View Hotel — was very keen to distance herself from Mary Ann Cotton, and suggested that she had lived elsewhere.[1] Whitehead also suggested that Seaham Harbour was "perhaps the most unhealthy place in the county of Durham",[2] partly to support his theory that several of Cotton's victims died naturally of typhus fever. Indeed, the second Margaret

---

1. On the other hand, there has been no such distancing by the town of Lord Byron — despite the fact that he seemed to have been less than happy to have been in the area, and in any event was there for less time than Mary Ann. The town's shopping centre is located in "Byron Place", and there is also a well publicised "Byron Walk". However, Yvette Adamson, the current owner of the Seaham Habour View Hotel — whom I interviewed in 2011 — knew all about Mary Ann Cotton, and was especially dismissive of the town's attempt to claim Lord Byron.
2. Whitehead, *op cit*, p.22.

Jane Mowbray was to die at Seaham Harbour on 30th April 1865, and the cause of her death is recorded as "typhus fever". Typhus fever would have been unlikely to have been confused with gastric fever, which was what Appleton—without having seen the death certificate—had claimed was the cause of Margaret Jane's death, and which had led him to speculate that the child was murdered. In any event, Margaret Jane's death may have prompted Mary Ann's mother—by now re-married to George Stott and living close by at New Seaham—to temporarily look after the remaining child, Isabella Jane, who was to lodge with the Stotts until the death of her grandmother in March 1867. This move undoubtedly prolonged Isabella Jane's life—she lived until she was nine-years-old—but died of "gastric fever" in April 1867, shortly after having being brought home by Cotton, and a few months prior to her marriage to James Robinson in August of that year.

Records and Registers

Here we would do well to consider Whitehead's defence of Mary Ann, especially as his support is largely based on what has been recorded on the relevant death certificates—and other formal registers of social life from the Victorian era—which Appleton did not use, or was simply not aware that they existed. Whitehead's defence centres on the fact that typhus fever and typhoid fever are not one and the same thing, and that typhus fever produces a distinct rash that should have been "obvious" to a Victorian doctor. Whitehead is therefore particularly keen to draw attention to the fact that it is "typhus fever", which is recorded, along with "diarrhoea", as having killed William Mowbray, as well as the second Margaret Jane. In fact, Whitehead categorically states that the symptoms of typhus "cannot be mistaken for anything else".[3] This is important for typhus fever would not mimic the most common underlying symptoms of arsenic poisoning—such as vomiting and diarrhoea (also recorded on William's death certificate)—whereas typhoid fever would.

Typhus fever—which was sometimes known as "gaol fever"—is an infectious disease caused by the organism *rickettsia prowazekii*, and is

3.   Whitehead, *op cit*, in the *Introduction*, p.18.

transmitted to humans by lice. The lice feed on human blood, and then defecate when they are feeding. It is the faeces which contains the typhus fever bacteria, which gets transmitted by being rubbed into small wounds, such as those caused by a child, or indeed an adult, scratching any lice-infected areas. So it is the faeces, not the bite of the louse that transmits the illness to humans. Symptoms of typhus fever usually appear within one, or two weeks of exposure. Common symptoms include fever, headache, weakness and muscle aches, as well as a rash which starts on the back, chest and stomach, before spreading more widely. Whitehead is certain that Dr Gammage—who certified William Mowbray's death—"would have seen hundreds, perhaps thousands, of cases of typhus in his career", and so "could not possibly have made a mistake regarding the tell-tale rash".[4]

Typhoid fever is caused by salmonella bacteria, and the main sources of infection are contaminated water, or milk. In short, typhoid fever was a disease of poor sanitation, while typhus was a disease caused by overcrowding. Of course poor sanitation and overcrowding often went hand in glove during the Victorian era. Symptoms of typhoid usually begin with a headache, and about ten to 14 days after infection would also include a high fever, diarrhoea and rose-coloured spots on the abdomen, and chest. Patients are often emaciated and exhausted, and can sometimes become delirious, during which state they may have convulsions.

Other death certificates discovered by Whitehead list such causes of death as: "*scarletina anginosa* and exhaustion" (the first Margaret Jane); "diarrhoea" (several children); "hepatitis" (Cotton's mother); "continued fever" (James Robinson); "gastric fever" (several children, including Frederick Cotton junior); "convulsions" (John Robinson and Margaret Isabella Robinson); "typhoid and hepatitis" (Frederick Cotton senior); "teething and convulsions" (Robert Robson Cotton); "typhoid fever" (George Ward and Joseph Nattrass); and simply "fever" (Charles Edward Cotton).

The distinction between typhoid and typhus had only been clinically established in England by Sir William Jenner between 1847 and 1851, after his series of investigations into what was known to the Victorians as "continued fever" at the London Fever Hospital. However, despite Jenner's

---

4. *Ibid.*

best efforts, Victorian doctors regularly confused typhus with typhoid, and some tended to use these descriptions interchangeably. It is also the case that several presenting symptoms are common — such as fever and headache — and that both diseases also produce a rash. Indeed, one contemporary medical text — *Smith's Family Physician* — published in 1873 by William Henry Smith, specifically suggested that typhoid fever "resembles in many respects Typhus Fever", and also that "a striking characteristic of typhoid fever is the prevalence of diarrhoea". As the late British medical historian Professor Roy Porter has put it, "industrial towns bred myriad fevers. Some were readily identifiable", and in this category he placed smallpox, diphtheria, measles and chickenpox. However,

> Other maladies, including what we now call typhoid and typhus were harder to distinguish amid the ceaseless surge of fevers which, in a time of pre-bacteriology, passed under names like "putrid fever". Involving severe diarrhoea and dysentery, "enteric fevers" were associated with the urban poor.[5]

In short, despite what Whitehead claims on behalf of Dr Gammage, it was perfectly possible for doctors to get their diagnosis wrong, and for them to have regularly confused typhus fever with typhoid fever. Perhaps all of this would suggest that Dr Gammage was actually dealing with a case of typhoid fever, rather than with the typhus which he had listed as the cause of William's death, given that diarrhoea is also specifically mentioned on the death certificate.

We should also note that the cause of death listed for James Robinson — who would die in April 1867 — was recorded as "continued fever", which was another generic term sometimes used by the Victorians for both typhus and typhoid, although the other death certificates would seem to indicate that the various doctors who attended Mary Ann's dying family members suspected typhoid, and not typhus. They had compelling, local reasons for doing so. Even as late as the 1890s, it was specifically mentioned in various contemporary medical commentaries that typhoid — not typhus — was unduly prevalent in "that tract of ground that runs along the

---

5.   Porter, R. (1997), *The Greatest Benefit to Mankind: A Medical History from Antiquity to the Present*, London: Fontana, p.402.

east side of Northumberland and Durham, from Morpeth in the north to Middlesborough and Guisborough in the south."[6]

Looked at this way, it would seem that defending Cotton on the basis of what was recorded on William's, and the second Margaret Jane's death certificates is not as strong a defence as Whitehead imagines, and that it was perfectly possible for Dr Gammage to have simply made a misdiagnosis—even if he was adamant about that diagnosis. He would not be the first, nor indeed the last Victorian doctor either to use the terms "typhus fever" and "typhoid fever" interchangeably, or to have believed that typhus was actually typhoid. Added to this we know that the north east remained one of the few places in the country where typhoid fever was still prevalent well into the 1890s. The benefit to Mary Ann of this continued and marked presence of typhoid fever in Northumberland is obvious. Most doctors would suspect typhoid fever when they encountered a patient with a rash, high fever, convulsions, diarrhoea and vomiting, when in fact Cotton was using arsenic.

There is one further issue to consider about Whitehead's steadfast defence of Cotton. Namely, the deaths that he is prepared to see as simply those that might have occurred naturally had very clear benefits to Mary Ann. They did not happen at inconvenient times, as one might have expected if we were dealing with random events. A child, a lover, or a husband always died at the most opportune moment—at least as far as Cotton was concerned. In other words, a death occurred when Mary Ann wanted to move on with her life, and felt that her current husband, lover, or even her children were getting in her way. The second Margaret Jane died in April 1865, and was more than likely murdered so that Cotton could try and cement her relationship with Joseph Nattrass, who would have been less likely to have taken Mary Ann as a partner if she had two children in tow. No doubt Isabella Jane would have gone the same way had not Cotton's mother offered to look after the child. And is there not something tragic about Isabella's short life in that, when she once again returned to live with her mother—who by then had started another new relationship—it was only a matter of some six weeks before she succumbed

---

6.   Quoted in Hardy, A (1998), "On the Cusp: Epidemiology and Bacteriology at the Local Government Board, 1890-1905", *Medical History*, 42: 328-346, p. 332.

to "gastric fever"? If Isabella is the "my Dear Child" referred to in her letter to Henry Holdforth, Cotton's ability to reshape the past to suit her
needs is frankly breathtaking. Even so Whitehead, rather too forgivingly,
suggests that Isabella's murder is "not proven".

Back to Sunderland as a Nurse

Mary Ann only lasted a few months in Seaham Harbour. Whatever had
attracted her there in the first place did not live up to its original promise,
and it is very clear that what didn't develop, at least at this stage, was her
relationship with Joseph Nattrass. When she moved from Sunderland,
she may, or may not have realised that Nattrass was already married to
Catherine Tempest (whom Appleton wrongly identifies as Mary Thubron),
and who according to the 1861 census was living with his wife at Pattison's
Buildings. Perhaps Mary Ann had simply thought that by being in the
same town as Nattrass—and without any children around to cramp her
style—it would have been easier to have cemented their relationship. This
does not seem to have worked, and in any event Nattrass and Catherine
moved to the Shildon area to find work. Catherine was to die three years
later, and her death was once more to open the door for Nattrass to link up
with Mary Ann. Catherine died childless, and perhaps this is significant.
Could it have been that Mary Ann's fecundity had been an attraction to
Nattrass, for there would have been three children in her house in Sunderland when in all likelihood he first met Cotton? He may not have wanted
these children, but perhaps he did want his own. In any event, at Seaham
Harbour, the relationship between them did not progress.

There is some evidence to suggest that, in the brief time that she had
lived in Seaham Harbour, Mary Ann had tried to make her living as a
dressmaker, and Whitehead speculates that she may also have worked as a
nurse at the local hospital, which at the time existed in North Terrace. He
further suggests that she may have worked as a prostitute too. While there
is no evidence to support this, Mary Ann would not have been the first,
nor indeed will she be the last woman to resort to selling sexual services
in a port town to make some money.[7] What can be substantiated is that

7.   In a report in the *Northern Echo* of 22 March 1873, for example, there is a discussion about
     the identity of the father of the baby daughter that Mary Ann had while she was in

in the early summer of 1865 she returned to Sunderland, where she took a job as a nurse at the hospital which then existed in Chester Road—which was a former workhouse, and which had been designed to administer to the infirm and elderly poor, but in due course would become the nucleus of the old Sunderland General Hospital.

It is at this stage that nursing enters Mary Ann's story in a more formal way (she had already been a nursemaid), although Whitehead suggests that a nurse was "in truth little more than a skivvy and not regarded as a trained professional."[8] There is some truth in this, but we should also qualify his judgement. First, all Victorian nurses—whether trained or otherwise—were required to undertake a great deal of housework in hospital, given that an emphasis on sanitation demanded cleanliness and discipline. As a consequence women who had had experience of domestic service were naturally drawn to nursing, and the gradual change in the social origins of nurses really only came towards the end of the century.[9] Even so, partly through the admiration of the Victorians for Florence Nightingale as a result of the work that she had done during the Crimean War (1854-1856), nursing was becoming more professionalised, and increasingly nurses were seen as having status. Indeed the view that nurses were old, weak, drunk, dirty and too disreputable to do anything else, and that nursing was not a respectable profession that decent women should follow, was largely exaggerated by Nightingale and by her fellow reformers so as to reinforce, and enhance the changes that were ushered in during the 1850s and 1860s.

Nightingale's *Notes on Nursing* was published in 1859, with its emphasis on the need for nurses to have a thorough training in nursing theory and practice, and in which she argued that nursing was not "little more than the administration of medicines and poultices", but should "signify the proper use of fresh air, light, warmth, cleanliness, quiet, and the proper

Durham gaol. The paper suggested that "rumours point to men yet living in the neighbourhood who are supposed, not without reason, to have been 'over kind' to use the old phrase, with Mrs Cotton, who, as all know by this time, was by no means too strict in her notions of modesty." The paper does not identify these men, nor provide evidence to support this allegation, but the idea that Cotton had been "by no means too strict in her notions of modesty" is a recurring rumour after her arrest, trial and sentence.

8.   Whitehead, *op cit*, p.24.

9.   Granshaw, L (1992). "The Rise of the Modern Hospital in Britain", in A Wear (ed.) *Medicine in Society: Historical Essays*, pps. 197-218. Cambridge: Cambridge University Press.

selection and administration of diet".[10] The nurse was the key weapon in the hygiene war, and specifically in the fight against dirt, which was seen as the cause of disease. In 1860 the first nurse training school was set up in St Thomas's Hospital in London, and was established in part with donations from members of the public who wanted to pay tribute to Nightingale's work at Scutari.[11] Of course, the changes being advocated by Nightingale, and the gradual and growing professionalism of nursing would take time to become widespread, but as the hospital increasingly moved from the margins to the centre of health care, more nurses were recruited, and nursing was increasingly seen as a suitable vocation for a woman. These changes were undoubtedly underway by the time that Mary Ann returned to Sunderland.

Second, it was not just nurses, but the medical profession more generally which had to fight to become accepted in the eyes of the Victorians. Doctors, for example, were not accorded the same social status as lawyers, and Porter has described them at the time as "self-employed petty capitalists" in a market that was competitive, and insecure. He also argued that "the small-time practitioner might not be very different from the shopkeepers he looked down upon—indeed he might actually call the practice his 'shop', earning his daily bread by dispensing brightly coloured medicines".[12] These observations are worth bearing in mind when considering other aspects of Mary Ann's story, both in Sunderland and in West Auckland when she would come into contact with doctors, and challenge their conclusions.

Finally, the growing acceptance and professionalism of nursing specifically, and medicine more generally, was intimately bound up with changing Victorian attitudes towards the institution of the hospital. Rapid industrialisation and urban expansion meant that the hospital increasingly became central to how people were treated. Whereas the pre-Victorian generation would have expected to have been treated in their own home—especially if they had money—by the end of Victoria's reign most people who were sick would have gone into hospital. They would also have expected to have come out again, having been cured. This was a remarkable change in a

---

10. Quoted in Porter, *op cit*, p.378.
11. Mitton, L (2010), *The Victorian Hospital*, Oxford: Shire Publications.
12. Porter, *op cit*, p.348.

relatively short period of time. Hospitals used to carry a social stigma to the Victorians, and there was a very clear understanding that the "undeserving poor" who were sick would have to go into the workhouse infirmaries. On the other hand, the "deserving poor"—those who could work—would be admitted to a "voluntary" (in that they were not being compelled to be there) hospital. These latter types of hospitals were often established by local dignitaries as a public way of demonstrating charity—possibly in the hope of buying salvation in the hereafter, and more immediately social status in the here and now—and were run by an elected Board of Governors of local worthies. Patients would receive their treatment free of charge, but would first have to find a benefactor who would issue them with an admission ticket, and so it was the governors and not the doctors who decided who should admitted.

The hospital where Mary Ann worked in Sunderland grew out of the reforms generated by the 1834 Poor Law, and more specifically the Bishop-wearmouth Workhouse at Gill Bridge Avenue. As Sunderland developed as a mining, boat building and railway centre, the old workhouse and its infirmary soon proved incapable of meeting the demand for places as those who could not compete with the demands of industrial capitalism fell by the wayside, or who by force of circumstance did not have labour to sell. Land was therefore purchased in Hylton Road, and a new institution was opened in 1857 with beds to cope with up to 300 elderly poor and infirm. The Hylton Road buildings gradually spread along Kayll Road, until a new entrance in Chester Road was opened.[13] In short, Cotton worked in what had once been a workhouse infirmary, where doctors were salaried, and conditions were often grim. Appleton notes that the full title of the hospital was The Sunderland Infirmary, House of Recovery for the Cure of Contagious Fever, Dispensary and Humane Society, and that Mary Ann worked in the House of Recovery—the "fever house"—which had 20 beds.[14] There was in fact an outbreak of typhoid fever in 1865. He goes on:

> Patients paid one-and-sixpence a day; the parish paid for paupers. Bedsheets
> were changed once a fortnight, and patients' linen every four days. There were

13. Corfe, *op cit*, in *Chapter 1*, pps. 72-73.
14. Appleton, *op cit*, in the *Introduction*, pps. 54-55.

no baths, and, when possible, patients were taken in cabs to the public baths. A nurse was paid a shilling a day, plus board and lodging when on duty. She had to wash out her ward by seven in the morning during the summer, and by eight in the winter, and serve breakfast within the next hour. Beverages, even for children, were beer, beer gruel, barley gruel and water. There was a small isolation ward. There was a small room upstairs for operations. Medicines were left in this room for the nurses to collect, at any time of the day or night.[15]

Husband Number Two — George Ward

It was while she was working at the hospital that Mary Ann met her second husband. George Ward was an engineer, a single man, and described by Appleton as "well built and [a] normally strong man".[16] The description "engineer" should not be taken too literally, and on their marriage certificate — reproduced by Whitehead — Ward was obviously illiterate, and so signed his name with a cross. He was likely to have been one of the "deserving poor" — a manual labourer, perhaps a stoker who looked after an engine (on his death certificate he is described as "an engine driver in a steam tug") — and who would normally have been able to have found work. Mary Ann, on the other hand signed her own name, although the section beside her for "Rank or Profession" was left blank. Clearly, Nightingale's reforms had not yet reached Sunderland, either that or Cotton — perhaps even the Church authorities themselves — did not regard nursing as a profession. Even so, several doctors were impressed by her work at the hospital, and during the typhoid outbreak in 1865 the doctor in charge had praised Mary Ann's skill, describing her as one of the best nurses. Perhaps that skill had also impressed Ward.

The couple were married on 28th August 1865 at St Peter's in Monkwearmouth, although no one from Cotton's family attended the service. James Potts, the groom from the preceding ceremony, had to act as their witness. It is interesting to speculate as to why Mary Ann didn't ask her mother (who at this time was still looking after Isabella Jane), or anyone else from her family to attend, especially as this was her first church wedding — her marriage to William Mowbray having taken place in a register

---

15. *Ibid*, p.55.
16. *Ibid*, p.55.

office in Newcastle. Perhaps this was simply a marriage of convenience; a way of bouncing back after the disappointment of Nattrass? After all, it was only a matter of a few months since she had been living and working in Seaham Harbour. Both George and Mary Ann gave their address as Dame Dorothy Street, near to the church, but they soon moved to 5 Ettrick Place in the heart of old Sunderland, which was destroyed during the Second World War. After her arrest, neighbours remembered that Cotton had worshipped at the Methodist Sans Street Mission Hall, which was within walking distance of Ettrick Place.

It does not seem to have been a happy marriage, and significantly Mary Ann had no children by Ward. Nor is he mentioned in her cast of characters in her letter to Henry Holdforth. Appleton and Whitehead speculate as to what might have been the source of this unhappiness, and both suggest that Ward "was a disappointment sexually".[17] This conclusion clearly feeds into the popular stereotype of female offenders being sexually voracious, and thus "doubly deviant". In other words, they break gender stereotypes by offending, and by being interested in sex which, presumably, is viewed as something that only men are, or should have interests about. However, as far as Cotton and Ward are concerned, how can the nature of their sexual relationship be proved one way or another? Of course, the source of their unhappiness might simply have been that, after his illness, Ward found it impossible to work, and that Cotton grew increasingly frustrated at having to look after her new husband. We do know that Ward was receiving four shillings a week poor relief, and therefore money must have been tight. In any event, George died at the age of 33 on 20th October 1866, and the cause of his death was listed as "English Cholera and Typhoid Fever". He and Mary Ann had been married for only 15 months.

During their time together there were a number of incidents that are worth considering further, as they reveal a little about Mary Ann's abilities as a murderer, and also her willingness to challenge people in authority—in this case doctors. Given Ward's continuing ill health he was seen by a number of doctors, including Dr Dixon, our old friend Dr Gammage, and Dr Maling, who was a doctor at the hospital where Mary Ann had

---

17.   Appleton, *op cit*, p. 56; Whitehead, *op cit*, p.25.

worked. The doctors were puzzled as to what was causing Ward's ill health, although his symptoms, which included diarrhoea, stomach complaints and tingling to the hands and feet, were consistent with arsenic poisoning. Dr Dixon in particular gave Ward a thorough examination, and saw him on three consecutive days. This close attention must have scared Mary Ann. Dixon thought that George's liver was enlarged and congested, and suggested to Mary Ann that she should apply 12 leeches, which, given her nursing background, she was able to do. The following day Dixon sent his assistant to check on Ward's condition, and he discovered that the leech bites had bled quite heavily. As a result the assistant changed the dressing, and the following day Dixon himself went back to check on Ward. When he arrived at Ettrick Place he discovered that Dr Maling was already there attending to Ward, and Mary Ann tried to explain that a neighbour had gone to fetch Dr Maling, and that no sleight was intended on Dr Dixon's competence.

Dr Dixon did continue to see Ward for a number of days, but he gradually withdrew his services as it was obvious that Mary Ann preferred Dr Maling, although Maling too would eventually stop treating George. In May 1866 George complained to one of the relieving officers who were responsible for administering the poor relief, that he blamed Dr Dixon, and in particular his inattention to him at the time of the application of the leeches, for his continued ill health. He also implied that if Dr. Maling had not attended to him, and stitched up the leech holes that he might have died. The relieving officer took this matter seriously, and the complaint was discussed at the Sunderland Board of Guardians meeting.

Boards of guardians had been set up by the 1834 Poor Law to oversee the running of poor relief in the community, and acting as a guardian — which was an elected post — offered local tradesmen the opportunity to make useful social and business contacts. We should also remember Roy Porter's observation that doctors at this time were self-employed petty capitalists in a competitive and insecure market, and therefore a complaint of this sort — and the scrutiny that it would attract — could cause a great deal of trouble for Dr Dixon. Indeed, the whole matter was picked up by the local press, and Dixon was forced to make a longish statement called "Facts in the Case of George Ward". The complaint made against Dixon was eventually dismissed, and as a result George lost a great deal of local sympathy, prior to losing his life.

Had Dr Dixon been on the cusp of discovering what was really causing George's illness? Appleton certainly thought so, although Whitehead questions why Mary Ann would have called in two other doctors if she had been poisoning George—Drs Maling and Gammage—and suggests that Cotton was merely attempting "to rally medical help to her dying man".[18] In trying to understand her actions, we can compare Mary Ann's behaviour with that of another nurse—Beverly Allitt—who murdered four children, and attempted to murder nine others in 1991 at Grantham General Hospital.[19] Allitt was able to repeatedly kill, and attack the children in her care, while all the time the doctors and the other nurses around her remained baffled as to what was causing these illnesses, and deaths. Like Drs Dixon, Maling and Gammage before them, the staff at Grantham never suspected foul play until tests proved that the children had been injected with large quantities of exogenous insulin, which pointed to the fact that there was a killer at large on the ward.

We now know that Allitt suffered from Munchausen Syndrome—a term coined in the 1950s to describe a particular form of hospital addiction. The sufferer often visits hospital with stories of medical disorder, usually supported by pathological evidence, which has often been falsified. So too there is Munchausen Syndrome by Proxy, a term introduced in 1977 by Professor Roy Meadow, whereby the fictitious injury, or manifestation of illness is inflicted on others—usually a child. About a quarter of those who are subsumed under the label Munchausen Syndrome by Proxy have themselves Munchausen Syndrome. It is not being suggested that Cotton had Munchausen Syndrome, but Allitt's case does demonstrate that another female serial killer who also worked as a nurse, was equally prepared to commit her crimes in full view of the medical authorities. This must also have given Allitt, and her Victorian fore-runner Cotton, a great sense of power; a feeling that they were invincible. They could kill, but remain undetected, and in Cotton's case she also benefited both financially and socially, given that the deaths of her loved ones would have attracted a

18. Whitehead, *op cit*, p.25.
19. Wilson (2009), *op cit*, in the *Introduction*, 234-244.

great deal of public sympathy.

Husband Number Three — James Robinson

Just a month after George's death, 27-year-old Hannah Robinson also died, leaving behind her husband James, and their five, young children. The children ranged in ages from nine-years-old, to nine months: William, the eldest; Elizabeth, aged eight; James, who was five-years-old and named after his father; the toddler Mary Jane who was two-years-old; and, finally, the baby John. James Robinson was a shipwright and shipyard foreman in the Sunderland suburb of Pallion. While he had three sisters, it was also clear that he would need some help in bringing up the children. He advertised for a housekeeper. Mary Ann applied for and got the job, and moved into his house in Grace Street, Pallion a few days before Christmas 1866. By the end of April the following year, Mary Ann was pregnant with Robinson's child, her mother had been murdered, and John, James and Elizabeth Robinson had all been killed, as had Cotton's own daughter Isabella Jane. As is obvious from what she would write to Henry Holdforth, events at Pallion were to remain a source of anger and irritation to Cotton for the rest of her life, perhaps because James Robinson was the only one of her four husbands who would survive her.

The first child to die was the baby John Robinson, but given what his father would later tell the police—which was widely reported in the local press—this has led to some debate as to whether Mary Ann was actually responsible for this death. According to an interview given by James Robinson prior to Cotton's trial and execution, he indicated that Mary Ann had moved into their house on the 20th December, and that John was dead by the following day. Whitehead suggests that Mary Ann could not have been responsible for this death as she "barely had time to get her coat off never mind pulling off such a killing undetected and the child was attended by a doctor who neither saw nor suspected anything amiss".[20] However, as the previous discussion about Beverly Allitt has shown, some serial killers are quite happy to kill in full view of doctors, and, more than this, Allitt would often attack during the few moments that the doctor

---

20. Whitehead, *op cit*, p. 26.

and other nurses had left the attending room, leaving her alone with the child. Britain's most prolific serial killer—Dr Harold Shipman—killed his first victim, Eva Lyons, in March 1975, within five minutes of visiting her in her home, and all the time maintaining a conversation with her husband.[21] Finally, we should note that John's cause of death was registered as "convulsions", which is one of the classic signs of arsenic poisoning.

Why would Cotton want to take a risk of this kind, especially as she had literally only just started to work for her new employer? Nor would she have benefited financially from John's death, for if he had been insured what little monies that would have accrued would have gone to his father. However, we need to remember that for Cotton taking John's life would not have been a "risk"—murder was by this stage a pattern of behaviour that she was comfortable with, and had become a technique to manage the circumstances that she found herself in; one, moreover, which she had all but perfected. And would not the fact that she had just arrived in the Robinson household have provided her with the perfect cover? Rather than have to deal with a no doubt demanding infant, and an all too real reminder of his recently departed mother, far better to dispatch him quickly, and in doing so make her working life that much easier. Murder had simply become the way of managing, and ordering, the world around her so as to best satisfy Cotton's needs, and what she thought of as her interests. In much the same way that Harold Shipman was to become one of the most popular doctors in Manchester, because of his willingness to visit his patients in their own homes, rather than ask them to come to his surgery, Cotton arrived as Robinson's housekeeper, and provided him with her own solution to restructuring his home and his family.

Mary Ann must have been persuasive and plausible, for by February 1867 she was pregnant with Robinson's child. Given the social conventions of the day, this would have meant that it was almost inevitable that she would become Robinson's wife, and therefore able to live in some comfort. The couple were duly married on 11th August 1867 at Bishopwearmouth Parish Church—when Cotton was five and a half months pregnant—and on the marriage certificate Mary Ann gave her surname as "Mowbray". By

---

21. Wilson (2009), *op cit*, p. 254.

now George Ward had been conveniently forgotten. No one from Cotton's family, or past life attended this service, and nor did Robinson's three sisters attend, given that they were clearly suspicious of Mary Ann. As she was later to write, "he [James Robinson] had 3 sisters i never Wos Looked on as i should be With non of them". Robinson's sisters had every right to be suspicious, especially after the events of March and April.

In early March, Mary Ann was contacted by her step-father to come and help him look after her mother, Margaret Stott, who had become ill, and was now living at Seaham Colliery, some five miles from Pallion. Mary Ann must have been slightly worried, given that she had just started her affair with James Robinson, and would not have wanted to have been gone for too long when she was in the process of cementing their relationship further. There was also the small matter of Isabella Jane Mowbray, who had been looked after by the Stotts since Mary Ann's move to Seaham Harbour. Had she told Robinson about this child? Given how she would later describe herself on her marriage certificate she does not seem to have mentioned George Ward to him, and so perhaps Isabella Jane was a mystery too. So Mary Ann must have had some mixed feelings as she went to nurse her mother, who died on 15th March 1867 from hepatitis, only nine days after Cotton had arrived. The death took several of the neighbours by surprise, and Mary Ann had in any event not endeared herself to them by prophesying her mother's demise, and laying claim to some bed linen and clothing. There does not seem to have been any love lost between her and her step-father George Stott, and there is some indication that he ordered Mary Ann out of his house, and to take Isabella Jane with her. George would next see his step-daughter in Durham Gaol, as he was Mary Ann's final visitor before her execution.

There was no *post mortem* conducted on Margaret Stott, but her cause of death is recorded as "hepatitis". Hepatitis is a disease of the liver, but would have presenting symptoms such as fever, abdominal discomfort, vomiting and diarrhoea, and these are similar to the symptoms produced by arsenic poisoning. We should also note that Margaret's neighbours were surprised by how quickly she died, with the implication that Mary Ann must have helped her mother on her way so that she could return to Pallion. It is also interesting to note that this is the first time that we have some record of Cotton prophesying the deaths of her loved ones. Was this just a mechanism to structure the expectations of neighbours, so that they would not become too suspicious when death subsequently occurred? And we should also remember that as a nurse Mary Ann's views might have been given greater credibility by those that she spoke to. Perhaps this prophesying is merely another manifestation of her belief in her power to shape the world according to her needs, and interests. In any event, she would later push this type of behaviour too far, and her prophecies about another death would become the basis for her arrest, trial and execution.

Mary Ann took Isabella Jane back with her to Pallion, but within a few weeks the child was dead. In fact, there were three deaths in the ten day period between 20th April and the end of the month, when Isabella Jane died of "gastric fever". James Robinson, by then aged six, died first of "continued fever", followed four days later by his eight-year-old sister Elizabeth, whose cause of death is recorded as "gastric fever" — the same cause as Isabella Jane. All three children had been insured for small sums of money, and all three were likely to have been poisoned. Mary Ann, as she had done with her mother's friends in Seaham Harbour, again prepared her neighbours in Pallion for what was about to happen, and once more committed these murders despite the fact that the children were regularly being seen by a doctor. Their symptoms included rolling about in bed, foaming at the mouth, and vomiting. We can only imagine the agony that they must have endured. As a result of these deaths, remaining in his house on the 1st May 1867 would have been James, Mary Ann, the oldest boy William Robinson, and his sister Mary Jane Robinson. It is hard not to reach the conclusion that Mary Ann was clearing the house of unwanted children, as she had done previously prior to her move to Seaham Harbour, and of course by that stage she was also pregnant with Robinson's child. Their baby was subsequently born on 29th November 1867, and baptised Margaret Isabella Robinson on 2nd February 1868. Like many of her brothers and sisters before her, she was dead as a result of "convulsions" within a matter of weeks. James and Mary Ann were to have another child together — a boy called George — who was born in June 1869, and who would be one of the two of her 12 children that would survive Mary Ann.

While Robinson's three sisters may have been suspicious of Cotton,

Robinson himself always steadfastly defended his wife, at least until his financial affairs took a turn for the worse in 1869. Mary Ann was first accused of doctoring a building society passbook belonging to James to the extent of £5. In effect she kept the money that she should have put into the society, and then altered the book to make it appear as if she had made the deposit. Initially James defended his wife, but it soon became clear that this was not Mary Ann's only fraud. William Robinson informed his father that his step-mother had regularly sent him out to pawn clothes and other household possessions, and the Home Office files also show that Cotton had taken £50 from James's bank account, and had run up other debts of £60. Inevitably there were rows, and according to Robinson, Mary Ann then tried to persuade him to insure himself and the three children. He refused—a refusal which probably saved his life and the lives of the children. For reasons best known to her, Mary Ann moved out of the house in Pallion, taking baby George with her, and there was some contemporary speculation that she may have been trying to raise the money that she owed from George Stott. This hardly seems likely, given the state of her relationship with her step-father. James boarded up their house, having decided to sell it, and temporarily moved in with his sister in Coronation Street, prior to setting up home in Rosannah Street.

However, there was one further twist in Mary Ann's involvement with Robinson. According to the Home Office file—in an account that differs slightly from that provided by Appleton—Mary Ann returned to Sunderland in December 1869 with baby George. We can't be certain why she did so, but she left George at a friend's house in Johnson Street, while she went out to "post a letter". She never returned, but the baby was eventually reunited with his father early in 1870. Later, while she was awaiting execution, she wrote to James asking him to visit her, and to bring the baby, but Robinson refused to do so. Who can blame him?

'I did not wish to part from him'

If we return once more to Mary Ann's letter to Henry Holdforth, there are some clues as to how Cotton interpreted the various events at the end of her relationship with Robinson. The relevant passage from the letter suggests:

…this last 6 years my Life has been miserable for i married A Man they call James Robinson he had 3 sisters i never Wos Looked on as i should be With non of them he and i not Ergree We had some Words About sum money and i Left the house fore a few days I did not wish to part from him As i had no home i went to south hetton stayed ther When i returned ther wos no home for me he had sold what he did not Want And tooke the othe things and Went to Live With his sister so i might go where i Liked …

If we ignore her editorial about the cause of her disagreement with Robinson—"We had some Words About sum money"—which is a rather partial account of what had actually happened, it is interesting to note that even though it was she who left their house in Grace Street, what she would later write indicates that she had also expected to return. Her phrase "i left the house fore a few days I did not wish to part from him", also helps us to understand one issue that rightly exercised Appleton and Whitehead—why did Mary Ann spurn this opportunity to change? Life with Robinson presented Mary Ann with the real possibility of establishing a comfortable and pleasant existence. Even so, through her own actions, she seems to have spurned what was on offer. However, if we accept that she had only gone "fore a few days", perhaps in the belief that matters would run their course and blow over, we are at least presented with behaviour that is rational to us, and which begins to make some sense. In other words, she had not wanted her relationship with Robinson to end, and that was why her last six years had been "miserable".

The phrase that "ther wos no home for me he had sold what he did not Want", also suggests that Mary Ann did indeed return to Pallion, and no doubt found her former home in Grace Street boarded up. Faced with this *fait accompli,* and perhaps also aware that James was now living with one of his sisters, with whom she did not get on, Mary Ann accepted her fate, and moved elsewhere. As she puts it "i might go where I liked".

But this type of reasoning only takes us so far, and there are other issues too that we need to consider about Mary Ann's time with James. In particular, why did she feel that she needed to steal money from her husband, and what did she actually do with the money that she had stolen? Cotton doesn't seem to have been a spendthrift, and perhaps the greatest luxury that we know for certain that she enjoyed was having other women clean for her. This indulgence could hardly account for the monies that she stole from Robinson, but there is no evidence of Cotton drinking to excess, buying clothes, gambling, or indeed saving the money for the proverbial "rainy day". Nor do we really know why she felt compelled to steal. However, perhaps we shouldn't really expect serial killers to make sense; we shouldn't expect them to be rational. Harold Shipman, for example, was caught because he made an obviously bungled attempt to forge the will of his last victim—Kathleen Grundy—whom he murdered on 24th June 1998. Kathleen's daughter, Angela Woodruff, was a lawyer, and she was suspicious of the will as soon as she saw it, and so took her suspicions to the police. Like Cotton, Shipman hadn't actually needed the money, and so perhaps we simply have to see these risky financial behaviours as a subset of the more general, risky behaviour of serial murder. After all, if you are repeatedly taking other people's lives and not being caught, it must be tempting to think that you can also take their money. Looked at this way, Cotton's thefts are merely another aspect of her feeling, and need for power, and invincibility.

There is one final issue that we should consider about Mary Ann's time with James. How did she choose the order in which to kill the children under her care? Why murder James and Elizabeth Robinson, but let William and Mary Jane live? After all, it must have been easier to have managed eight-year-old Elizabeth, than three-year-old Mary Jane, a fact that Whitehead draws attention to. Why abandon baby George, and then later ask to see him? Once again we should not necessarily think that there is any rational decision making going on behind these decisions, and that they might often have been simply the outcome of circumstances. William Robinson was also clearly useful to Cotton, in that he could be sent to the pawnbrokers, and run other errands for her too, which clearly the younger children could not. Perhaps she simply preferred Mary Jane to Elizabeth, or James had attracted her ire? Might she have thought that George was a pawn to use so as to get back together with Robinson?

The serial killer Dennis Nilsen, whom we have previously encountered observing his dead grandfather laid out in his mother's front room prior to his burial, would either kill, or allow his victims to survive an attack—sometimes for reasons that defied logic. For example, he murdered the Canadian tourist Kenneth Ockenden in December 1979, even though Kenneth was quite different to the other types of victims that Nilsen targeted, and who was accordingly very quickly reported as missing. On the other hand, Paul Nobbs and Douglas Stewart survived attacks. Paul was a student at the University of London, and the day after having been attacked by Nilsen, and still feeling unwell, went to see a doctor at University College Hospital who suggested to him that someone had tried to strangle him. Paul was amazed, but later gave evidence against Nilsen. So too Douglas reported Nilsen's attack on him to the police almost as soon as he left Nilsen's house, although no action was taken.[22] As with Cotton's choice of victims, we might also ask why Nilsen allowed Paul and Douglas to survive, but decided to kill Kenneth. None of these decisions makes much sense, but then again why should they? Serial killers are by their very nature both irrational, and often totally incomprehensible.

The Wandering Months

Mary Ann's story really begins again in West Auckland, where in all likelihood she moved to in April 1871. However, the intervening months between her leaving Robinson and April 1871 are not without incident, and are worth some scrutiny. After her arrest, local newspapers were filled with stories about Cotton surviving during this period by prostitution, or from the proceeds of crime. One story has her living with a sailor, and then stealing his possessions. However, there is no hard evidence for this. She may also have returned to Murton, or to South Hetton (as she indicates in her letter to Henry Holdforth)—and perhaps she even attempted to track down "gorge hall"? What is more certain is that we know that at the beginning of this period Cotton seems to have worked for the wealthy Quaker, Edward Backhouse—who would later plead with the Home Secretary for Mary Ann's life—at the Smyrna House Home for Fallen Women, in Borough Road, Sunderland, and Appleton believes that she may have been in charge of the laundry.[23] There is evidence to support this assertion in the form of testimony given by another "fever nurse" called

22. *Ibid*, pps.151-160.
23. Appleton, *op cit*, p. 64.

Isabella Smith, who had worked with Cotton in Sunderland, and would later give evidence against her at Mary Ann's trial. Isabella seems to have remained in contact with Mary Ann, and even visited her in Pallion.

Mary Ann was given a reference for this job by Dr. Maling, and so events over the death of George Ward had clearly been forgotten. We also know that she worked as housekeeper for Dr Hefferman, a naturalised German doctor who lived in Whitworth Terrace, Spennymoor, in mid-1870. Hefferman was pleased with Cotton's efforts—the house was neat and tidy—although Mary Ann, once again, hired help to clean the house. When she left Spennymoor, Dr Hefferman noticed that a watch, other jewellery, and some money was missing, although he blamed his groom for these thefts, rather than Mary Ann, and the poor man was sacked.

It was also during this period that Frederick Cotton appears on the scene. Mary Ann was introduced to Frederick by his sister Margaret Cotton, who was a friend from her time working in service at Edward Potter's house in South Hetton, when they both would have been in their teens, and when Mary Ann's surname was "Mowbray". Frederick Cotton lived at North Walbottle, which was a small mining community six miles west of Newcastle, with his wife Adelaide, and their four children: Margaret, aged eleven, and no doubt named after her aunt; nine-year-old Adelaide Jane; Frederick Jnr., aged eight; and five-year-old Charles Edward Cotton.

Mary Ann had nothing to do with the first few deaths in the Cotton household, even if they did create the opportunity for her to move in with Frederick. Margaret, the eldest child, died of "typhus fever" on 9th October 1869, and Frederick's wife, Adelaide, later died of "consumption" on 19th December. Their remaining daughter, Adelaide Jane, also died of "typhus fever" in January 1870. After Frederick's wife died, his sister, Margaret, gave up her work as a laundry maid at Stanhope Rectory, and came to help her brother out at Walbottle. The Rector of Stanhope would later state that Margaret, who had never married, had about £60 in the bank—which would pass to her brother if she died—and that she had regularly spoken about Mary Ann to the other servants.[24] Margaret was thus in the way if Mary Ann wanted to take over the Cotton household, and was clearly

24. *Ibid*, p.65.

also relatively wealthy.

Mary Ann visited Walbottle in early 1870, and by April of that year was pregnant with Cotton's child. Their child—Robert Robson Cotton—was born in January 1871. Frederick's sister Margaret died on 25th March 1870, at the age of 38, after severe stomach pains, and the cause of her death was listed as "pleuropneumonia". Of course, the primary symptoms of pneumonia would include a cough, rapid heartbeat, and the patient would have difficulty breathing, but other symptoms such as fever, nausea, and vomiting are also common in some people, and these symptoms are also produced by arsenic poisoning. Margaret Cotton's death was clearly advantageous to Mary Ann, because this would allow her to take charge of Cotton's affairs, and also begin to cement her relationship with Frederick. He would also have inherited his sister's money. However, she briefly left Walbottle at this stage to work for Dr Hefferman in Spennymoor. Why did she move? Was there gossip in the town about Mary Ann's behaviour? Walbottle must have seemed very small and parochial to Mary Ann after Sunderland, and even Seaham Harbour. Or, perhaps she simply identified a good opportunity to move on, and would have explained away her pregnancy when the occasion arrived. We can't be certain, but by the summer of 1870 she decided to return to Walbottle—no doubt with the items that she had stolen from her former employer.

Mary Ann did not go immediately to Cotton's house, but used the services of some of his friends—Joseph and Frances Gallon, who would later be witnesses at Mary Ann and Frederick's wedding—to help to renew their relationship. Perhaps this does imply that there had been some disagreement with Cotton in April, and that the move to Spennymoor had been forced on Mary Ann. In any event, Mary Ann and Frederick were married on 17th September 1870 at St Andrew's Church, Newcastle. Later, in her prison cell, this would be the only crime that Mary Ann would admit to—she had committed bigamy, given that she was in fact still married to James Robinson, and therefore not free to have married Cotton. A few weeks after their marriage, Mary Ann insured Cotton's two sons with the Prudential, although any monies would pass to their father—if he was still alive.

There is one further incident to consider that was reported as having happened at Walbottle, prior to the Cottons moving to West Auckland,

and which may also have helped to prompt their move. The Home Office files, and several contemporary newspapers, mention that a number of pigs belonging to a neighbour of Frederick's had died suddenly, and Mary Ann was seen as being the cause of these deaths. Walbottle was a small community, and no doubt Mary Ann had already scandalised the neighbours by having moved into the recently bereaved Frederick's household. Perhaps she — or indeed Margaret — had spoken too freely about the past, embellishing just too many details about her life in Sunderland for the more modest people of Walbottle. And, after all, Mary Ann was pregnant with Frederick's child, just four months after Adelaide's death. As an outsider, and as a newcomer, she was an easy target to blame for some pigs dying unexpectedly. Of course, something which the good people of Walbottle would not have been aware of, Mary Ann did also know how to access arsenic, and may even have brought some with her, courtesy of Dr Hefferman.

What can we conclude about these months after leaving Robinson? It's hard not to escape the conclusion that Mary Ann returned to doing what she knew best. She used doctors — including Dr Maling and Dr Hefferman — and set herself up as a housekeeper, first for Hefferman, and then for Frederick Cotton. She stole when the occasion presented itself, and may even have poisoned her neighbour's pigs. She also used her friends, and specifically Margaret Cotton, but also the Gallons, who would become the witnesses to her bigamous marriage to Frederick. We can also be fairly certain that she continued to murder when she felt that was helpful to her circumstances. Margaret Cotton was soon dispatched so that Mary Ann could begin to take over the Cotton household, and, of course, she ensured that she was pregnant with Frederick's child almost as soon as Margaret was out of the way. After her marriage, she was quick to have Frederick Jnr and Charles Edward insured with the Prudential — almost as if she was signing their death warrants. A restlessness to move on, pregnancy, theft, poisoning and murder were all strategies that by this stage Mary Ann was well used to employing.

In any event, sometime after April 1871, Frederick, Mary Ann, Frederick Jnr, Charles Edward, and the baby Robert Robson Cotton, packed up their belongings, and headed to West Auckland. They probably moved at Mary Ann's suggestion, for there was an old lover waiting for her.

Chapter Three

A Death Too Far

"Among other public buildings in the town of Mudfog, it boasts of one which is common to most towns great or small, to wit, a workhouse; and in this workhouse there was born on a day and date which I need not trouble myself to repeat, inasmuch as it can be of no possible consequence to the reader, in this stage of the business at all events, the item of mortality whose name is prefixed to the head of this chapter. For a long time after he was ushered into his world of sorrow and trouble…"

Charles Dickens, *Oliver Twist*, Chapter The First (1838).

Charles Dickens, arguably our greatest ever novelist, died in 1870. Had he lived he would undoubtedly have written about Mary Ann Cotton, given his life-long interest in prisons and prisoners and, more generally, about crime and punishment.[1] Partly because of his own personal circumstances, Dickens had always championed the cause of the poor in Victorian England, and in *Oliver Twist*—his second novel which was serialised in monthly instalments between 1837-1839—he satirised the then controversial "New Poor Law" which had been created by the Poor Law Amendment Act of 1834. Oliver was a child of the workhouse—the practical manifestation of the Poor Law—and he was introduced to the reader struggling

---

1. For a general introduction to Dickens and his interest in crime and punishment see Phillip Collins (1962), *Dickens and Crime*, Basingstoke: The Macmillan Press. Both Peter Ackroyd (1990), *Dickens*, London: Sinclair-Stevenson and Michael Slater (2009), *Charles Dickens*, New Haven: Yale University Press are useful biographies of Dickens. I have also written about Dickens and Victorian prisons in David Wilson (2002), "Millbank, The Panopticon, and Their Victorian Audiences," *The Howard Journal of Criminal Justice*, Volume 41, Issue 4, pp.361-381, September, 2002. I used the Penguin Classics edition of *Oliver Twist*, published in 2002, and which was edited by Philip Horne.

for breath, having been brought into life through the efforts of the parish surgeon, who was contracted to provide medical treatment to the inmates of the workhouse, and, as Dickens suggested, "It remained a matter of considerable doubt whether the child would survive to bear any name at all".

The workhouse — "an unloved institution"[2] — was a recurring theme in Dickens's novels, and so in *Our Mutual Friend*, written towards the end of his life, for example, Dickens has an elderly woman die at the roadside rather than enter the dreaded place. Even so, for all its many failings, the workhouse was an attempt to solve a seemingly intractable problem — what to do about those people who were so poor that they had to be looked after by the rest of society. The Victorians recognised two types of "poor": the "impotent poor" who were very old, very young, the sick, blind or insane; and the "able bodied" poor who merely lacked work, and therefore could not support themselves. Only a small proportion of those in receipt of poor relief would actually be lodged in a workhouse, and most would receive "out relief". In 1837, for example, only eleven per cent of those who received poor relief were actually in a workhouse, and by 1844 while that number had increased to 15 per cent. This figure represented only 180,000 people, compared to nearly a million who received "out relief".[3]

An entire Victorian bureaucracy was created to supervise the New Poor Law, under the overall control of the central Poor Law Commission. The Poor Law Commission was in effect the first modern government department, and existed from 1834 until 1847, when it was replaced by the Poor Law Board, and thereafter by the Local Government Board in 1871, which had responsibilities for both health and the distribution of poor relief. Key players in this emerging bureaucracy were local Boards of Guardians — elected from ratepayers within those parishes which would come together to form a "union" to administer a workhouse — and overseers of the poor who were responsible for the day-to-day management of poor relief within any given parish. Allocating poor relief, or putting someone into a workhouse was, for a number of reasons, not a decision to be taken lightly, and as one historian has described it, "Few fates were less enviable than that of a 'juvenile pauper' — the infant, child or adolescent brought

---

2.   Longmate, N (2003) *The Workhouse: A Social History*, London: Pimlico, p. x.
3.   *Ibid*, p. 118.

up in an institution designed for the supposedly work-shy adult."[4]

The Auckland Poor Law Union had formally come into existence in 1837, and was overseen by a 40-strong elected Board of Guardians, representing the union's 33 constituent parishes and townships. Three members of the Board of Guardians represented West Auckland, where Cotton had moved to. The first workhouse used by the union was the former parish workhouse in Newgate Street, Bishop Auckland, but in 1855 a new workhouse was opened on the west side of Cockton Hill, at a cost of £5,000, and a further extension was built in 1865. It would have been to this workhouse that Charles Edward would have been sent, had Cotton got her way—not so much a child born in the workhouse, but rather a child that Mary Ann had wanted to be placed there—a move resisted by workhouse officials in the community—and which led directly to his death.[5] In any event, like Oliver, events surrounding Charles Edward and the workhouse, his troubles and his sorrows, and the various doctors and parish officers created by the Poor Law Amendment Act—and who would now come to dominate Mary Ann's story—have ensured that his name too has lived on in history and, more crucially, that Cotton's murderous ways came to an end.

West Auckland and the Murder of Joseph Nattrass

There were five Cottons who moved the 40 odd miles south from Walbottle to West Auckland—Frederick, Mary Ann, Frederick Jnr., Charles Edward, and the baby Robert Robson Cotton. Just over 12 months later the only Cotton still alive was Mary Ann. The family initially stayed at 20 Johnson Terrace, which has now been re-named as Darlington Road, and Frederick found work as a hewer at the West Auckland Colliery. As if by chance, Joseph Nattrass also lived in Johnson Terrace—where he lodged with a family by the name of Shaw—and like Frederick he too worked as a hewer at the West Auckland Colliery. We can be certain that Frederick knew nothing of his wife's previous history with his mining colleague Nattrass, but that the move south had in all likelihood been suggested by

4. *Ibid*, p. 165.
5. For an account of the early days of the new Bishop Auckland Workhouse, see Rose, D., (1970) "Bishop Auckland Poor Law Union, 1863-1866", *Durham Local History Society Bulletin*, pp.2-7.

Mary Ann so that she could renew this relationship. We also have to marvel both at how adept Mary Ann was in keeping track of her various friends and lovers in an age before the development of the telephone, and at her *sang froid* in believing that she could keep this relationship secret from her husband, and her neighbours. We can also safely assume that when she packed up her belongings to begin the move south, she would have known that it was only a matter of time before she would start to kill again.

Frederick Cotton was the first to die—on 2nd September 1871—and his cause of death was listed as "typhoid and hepatitis". He was only 40-years-old. Three months later Nattrass moved into 20 Johnson Terrace, and it was understood in the village that the couple were to marry, although we should also remember that in fact at this time Mary Ann was still married to James Robinson. This small detail notwithstanding, all of this might have been seen as the culmination of everything that Mary Ann had been plotting and planning since her first move to Seaham Harbour in January 1865; she had, at last, found a way to be with the man that she had been coveting for at least six years, and probably for much longer. In short Nattrass's attentions had finally been legitimately obtained, and this should have provided Mary Ann with the opportunity to "settle down". However, by this stage, it is obvious that Mary Ann didn't really know what she wanted, and that the attractions of murder had taken over her life.

Prior to Nattrass moving in with Mary Ann, she had advertised her services as a nurse, and was soon contracted to look after a bachelor called Quick-Manning (his first name has been lost to history), who was recovering from smallpox. Quick-Manning lived in Brookfield Cottage, which was also in Johnson Terrace, and he was employed as an excise officer at the local brewery. In other words, he was not a miner, and instead was shaped in the same social and economic mould as James Robinson. Nor did he have any children that needed to be looked after. Clearly Mary Ann did not want to pass up this further opportunity to move onwards and upwards in the world, but there was the small problem of Nattrass to deal with, and also the remainder of the Cotton family.

Between 10th March and 1st April 1872 Mary Ann struck three times, although it is likely that she would have been poisoning all three of her victims at the same time. Of course she would not have wanted all three to have died on the same day—it would have been too obvious and suspicious—and so she had obviously learned how to administer sub-lethal does of arsenic to her victims, and carefully calibrate how much was necessary to prolong, and also to end life.

Frederick Cotton Jnr. was the first to die—his death was attributed to "gastric fever"; next the baby Robert Robson Cotton, whose death certificate suggests that he died of "convulsions from teething" on the 28th of March; and then finally Nattrass himself was dispatched on the 1st of April, although his death was recorded as "typhoid fever". We know a great deal about the death of Joseph Nattrass because accounts of what happened to him featured in the evidence given by a number of Cotton's neighbours at her various magistrates' court appearances (evidence at Durham Assizes was only taken in relation to Charles Edward's murder), which in turn appeared in contemporary newspaper accounts, and there is also evidence about these court appearances in the National Archives at Kew. And, of those neighbours who gave evidence about the death of Nattrass it is perhaps Jane Hedley's account which is most moving, given that she was present when Joseph actually died. Under oath Jane stated that:

I lived at West Auckland and was very friendly with the Prisoner. I assisted her about her house backwards and forwards. I assisted during the time of the illness of Joseph Nattrass. I saw him several times during his illness. The Prisoner waited on him and was constantly about him. I saw no one else wait on him. The Prisoner gave him anything he required. Nattrass was several times sick and purged. This [sic] was occasionally he complained of pain at the bottom of his Bowels. I saw him have fits, he was very twisted up and seemed in great agony. He twisted his toes & his hands & worked them all ways. He drew his legs quite up. He was throwing himself about a good deal & the Prisoner held him & had to use great force. He was unconscious when in the fits. After the fits were over he sometimes said it was a very strong one and sometimes said it was not. Robert Robson Cotton died on the Thursday before Easter & was laid out in the same room where Nattrass was.

On the Friday before Nattrass died I was in the Prisoner's house with Dr Richardson, Nattrass & the Prisoner. Dr Richardson asked him if the pain had left him. He said no. Dr Richardson then said if he could stop the purging he thought he would get better. Nattrass said it is no fever I have. The doctor said if he knew better than him it was no use his coming. He then asked Nattrass if he had taken the medicine & he said no. I was present just at the time of Nattrass's death. He died in a fit, which was similar to the previous ones. The Prisoner was holding him down. I did not say anything about Nattrass having proper support. I have seen her several times give him a drink.

On the Thursday before Nattrass died the Prisoner told me that Nattrass had said she, the Prisoner, was to have his watch and Club money, as she had been his best friend. On the same day the Prisoner asked me to get a letter written for the Burial money from the Club of the deceased. I lived about half a dozen houses from Prisoner at this time. Shortly after Nattrass's death, namely about a week, the Prisoner was in my house assisting to clean. She sent me to her house for a pot that stood of the pantry shelf. She said there was soft soap & arsenic in this pot. I went for and got this pot and showed it to the Prisoner. She said it was the right one & what she got to clean beds with...I got the pot from the top shelf in the pantry of Prisoner's House and which was the place where Prisoner told me it was.[6]

There is much to consider in this account, even accepting that what Jane said was constructed via questioning at the magistrates' court for the purposes of convicting Cotton. As a result, some issues are emphasised by the prosecution (for example Mary Ann's access to arsenic), while others are rather superficially discussed, and we have no "defence" to counter these allegations as Cotton refused to say anything. However, what emerges from a close reading of this evidence is a much clearer understanding of how Cotton operated within a community to make friends of her neighbours, and how she murdered her victims. We can also glimpse just a little of the pain that her victims had to endure before they finally succumbed to her poison.

If we consider the first of these issues, it is interesting to note that Jane described herself as "very friendly" with Mary Ann. So, by this description, not just friends, but good friends. Here we need to remember that Cotton had only relatively recently moved to West Auckland, and if we

---

6. The relevant records are held at Kew in the National Archives. See Home Office (HO) Box 140/21.

can presume that she was not previously acquainted with Jane, it suggests something of her ability to seduce; it is a description that tells us a little about how plausible Mary Ann must have been to other women that she met in these mining communities. Perhaps this charm offensive was also helped by the cachet that came with being able to describe herself as a nurse, or as a Sunday School teacher. These are roles that would have made her appear skilled, different, respectable, capable and worldly. Added to this, she also seems to have employed Jane as a cleaner, as she had employed other women in the various towns and villages where she had lived. How could she afford to pay for such assistance? After her arrest there were a number of press reports that she owed money at various stores in the towns where she had stayed, and this perhaps suggests that Mary Ann may have financed her cleaners through borrowing goods or monies, as well as using some of the income that she derived from the insurance that she received after the deaths of her victims.[7] She also seems to have cleaned for Jane, and so we cannot also rule out the possibility that there were informal reciprocal relationships between very good friends.

And what of Cotton's abilities as a killer? We can see in this account how Mary Ann had developed as a murderer since she poisoned George Ward in October 1866. Six years previously she had almost been caught by the close attentions of Dr Dixon, and Mary Ann clearly felt that she may have pushed her luck too far in challenging the doctors who had attended to George, and which resulted in Dr Dixon writing his defence— *Facts in the Case of George Ward*. So, during Joseph's illness, there is no mention of Mary Ann challenging Dr Richardson, but instead it is left to Nattrass to say—accurately as it turned out—"It is no fever I have". Rather peevishly Dr Richardson is forced to reply that if Joseph knew better than him "it was no use him coming". We can almost hear Mary Ann in the background encouraging Joseph to raise his concerns, and not to take any medicine. She would have done this not because she wanted to be caught, but rather because she would have spent her time convincing Joseph that doctors were essentially useless, and that the medicine wasn't going to save

---

7.   For example, see the report in the *Northern Echo* of 22 March 1873 which suggested that Mary Ann had contracted debts of 30 shillings at the store of Mr Riley before her credit was stopped.

him. And, of course, in downplaying the skill of Dr Richardson she was, by implication elevating her own abilities as a nurse and as a carer. This strategy clearly worked, for Joseph described her as his "best friend", and left to Mary Ann his watch and "Club money". Nor did Dr Richardson suspect anything untoward.

There is another feature of Mary Ann's abilities as a killer on view in Jane's evidence. Note how attentive she was of Joseph's needs. She was "constantly about him", and gave him "anything he required". This would be important for the prosecution to establish so that they could demonstrate that Cotton alone could have carried out the killing, but in effect what Mary Ann was doing was carefully controlling who had access to Joseph, and perhaps because of her nursing background Jane did not think to ask why Joseph wasn't getting "proper support". So Mary Ann was able to ply Joseph with drink — which undoubtedly contained the arsenic which would kill him — whilst all the time appearing as if she was being attentive and caring. In effect Mary Ann was performing Victorian femininity, whilst in actual fact she was committing murder.

Mary Ann also held Joseph down when he was having his fits, and when he was clearly in agony — an agony that she had created. How might this have made Cotton feel? Did she enjoy this physical control over her victims? Did she perhaps seek out these very circumstances that would allow her this practical manifestation of her murderous ways? Is this a symbolic counter to the idea that Cotton was simply "purpose-orientated", and that she might have instead rather enjoyed this sado-masochistic behaviour; this subtle form of torture?[8] But not only was Mary Ann physically controlling — of Joseph and over which people would get access to him — she was also controlling psychologically. The body of her dead child — Robert Robson Cotton — was left in the same room as Joseph, as an awful foretaste of the fate that was about to befall him. Joseph must have realised that her failure to bury the dead baby was because his "best friend" had calculated that he hadn't that much longer to live, and that it would be better to save on the costs of the funerals. So, instead of paying for two, much better — in other words cheaper — to have one instead. And, almost inevitably, when

8.   See the *Introduction* under 'Thinking about Female Serial Killers' for a discussion of the motivations of female serial killers.

the end did come, Joseph died being held down by Mary Ann.

Finally, Jane's testimony provides us with an account of where Mary Ann kept her arsenic, and how she used it — to clean beds, or at least that is what she claimed. Clearly this was of crucial importance to the prosecution, although Jane was never called to give her account at the Durham Spring Assizes, given that Joseph's murder would be left on file after Mary Ann had been found guilty of murdering Charles Edward. However, there is no doubt from what is revealed that Mary Ann had access to arsenic, and that she kept the poison in her home — in a pot, on the top shelf of the pantry — even if a search of her house after she had been arrested failed to turn up anything significant. In a pot, on the top shelf, in the pantry; the everyday descriptions of where one might find an indispensable household item. It all sounds so perfectly ordinary; so perfectly domestic; and so very Victorian.

Arsenic

Arsenic was everywhere in the Victorian world, and there was a recurring tension between its presence as an everyday household staple, and the means to commit murder. Arsenic could be found in playing cards, fireworks and rat poison, to much more ominously lurking in such household furnishings as curtains, cushions and wallpaper. It was even present in a range of medicines, such as Dr Fowler's Solution which became regarded by the Victorians as a sort of "cure-all".[9] People took arsenic "with fruits and vegetables, swallowed it with wine, inhaled it from cigarettes, absorbed it from cosmetics, and imbibed it even from the pint glass", and it quickly became an "inescapable element of daily life".[10]

However, when people say "arsenic" they are in fact usually meaning its oxide, which has the chemical symbol As_2O_3 and is what chemists call "arsenic trioxide". Arsenic trioxide was also known as "white arsenic". It has no distinctive smell, taste or colour and, as the name implies, since it

---

9.   See Emsley, *op cit*, in the *Introduction*, pp.105-106. Emsley advises that Dr Thomas Fowler's Solution, which contained 10g of arsenic trioxide and 7.6g of potassium hydrogen carbonate, first appeared in 1809, and that Queen Victoria's doctor, James Begbie, who was also the vice-president of the Royal College of Physicians, endorsed it's benefits. It was only stopped from being sold in the 1950s.

10.   Whorton, *op cit*, in the *Introduction*, p. x and xii.

resembles flour, baking soda, or even sugar it could mistakenly be added to food. White arsenic was also soluble — much more so in hot rather than in cold water — and therefore would dissolve more effectively if added to tea or soups. Finally, it was also cheap to buy and widely available, even after the rather ineffectual Arsenic Regulation Act 1851 and Pharmacy Act 1868 limited the sale of arsenic and other poisons to trained chemists and druggists. In short, white arsenic rapidly became the accidental killer of the Victorian world.

Accidents, of course, are always to be regretted, but some Victorians could also use white arsenic more deliberately to get rid of rivals, enemies, or unwanted loved ones. The temptations to do so were many and various, but the development of the insurance industry, and the rise of so-called "Burial Clubs" — which would pay out on the death of a family member so that a "pauper's grave" could be avoided — clearly opened up a less scrupulous market. Children, in particular, were often the victims of murder so that their parents might profit from the monies that could be generated by their deaths. So worried did Parliament become due to this deadly business that in 1850 they limited to £3 the amount that a child under ten could be insured for, in the hope that this might discourage parents from taking the lives of their offspring. Even so, as late as the 1880s, 60 per cent of all homicide victims were less than 12 months old.[11] Some measure of the malevolent role of white arsenic can be gleaned from the fact that in the 1840s — when there was more generally a moral panic about murder by poisoning — there were 98 trials of criminal poisoning in England and Wales, and 70 per cent of these related to arsenic.[12] Murder through using white arsenic became so commonplace that people

11. Rose, L (1986), *The Massacre of the Innocents: Infanticide in Britain, 1800–1939*, London: Routledge & Kegan Paul, p. 8. This dreadful statistic has remained a stubborn feature of the British murder landscape, and even now two children a week die at the hands of their parents or carers, although these children are rarely killed by poison.

12. Female poisoners played a major role in this panic, and a number were executed throughout the 1840s. For example, Mary Gallop was executed in 1844 for murdering her father with arsenic; Mary Milner took her own life in her cell prior to being executed in 1847 for poisoning three family members for the burial club money; "countless numbers" turned up to watch Rebecca Smith hang in 1849 for poisoning her children; and an estimated 7,000 people turned up to watch Sarah Chesham — dubbed "Sally arsenic" by the press — hang in 1849 for murdering her husband, after having previously been acquitted of poisoning her children two years earlier.

joked about "white powdering" their enemies, or unwanted children, and women in particular would threaten to "season a pie" for their ungrateful husbands, or "give them a dose".[13]

As little as 300 mg of white arsenic could prove to be fatal, depending on the age or underlying health of the victim.[14] The skilled poisoner would also quickly learn to assess whether or not to deliver an acute dose of white arsenic—which would mean that death would come within a matter of a few days—or if instead smaller, sub-acute doses would be preferable. The advantages of delivering sub-acute doses were related to the fact that the victim would linger for that much longer before expiring, and thus provide the poisoner with an opportunity to prepare friends, neighbours, other family members, or even the local doctor for the inevitable. A sudden death of a basically healthy adult or child, on the other hand, would start tongues wagging, and draw too much attention to the poisoner. But the greatest advantage in using white arsenic as a poison was that it mimicked the symptoms of a number of other illnesses that were all too common to the Victorians.

White arsenic is an irritant poison, and so it inflames the internal organs. With an acute dose the victim's stomach would be very painful to touch; he would have great thirst but would find it difficult to swallow; he would be nauseous, and his nausea would be followed by vomiting and diarrhoea, which the Victorians described as "purging". When this purging ended the victim would suffer from tenemus—a spasm of the anal sphincter, which would create in the victim the sensation that he still needed to defecate. Sub-acute doses would ultimately create the same symptoms, but might start with the victim losing their appetite, and feeling tired and weak. They would also suffer from vomiting and diarrhoea, and might have a number of other symptoms such as skin eruptions, muscular pain, and numbness to the hands and feet. Some victims might also have convulsions, and fall into a coma before death occurred. These symptoms could all easily be

---

13. Whorton, *op cit*, p. 39. A woman's threat to "white powder" a family member—especially a husband—would eventually be countered after 1888 with a husband's retort to "whitechapel" his wife.

14. The Victorians measured their arsenic in "grains". There were 480 grains in an ounce, and 15 and a half grains in a gram. 1 grain was therefore the equivalent of 64.8 mg and 4-5 grains would prove to be lethal.

confused with cholera, typhus (see *Chapter 2*) or with gastric fever, and a Victorian doctor would be much more likely to ascribe a death to any of these illnesses, rather than suspect that his patient had been poisoned.

Look again at Jane Hedley's account of Joseph Nattrass's death. Her descriptions of his symptoms are almost exactly what one would expect of someone suffering from white arsenic poisoning—delivered no doubt in the tea that Cotton served to him to assuage his thirst. Jane advises, for example, that Joseph was "several times sick and purged", and that he had pain in his bowels. This was in all likelihood tenemus. So too he had fits and convulsions, and was particularly troubled by muscle spasms. The cause of his death was listed as "typhoid fever", although as he stated "It is no fever I have". We should also consider the speed with which Mary Ann murdered Joseph. We cannot be certain when Cotton started to administer the poison to him, but death came within a few weeks, which suggests that almost as soon as she realised that Quick-Manning needed a nurse she decided to get rid of Joseph.

The balance against the poisoner was tilted a little back in favour of the victim with the development of medical jurisprudence within universities, which in turn saw the publication of textbooks on poisons, and the gradual growth of forensic toxicology as a discipline. The Spaniard Mateu Orfila (1787-1853) published his *Traite des Poisons— Treatise on Poisons*—in 1814, and in Edinburgh Robert Christison published his own *Treatise on Poisons* in 1829. Slowly, but surely the toxicologist would become as indispensable at Victorian criminal cases, as the forensic scientist has become to our own. Their role was enhanced when they were able to demonstrate scientifically the presence of poison in the body of the victim, and how it had operated to kill, although the toxicologist's ability to do this was never as clear cut as it might appear, given that arsenic was present in numerous domestic products, and was even used in medicines. Clever barristers often used this ambiguity in constructing a defence for their clients, albeit with varying success.

The first test for arsenic was developed by James Marsh in 1836, and the more common (largely because it was so quick and easy to do) Reinsch Test was first used in the1840s. The Reinsch Test—named after the German chemist Egar Hugo Reinsch—was much simpler than the Marsh

Test and involved simply cutting, for example, a thin strip of the stomach of a suspected poison victim, adding water and hydrochloric acid to the strip, and boiling the mixture for about half an hour. A sheet of copper foil would then be added to the mixture, and any arsenic present would form a grey/black coating to the sheet. Christison was a great advocate of the Reinsch Test—stating that "Nothing could be more easy than the method of Reinsch"—and he was the first to use it in Britain in the 1844 trial of an Edinburgh woman convicted of murdering her husband with arsenic.[15] Indeed Christison would devote nearly 100 pages of his *Treatise on Poisons* to arsenic, which also reveals how important arsenic was to the toxicologist. Mary Ann especially would also come to rue the growing use of the Reinsch Test.

Business as Usual

With Joseph out of the way, Mary Ann did two things. First, she made contact with Charles Edward's uncle who lived in Ipswich, and asked him to take charge of the boy. This he refused to do. Second, she moved with Charles Edward from Johnson Terrace to a small, three storey house at 13 Front Street, West Auckland in early May. Appleton also suggests that by this stage Mary Ann was pregnant with Quick-Manning's child. This may very well have been true.[16] In any event it was this child that she would give birth to on 10 January 1873 while imprisoned in Durham Gaol, and the father could only have been Quick-Manning or, at a push, Nattrass. Mary Ann named the baby girl Margaret Edith Quick-Manning Cotton, which would seem to suggest that as far as Mary Ann was concerned, the excise officer was the father.

Quick-Manning did not visit Mary Ann in prison, and nor is there any evidence that he provided financial support for Margaret Edith. However, it is hard not to come to the conclusion that it was Quick-Manning's needs that were prompting Cotton's behaviour at this time. Most obviously she

---

15. Quote taken from Whorton, *op cit*, p. 95. The Reinsch Test was capable of detecting as little as a tenth of a microgram of arsenic.
16. While this would appear to be the case, a number of local newspapers questioned the identity of the father of Mary Ann's baby. See, for example, *Northern Echo* 25th and 28th March 1873.

was trying to get rid of Charles Edward to his uncle, perhaps because Quick-Manning did not want to become responsible for another man's child. Mary Ann also stopped taking in male lodgers, which had been a steady source of income — and no doubt lovers — for her over the years. She told William Lowrey, her final lodger, for example, that he had to leave his lodgings with her in Front Street because the gentleman that she was going to marry did not like her taking in men. Lowrey would also eventually take possession of some of Mary Ann's property, and would later write to her in prison explaining that these possessions had subsequently been collected by her lawyer to pay for her legal bills.[17] Lowrey also wrote to the *Northern Echo* on 19 March 1873 on her behalf, and may have acted as the intermediary which saw Margaret Edith adopted by Mary Ann's former neighbours, William and Sarah Edwards.[18]

So, by early summer 1872, Mary Ann was living in Front Street with Charles Edward, pregnant with Quick-Manning's child, and seemingly forbidden by him from taking in male lodgers. As a consequence, while clearly awaiting her next marriage proposal, Cotton continued to advertise her services as a nurse, and local knowledge about her nursing skills meant that customers also came to her.

On Saturday 6th July, Thomas Riley enters our story, and it was his entry that was to prove to be decisive. Riley ran a corner grocer's store in West Auckland — he was described in the 1871 census as a draper, druggist, grocer and farmer–and he too lived in Front Street, and so we can presume that he knew something of Mary Ann and her circumstances. He was also the assistant overseer of poor relief, and we should also remember that at this time Mary Ann would have been in receipt of a little money to support

17. Lowrey was to be Mary Ann's last lodger, and a letter dated 22 February 1873 exists from Lowrey to his former landlady explaining that George Smith — her lawyer–took her possessions from him and then sold them for £13.
18. This letter was published on 21 March 1873, and begins "I am a constant reader of your valuable paper", and while Lowrey was ostensibly writing to garner support to petition for Mary Ann's life, he also admitted "there would be no chance for her". Again we might note that someone who knew Cotton only very slightly was willing to write on her behalf, and in doing so become involved in her life, which suggests something of her powers of persuasion and her superficial charm. Lowrey also stated that in his final conversation with Mary Ann in her condemned cell that she had once again denied killing Charles Edward, and that he had become accidentally poisoned through taking arrowroot.

Charles Edward. On this particular Saturday Riley went to see Cotton to ask if she could look after another smallpox patient. The conversation that followed between the pair—which is recounted in Riley's court depositions, and was widely reported in a number of newspaper accounts[19]—was the basis on which Riley became suspicious about Mary Ann's dealings with Charles Edward, and led directly to her arrest.

In the presence of Charles Edward, Mary Ann stated that she could not look after any further patients as she was "much tied" by the boy, whom she was keen to point out to Riley was only her step son, therefore implying that this burden on her was unfair. She is then reported to have asked Riley to give her an order to have Charles Edward put into the Bishop Auckland Workhouse, but Riley refused unless Mary Ann was prepared to go with the boy. Cotton replied that she would "never go into such a place", and then seems to have pressed her claim further by stating that the boy was preventing her taking in a respectable lodger. Riley then laughingly suggested that he presumed she was implying Quick-Manning, as there were rumours in the village that the pair were to marry. Mary Ann is reported to have smiled at this suggestion, and said, "It might be so, but the boy is in the way". And then, in the crucial exchange, Mary Ann stated, "Perhaps it won't matter, as I won't be troubled long. He'll go like all the rest of the Cotton family".

Riley, clearly aware and perhaps also embarrassed that this conversation was being held in front of Charles Edward, stated that he then said, "You don't mean to tell me that this little healthy fellow is going to die?" and to this question Mary Ann replied, "He'll not get up". Riley interpreted this observation as Mary Ann meaning that Charles Edward would not reach manhood.

Six days later, Riley passed Mary Ann's house, and he saw her standing in her doorway. She seemed distressed, and then she told him that Charles Edward was dead. Mary Ann asked Riley to come in and view the body, but this he refused to do. Riley was clearly shocked and highly suspicious abut this turn of events, given their previous conversation, and immediately went to report his suspicions to the local police officer

---

19. See, for example, the account given in the *Northern Echo*, 6 March 1873.

Sergeant Tom Hutchinson, and then to Dr William Kilburn—who had been attending to the boy.

Here we would do well to pause and reflect on Charles Edward's death, and the exchange that took place between Mary Ann and Riley before the boy's demise. After all, Mary Ann seems to have drawn attention to herself in a way that was reckless and cavalier. There is also an element of prophesy and grandiosity in her speech, as there had been when she foretold of the imminent death of her mother in March 1857. Some might suggest that this indicated that she wanted to be caught, although this is hardly likely given that she had been happily planning her next marriage to Quick-Manning. However, she had clearly miscalculated Riley's reaction. Perhaps by this stage she had become so used to conning the various doctors who had attended to her ailing family members that she simply presumed that she could con Riley too. Riley proved to be of sterner stuff, perhaps because as an overseer of poor relief he was more used to people trying to pull the wool over his eyes than a doctor would be.

We should also note Riley's joke about Quick-Manning, which surely reveals that there was gossip about Cotton in the village. How might Mary Ann have interpreted Riley's humour? Perhaps she saw it as a challenge to her authority and control; a challenge that had to be resisted and overcome. We should certainly note that their exchange took place in Charles Edward's presence, and that he would have heard Mary Ann state that she wanted to put him in an institution where she herself "… would never go", and that he was going to die young. This was callous and unfeeling in the extreme, and a verbal manifestation of the very same cruelty that had allowed her to keep the dead body of her baby in the same room as her lover Joseph Nattrass, when the latter was struggling for his life. Indeed it is tempting to view these behaviours as symptoms of Mary Ann's underlying psychopathy—an issue which will be discussed later.

It is also interesting to reflect that many serial killers are caught not because of the efforts of the police and good detection, but through sheer luck. Dennis Nilsen, for example, was caught because the house which he shared had blocked drains as a result of the body parts that he had attempted to flush away, and other tenants called out the Dyno-Rod engineer; Harold Shipman was caught because of the efforts of his last victim's daughter, who was a lawyer, and who would not accept that her mother would have changed her will in favour of the GP; and Robert Black's murderous career came to an end when a neighbour of his last intended victim noticed that the little girl that Black had abducted into his van had disappeared, and promptly called the police. To his amazement, the van that he had noticed only minutes earlier re-appeared in the village with Black in the driver's seat. In short, good policing rarely brings a serial killer to justice.

Even so it was Sergeant Hutchinson who, at the time of Cotton's arrest and execution, was elevated almost to heroic status, rather than Thomas Riley. As might be expected, the *Illustrated Police News* was fulsome in its praise of the sergeant, describing him as "acute", "intelligent" and "energetic", and that he had had "the case in hand from the commencement"; a picture of Hutchinson appeared on various handbills about the West Auckland poisonings; and the *Northern Echo* was even moved to describe Hutchinson as "worthy", and "to whom is due the credit for working up and unearthing the dread tale of horror which will soon be brought to a fitting conclusion by the execution of its central character".[20] However, the credit for bringing Mary Ann to justice really belongs to Riley, although there does seem to have been feeling against Riley in the village—he was after all responsible for the administration of the poor relief—and this continued before, and especially after, Cotton's execution.[21]

Mary Ann certainly disliked Riley. In one letter that she wrote to a neighbour in West Auckland, dated the 11th March 1873 and published in the *Northern Echo*, she suggested that "as fore Riley god Will juge him, not A orthely Juge", which gives a flavour of her particular hatred for him. Of course, her intense dislike really stemmed from the fact that it was Riley's suspicions, and then his persistence to act upon these suspicions which had brought Cotton to justice. Riley had nothing to fear from being judged by God, or indeed anyone else, but it is clear that there were people in the village who were prepared to unfairly judge him.

20. See accounts in the *Illustrated Police News*, 31 August, 16 and 30 November 1872; the handbill which has Hutchinson's appearance on it is reproduced by that publication as their front cover on 16 November 1872—and this in turn becomes the front cover of Appleton's book; the quote from the *Northern Echo* taken from a story entitled "West Auckland Poisonings", 22 March 1872.
21. See report in *Northern Echo*, 22 March 1873.

Some insight into how Riley was perceived locally can be gleaned from a very interesting contemporary account, which had a reporter from the *Northern Echo* travel to West Auckland on the weekend before Mary Ann was executed. This unnamed journalist wandered about the village interviewing the people that he encountered, and more generally testing out people's thoughts and feelings. His report, which was published on Saturday 22 March 1872, described how Riley had been ordered out of the home of William and Sarah Edwards — the couple who had fostered Margaret Edith — "in a very peremptory manner", and the reporter concluded that Riley had "much better stay away from Johnson Terrace".

Nothing much is known about Riley after Mary Ann's execution, or whether he took the journalist's advice. However, as a shopkeeper who needed customers to survive, he no doubt found various ways of later rebuilding his relationships in Johnson Terrace, and elsewhere within the village. Thomas Riley may have had to endure some local animosity at the time, and thereafter has almost been lost to history, but had it not been for him there is every chance that Mary Ann might once again have evaded justice. Even so, and despite all of his persistence, there was one final hurdle that had to be jumped before Cotton was arrested.

The Coroner's Inquiry

Coroners inquire into any death that is suspicious, accidental, violent or otherwise unnatural, and from 1830 to 1926 between five to seven per cent of all deaths were made the subject of a coroner's inquiry.[22] These inquests are investigatory rather than adversarial, and their goal is to establish a satisfactory cause of death. One historian has described Victorian coroner's inquiries as a "rough and ready", open form of public justice, given that the actual inquiries were often held in public houses — one of the few public buildings that every Victorian had access to, and which were therefore regularly pressed into service for a range of civic duties.[23] Coroners did

---

22. Burney, I (2000), *Bodies of Evidence: Medicine and the Politics of the English Inquest, 1830–1926*, Baltimore: The John Hopkins Press, p.3.
23. *Ibid*, p.81. It would not be until the passage of the Public Health Act 1875 — which enabled the construction of public mortuaries and coroner's courts out of public funds — that the public house gradually lost this rather gruesome role. However, Burney states that pubs were still used to house coroner's inquiries as late as the 1920s. Dickens disliked coroner's

most of the talking during these inquiries—most had had a legal training, and after the Coroners Act 1860 the coroner, who was appointed for life, was paid a fixed salary. Usually, an inquiry was triggered by the police, a doctor, a local registrar of deaths, or in exceptional circumstances if there was great deal of local gossip about a particular death or deaths.

A Victorian coroner's inquiry would follow a common set of procedures, with a jury of between 12-24 local men summoned to serve by coroner's order, who would view the body, listen to witnesses, and assess any medical evidence that was available. Initially doctors were not paid to give evidence, but after 1836 they would receive two guineas out of the rates if their evidence involved a *post mortem* on the body of the deceased, and one guinea if it did not. In other words, cost could often dictate the thoroughness of what was presented at the inquiry, and inevitably some of those responsible for suspicious deaths could escape justice. Even so, as the Victorian era developed it was increasingly the medical "expert" who took centre stage—a development that helped to make the inquiry more professional, and less sentimental, or prurient.

The first that Mary Ann knew formally about Riley and his suspicions was that Dr Kilburn—who, along with his assistant Dr Archibald Chalmers, had been attending to Charles Edward in the weeks before his death—postponed making out a death certificate. This must have been a blow to Cotton, for without a death certificate she would not be able to make a claim for the £4 10s that Charles Edward's life had been insured for with the Prudential. As Kilburn was not prepared to make out a death certificate, Sergeant Hutchinson reported the matter to the coroner, and an inquest was scheduled for the following day—Saturday, 13th July. Dr Kilburn also requested permission from the coroner to carry out a *post mortem* examination. Kilburn's request was granted. Sergeant Hutchinson then reported all of these developments to Mary Ann, but she seemed

---

inquiries being held in public houses. In *Bleak House*, for example, he comments that the coroner "frequents more public houses than any man alive. The smell of sawdust, beer, tobacco-smoke, and spirits is inseparable in his vocation from death in its most awful shapes", and at an inquest in the Sol's Arms within the book he has the coroner struggle to make himself heard over the noise in the pub. I used the Penguin Classics edition of *Bleak House*, published in 1996, and which was edited by Nicola Bradbury. The quote about the coroner can be found at page 174.

unfazed and repeatedly maintained her innocence to him, and to anyone else who was prepared to listen.

The inquest was held before Thomas Dean, the deputy coroner, at the Rose and Crown public house, which was next door to Mary Ann's house on Front Street. As the jury gathered in the pub, Kilburn began his *post mortem* of Charles Edward—on a table in Mary Ann's house—but he didn't have enough time to conduct this thoroughly, and so he eventually arrived at the inquest hesitant as to what had actually caused Charles Edward's death. He suggested to the jury that the boy may have died of gastroenteritis. He was pressed a little by the coroner, but Kilburn speculated no further at this stage, and so the jury retired for an hour. When they returned they gave their verdict as death by natural causes. And with that it looked as if, yet again, Mary Ann had escaped justice. Never one to miss an opportunity, she promptly wrote to Riley demanding that the overseer should pay for Charles Edward's funeral expenses from the rates, as she had no money. This was done, and Charles Edward was buried on Monday 15th July.

Mary Ann must have thought that with Charles Edward dead and buried she would now be able to get on with her life, and, specifically, to go back to cementing her relationship with Quick-Manning. However, two things would prevent her from doing so. First, the local and regional papers covered the coroner's inquiry into Charles Edward's death extensively[24] and this stirred up rumour and gossip. Second, and more important, Riley continued to press for action, and clearly used his social position within the West Auckland community to make his views and opinions known and acted upon.[25] All of this press interest in the case, and local feeling

24. The *Newcastle Courant* of 19th July 1872 for example, states that there had been a "sudden" and "unexpected" death of a boy at West Auckland (it also rather uncharitably describes Charles Edward as "scrofulous") and noted that Mary Ann, "though a comparatively young woman, has had three husbands". All of this was clearly meant to convey that not only was something amiss with how Charles Edward had died, but also that suspicions centred on his step-mother—Mary Ann Cotton. No doubt that name would have been familiar to other people in the wider community, and slowly but surely rumours of the deaths of other children, husbands and lovers would have started to circulate and the noose would have started to tighten around Mary Ann's neck.

25. Whitehead suggests that Riley may even have been related to Dr Kilburn, although he does not supply any convincing evidence to support this statement. Whitehead *op cit*, in the *Introduction*, p. 40.

and gossip within West Auckland must have frightened Quick-Manning, and it is clear that he did nothing thereafter to support Mary Ann. In an echo of her relationship with James Robinson, she was abandoned by the man on whom she had pinned much of her hope and aspiration. Mary Ann was therefore penniless and unpopular at a time when, in all likelihood, she would have wanted to get out of the village, but quite simply she didn't have the means to do so. So she sold a little of her furniture to her lodger Lowrey to raise money, but then took to her bed with a sore throat. Unbelievably, given everything that had just happened, she asked Mary Ann Dodds, a neighbour from Johnson Terrace to have either Dr Kilburn or Dr Chalmers to come to attend to her. They both refused, and advised her find another doctor.

Dr Kilburn did more than reject Mary Ann's request for medical assistance. Late on Wednesday 17th July, probably as a result of Riley's insistence, Dr Kilburn finally got round to conducting various chemical tests on the contents of Charles Edward's stomach — which he had kept at his surgery in a jar, and on his other internal organs (some of which he had buried in his garden, but which he had been unable to analyse prior to the Saturday inquest). Dr Kilburn set up his equipment, and then proceeded to submit Charles Edward's viscera to Reinsch's test. Thirty minutes later he discovered that Mary Ann had indeed given Charles Edward a "dose"; that he had been "white powdered"; that the boy had in fact been murdered by his step-mother, rather than having succumbed to gastroenteritis. Some would also later question whether Dr Kilburn and his assistant should have been able to have detected what was going on much earlier, and which might have saved Charles Edward's life. Perhaps Dr Kilburn felt that too. In any event, near midnight, he made his way to the police station in Bishop Auckland, and told Superintendent John Henderson about what he had found, but had previously been unable to share with the inquest.

The following day Mary Ann was arrested in Front Street, and taken to Bishop Auckland Police Station, while her house was searched. The search produced very little, except some pills, powdered red lead, a little of another form of powder, and some arrowroot, which was no doubt used in baking as a substitute for flour, or boiled with some flavouring and then served. Mary Ann remained in police custody on the 18th and on the 19th July she was formally remanded in custody. On the same day, the clerk to the justices at Bishop Auckland wrote to the Home Office seeking permission to exhume Charles Edward's recently buried body—a process completed on 26th July, in front of Drs Kilburn and Chalmers, and Superintendent Henderson and Sergeant Hutchinson. Dr Kilburn put some of the viscera that they obtained from Charles Edward's body (and the remnants of the stomach that he had stored in his house) into some clean bottles, which he then corked, sealed, signed and labelled and sent off for analysis to Dr Thomas Scattergood, lecturer in forensic medicine at Leeds School of Medicine. Scattergood, who would become the crucial witness at Mary Ann's trial, found evidence of arsenic everywhere in these samples, and so soon there were more exhumations, and further charges. Meanwhile Mary Ann continued to protest her innocence.

Chapter Four

A Series of Court Appearances and a Trial

"… it is not the case that the defence suggests the scientific findings are wrong…
The defence challenge the assertion that these findings illustrate that [Wright]
was responsible for their deaths as opposed to someone who had sex with them
…You will have noted more than once in the case of the opening speech, the
prosecution counsel suggested that another person or others may, they say, in
addition have been involved in the deaths and disposals. This is a matter to
which you will no doubt pay close attention. You will have to consider the evidence, for example, from the scientists as to the real possibility of someone being
able to kill the victims without leaving any trace on the bodies of the victims":

Timothy Langdale QC, defending the serial killer,
Steve Wright at his trial in January 2008.

Forensic science has, of late, become the "star witness" at most trials involving serious crime—especially murder and serial murder. Scattergood would
no doubt have approved of this development. In particular, Deoxyribo-
Nucleic Acid, which is more commonly known as "DNA"—the genetic
material of a cell—is a recurrent feature of more recent high-profile murder cases. The reason for this is quite simple. Since DNA is unique within
any species, and to any individual within that species, it can be used as a
form of identification. This process is sometimes called "DNA profiling"
or "DNA fingerprinting", and it was first used to catch a killer in 1987.
Eight years later Britain established the first national DNA database in
the world, with some five million people now registered on it. When it
was first established only those with a criminal record were added to the
database, but now anyone who is arrested for an offence which might
lead to imprisonment is subject to a mouth swab, the results of which will

then be added to the database. So, as a result, forensic science has come to dominate the narrative of most murder cases, with various forensic experts used to bolster, or destroy, the prosecution, or defence, cases.

Forensic science certainly dominated the course of the serial killer Steve Wright's trial — the opening moments of his defence are quoted at the start of this chapter — from the first day until the close. Hardly a day passed without evidence from one scientific expert being offered, and what Timothy Langdale QC was trying to do on Wright's behalf was not to imply that the various forensic scientists who took the stand had got things wrong, but rather that they had placed too much emphasis on certain findings, and had not paid enough attention to other possibilities. Mr Langdale was less concerned with prejudice, conjecture and error, but much more with omission. Specifically, that the forensic scientists had not paid enough attention to the possibility that Wright's five victims had been killed by someone else.

Wright's DNA was on the national database as a result of his having been arrested and convicted of stealing £80 from a former employer, when he was working as a barman at the Brook Hotel in Felixstowe. Little did he realise then just how important that theft would become, and how it would later help to convict him of five murders.[1]

At Mary Ann's trial, forensic science was still in its infancy, but it would prove as crucial to convicting her as it did in bringing Steve Wright to justice. DNA might have been over a century away from first being used in an English court case, but the Victorian forensic expert — in the guise of Dr Thomas Scattergood — also had some scientific tricks up his sleeve to convince the jury of the guilt or innocence of a suspect, especially in cases of poisoning. We have already seen how Dr Kilburn used Reinsch's Test on Charles Edward's viscera, and then carefully sealed samples to send to Scattergood for further analysis. It was Scattergood's opinions that would become central in securing a conviction, but like Timothy Langdale QC

---

1.   For an account of Wright's case see Harrison, P and Wilson, D (2008), *Hunting Evil: Inside the Ipswich Serial Murders*, London: Sphere, and Wilson, D (2011), *Looking for Laura: Public Criminology and Hot News*, Winchester: Waterside Press, pp.45-52. I sat through the whole of Wright's trial in Ipswich Crown Court from 14 January 2008-21 February 2008. The jury would eventually take only six hours to find Wright guilty of all five murder charges.

defending Wright, Thomas Campbell Foster QC—Mary Ann's defence barrister—would also argue that too much emphasis was being placed on certain findings by this Victorian expert witness, and not enough attention to other possibilities. Specifically, he would argue that Charles Edward had been accidentally poisoned—a suggestion that Scattergood utterly rejected, and which he then carefully recorded in his notebooks. However, unlike Wright, who took the stand at Ipswich Crown Court, Cotton continued to resolutely refuse to say anything at all.

Magistrates' Hearings

It was now time for the law to take its course, and so Mary Ann duly appeared twice before the Bishop Auckland magistrates: first on 21st August 1872, and then again for several days in late February 1873. It was the duty of the magistrates to assess the evidence being presented against Mary Ann, and then to decide if the case should thereafter be heard at a higher court.[2] On the first occasion she faced a charge of the wilful murder of Charles Edward Cotton, by administering arsenic to him, or causing it to be administered, and on the second she was charged with the murders of Joseph Nattrass, Frederick Cotton Jnr, and her 14-month-old son Robert Robson Cotton. These new charges flowed from permission granted by the Home Office to have the bodies of her three victims exhumed from their graves, and tested for arsenic.[3] By the time of the second magistrates' hearing at Bishop Auckland, Mary Ann had given birth to Margaret Edith on 7th January 1873 while confined in Durham Gaol, and she breast fed the baby during these court proceedings. It was exactly the impression that she wanted to give to the public—a dutiful mother behaving as a mother should.

She had also by this stage engaged a Bishop Auckland solicitor called George Smith to look after her case—having previously tried to secure the services of Charles Chapman of Durham—but neither Smith, nor indeed

2. For an outline of the world of the Victorian prosecutor and the role of the magistrate's court see Emsley, *op cit*, in the *Introduction*, pps. 183-220.
3. The Home Office also agreed to have the body of Frederick Cotton Snr exhumed, but despite an extensive search of the graveyard—which involved a number of coffins being opened–his body could not be found. Poor Frederick had literally "disappeared".

Chapman, proved to be very useful. Smith in particular seems to have contented himself simply in finding ways of spending what little money Mary Ann had left, and he did not actually appear on her behalf at any of these court proceedings (he claimed that he had a "watching brief"), and nor does he seem to have instructed any barrister. This caused a great deal of gossip locally, and he was eventually hauled before the magistrates to explain himself for his lack of action. The normally measured Appleton is even reduced to describing both Chapman and Smith as "a deplorable pair—one scared and squeamish, the other conscienceless, concerned only with making what little money he could".[4]

Smith also seems to have convinced Mary Ann that she should say nothing in her defence at these hearings—a tactic that she was later to adopt at the Assizes too, although in my experience it is normal for serial killers to be silent, and to refuse to engage with the legal case that is being put against them.[5] Some might do this through shame, perhaps even remorse, but their silence has probably much more to do with arrogance. In other words, it is simply another way of expressing their contempt for those who want to bring them to justice. So while Cotton was eager to blame Smith for her actions at court, it is likely that in any event silence would have been her preferred tactic. After all, she could hardly tell the truth. Nonetheless, she wrote to a neighbour in the days before her execution that:

---

4.   Appleton, *op cit*, in the *Introduction*, p.37.

5.   For example, at the trial of the serial killer Stephen Griffiths—dubbed by the press "the Crossbow Cannibal"—at Leeds Crown Court in December 2010, I noted in my reflexive diary how Griffiths sat "arms folded aggressively across his chest, his eyes staring resolutely down at his feet, the defendant exuded a feeling of utter disdain for the court". It should be acknowledged that Griffiths did plead guilty to three charges of murder, although this plea was not so much about his remorse, but rather served to reduce his time in court—everything was over in 2 hours and 30 minutes. I wrote about Griffiths' trial in the *Daily Mail*, 23 December 2010. I also noted this same disinterest at the trial of the serial killer Peter Tobin at Chelmsford Crown Court in December 2009, who entered a plea of "not guilty" but then refused to take the stand, and he put forward no defence. All the way through the several days of his trial Tobin would sit impassively behind a glass screen, doodling on a notepad, and almost completely oblivious to what was happening around him. See David Wilson and Paul Harrison (2010), *The Lost British Serial Killer: Closing the Case on Peter Tobin and Bible John*, London: Sphere, p. 151-152.

Smith has lead me rong. He told me not to speake A single word if I Was Asked Ever so hard or Ever so mutch, I Was not to say it was Wrong, that Would All be don in durham. He was never brote forth Won Witness fore me, he new What they Ware Wanted fore, not only the childe, but for mysealfe. I do not Want nothing but the trouth of Every Won then ie Would have A Chance fore my Life… if it had not been for smith I should make 5 or 6 of them stand With thar toungs tyde.[6]

This is a quite extraordinary outburst — written just after her trial had ended—and is worth considering further. In particular three phrases stand out: "I Was not to say it was Wrong, that Would All be don in durham"; "I do not Want nothing but the trouth of Every Won"; and finally, "I should make 5 or 6 of them stand With thar toungs tyde". In all of this Mary Ann is clearly trying to suggest that quite apart from Smith leading her "rong", there was in effect a local conspiracy to have her found guilty (and no doubt in her mind headed by Thomas Riley). Indeed, her defence barrister had suggested that much of the prosecution's case against Mary Ann had been based on the "gossip" of old women in the village, and his defence of her on this point would still have been fresh in her mind when she wrote this letter. However, we should also remember that she actually said nothing while at court "in durham"— by which stage Smith was a recent, albeit unpleasant memory, and where she had by that stage had new legal representation appointed to defend her. Even so Mary Ann maintained her silence. Her abilities to persuade others did not come from having a stage, such as a witness box, but rather from being able to exert more inter-personal influences. Cotton preferred the cosy intimacies of life, where she clearly felt that she could maximise her influence, and use her honeyed-powers of persuasion to their best effect.

And who are these "5 or 6 of them" who would stand with "thar toungs tyde"? We don't really need to look further than those who gave evidence against her in Bishop Auckland and at Durham. This group included neighbours, such as Mary Ann Dodds, Phoebe Robson, Sarah Smith, Mary Tate and Jane Hedley (whom we have already encountered describing the

---

6. Printed in the *Northern Echo* on 21 March 1873, although the letter is actually dated 11th March. The same letter is also partially quoted in Appleton, *op cit*, p. 29.

death of Joseph Nattrass); the two doctors who had attended to Charles Edward—William Kilburn and Archibald Chalmers, as well as Scattergood; her nemesis Thomas Riley; and finally a Newcastle chemist's assistant called Thomas Detchon, who gave evidence at the second magistrates' hearing in February, 1873, though not at Durham.

We should think about these witnesses (and those other witnesses who testified) as performing different roles on behalf of the state. Thomas Riley, for example, provided the motive for her murder of Charles Edward—Mary Ann wanted the boy out of the way so that she could cement her relationship with Quick-Manning; the various neighbours who were called to give evidence were used to demonstrate the method that Cotton had employed to commit the murder; and finally the three doctors—in particular Scattergood—provided the scientific testimony that a murder by poisoning had actually taken place. Of course there was a problem—one which Smith, had he bothered to attend the magistrates' hearing, might have been able to have exploited on Mary Ann's behalf. In the police search of her house after her arrest, no arsenic had actually been found, and thus the evidence about this aspect of the case was circumstantial, and relied on Mary Ann's neighbours testifying that she had access to, and had used, arsenic within her house.

We have already seen how Jane Hedley testified about Mary Ann's use of arsenic in her account of the death of Joseph Nattrass—Hedley maintained that Cotton kept arsenic in a "pot [on] the top shelf in the pantry of Prisoner's House". So too, at the first magistrates' hearing, Mary Ann Dodds gave evidence that some six weeks before Charles Edward had died Cotton had sent the boy to Mr Townend's—the chemist shop in the village—to buy two pennyworth of arsenic and soft soap to rub into a bedstead, which Mary Ann claimed had bugs. Mr Townend had refused to serve Charles Edward—as he was required to do under provisions of the 1851 Arsenic Regulation Act which permitted the sale of arsenic only to an adult[7]—and so Mary Ann had then asked Mrs Dodds to go buy the substance on her behalf. This she did, and they subsequently used half of the mixture on the bed (they found two or three bugs in the mattress).

---

7.   For a discussion of the Arsenic Regulation Act, see Burney, *op cit*, in the *Introduction*, pps. 64-68.

The other half was, according to Mrs Dodds, put into a
then placed in the lumber room.[8] Whether the pint jug of
described by Mrs Dodds was the same arsenic mixture that
described in her account of Joseph Nattrass's death cannot b
proven one way or another, but both accounts would seem to confirm that
Mary Ann had access to the poison and that she claimed that she needed
the arsenic to clean the beds in her house.

Phoebe Robson and Sarah Smith's testimonies — like those provided by
Dodds and Hedley — merely confirmed that Mary Ann had looked after
her ailing family members, and would not let anyone else provide for them.
Mrs Smith also mentioned that she saw Mary Ann give Nattrass cups of
tea from two small teapots that Cotton kept on a table in her lover's room,
and we can infer that this was likely to have been the means by which she
poisoned her victims. So, in essence their testimony suggested that Mary
Ann had access to arsenic, and that she was very careful to control the
circumstances of who was able to attend to her victims while they were
dying. She clearly was not troubled by the presence of her neighbours — in
fact she probably wanted them to be there — but she did not want them
to play any active role in what was happening to those who were dying,
such as by bringing food, or drink that they had prepared.

Only one witness caused Mary Ann any disquiet — the Newcastle
chemist's assistant Thomas Detchon, who gave evidence at the second
magistrates' hearing in February 1873. We can judge that he had upset her
by the fact that he was the only witness that Cotton actually questioned.
Detchon worked for the chemist William Owen in Collingwood Street,
Newcastle, and he testified that he remembered a woman, who gave her
name as Mary Ann Booth coming into the shop in January 1869, and asking for soft soap and arsenic to help to clean beds. Mary Ann would have
been living in Sunderland at this time. Detchon claimed that he refused
to sell the woman arsenic, as he did not know her (again, as required by

8. A "lumber room" was more often found in larger Victorian houses than the one that Mary
   Ann lived in at West Auckland, and it was usually a place where discarded pieces of furniture were stored. If we accept that a pantry is also a store — one which usually contained
   food and kitchen utensils and materials such as pots and pans — Mrs Dodds may have
   been describing the same storeroom as Jane Hedley.

the Arsenic Regulation Act), but she later returned with a witness called Elizabeth Robson, and so he duly sold Mary Ann Booth the arsenic. He then stated that he subsequently recognised Mary Ann Cotton as Mary Ann Booth from a photograph published in November 1872, and thereafter went to Durham Gaol to identify her formally.

Mary Ann directed her only question during these proceedings to Detchon. She asked him at what time of day she was supposed to have visited the shop, to which Detchon replied "between two and three". In the end Detchon was not called to give evidence at Mary Ann's trial in Durham, probably because he had in fact confused her with someone who really was "Mary Ann Booth". Even so his evidence is odd, especially as it confirms many aspects of Mary Ann's story more generally, such as using soft soap and arsenic to clean beds. We should also note that Mary Ann Booth returned with a woman called Elizabeth Robson — which was Cotton's maiden name. Elizabeth Robson was eventually tracked down after this hearing, and she denied that Mary Ann Booth was in fact Mary Ann Cotton.[9]

Detchon had clearly got his facts wrong, although his story is of interest simply because of how Mary Ann responded. She chose to end her silence by asking him a rather ineffectual question, and was clearly put out by the evidence that he had given. We need to consider this carefully. After all she had sat impassively in court as friends and neighbours, and various doctors had given their evidence, but only chose to ask Detchon a question. Why should this have been the case? What had driven her to speak to Detchon, while the testimonies of how, for example she had held down Nattrass as he had writhed in his bed in agony, had left her silent? It is tempting to suggest that Mary Ann knew that she hadn't bought arsenic in Owen's chemist shop, and so was frankly indignant that this was being alleged. In other words, that she knew that this was a mistake, and so she broke her vow "not to speake A single word". Of course, the inevitable inference that we can also take from this specific piece of behaviour is that what was being said by all the other witnesses was accurate and correct, and therefore in the face of the truth, it was a far better policy for Mary

9.   See Appleton, *op cit*, pps. 44-45.

Ann to say nothing at all; it was only when something was said that was clearly untrue that Mary Ann wanted to intervene.

Doctors Chalmers and Kilburn also gave evidence before the magistrates, and the latter would be given a particularly hard time at Assizes by Mary Ann's defence barrister. However, the evidence that proved most impressive both before the magistrates and at Assizes came from Scattergood. It would be his evidence in particular that Mary Ann's barrister would want to challenge, and whilst we have already met the Dean at the start of his lecture about Charles Edward, perhaps we should now also get to know him a little more formally.

Dr Thomas Scattergood

Thomas Scattergood was born in Huddersfield in 1826, and he only re-appears in the historical record 20 years later when he was appointed as assistant apothecary at Leeds General Infirmary, where his aunt was already working as matron. He entered into general practice in the city, but also lectured in chemistry at the Leeds School of Medicine, and then took up the post of honorary surgeon to the Hospital for Women and Children in 1863. These roles suggest something of the esteem with which Scattergood must have been held within Leeds at the time—an esteem which culminated in 1884 when he was made the first Dean of the new Faculty of Medicine, a post which he held until his death in 1900. However his value to history was the result of a much more mundane role that he occupied.

From 1869 until June 1888 Scattergood lectured in forensic medicine and toxicology, and he has left for us not only the notes that he used to develop these lectures—which provide a glimpse of both the state of forensic science in the mid-Victorian period, and how forensic medicine was taught to the next generation of doctors—but also three notebooks about the cases that he worked on between 1856 to 1897.[10] These wonderful sources are rarely consulted, but they provide a marvellous insight into the professional development of forensic medicine and the growing connections between medical teaching, education and the legal procedures

10. The lecture notes and three volumes of Scattergood's notebooks are held in the Special Collections, Brotherton Library, University of Leeds. They are now quite fragile—they cannot be photocopied—but can be viewed by appointment with the library staff.

for investigating deaths.[11] And, as far as Scattergood is concerned, they are a first hand account of what a Victorian expert witness said and did, and how he went about his business of giving evidence and providing an opinion at court. They also throw further light onto the evidence that he presented at Mary Ann's trial.

Scattergood's lectures covered a variety of topics ranging from gunshot wounds and death by suffocation, to death by drowning or spontaneous combustion. They were often prompted by questions. "Which of two or more dead persons died first, or which survived the other?" "When was the injury inflicted?" "With what weapon was the injury inflicted?" "Was the injury accidental, suicidal or homicidal?" And, as he put it in his notes, "the question most important of all" — "What was the cause of death?" In relation to this last question he cited "Bichat's classification"[12] which he described to his students as death beginning at:

> The head, heart or lungs, and though these modes of death are mixed together
> in different cases, and the class[ification] is not exhaustive, yet as the natural
> cause of sudden death can be generally traced to some injury or impediment to
> the action of these organs, then distinguishing characters [sic] may be stated.

His lectures were clearly meant to help to train his students about how to give evidence in court, which also suggests that the notes which have survived to us were made after Scattergood himself had appeared as an expert witness. As a result he passes on advice about the police, lawyers, judges and, above all, the need to make careful notes both at crime scenes, and in the laboratory. After all, as he suggested to his students:

11. However, see M A Green (1973), "Dr Scattergood's Case Books: A 19th Century Medi-
     co-Legal Record", *The Practitioner*, Volume 21, pps. 679-684; Katherine D Watson (2006),
     "Medical and Chemical Expertise in English Trials for Criminal Poisoning, 1750-1914",
     Medical History, Volume 50, pps. 373-390. Watson's (2011) *Forensic Medicine in Western
     Society: A History*, London: Routledge is also very useful, although she does not mention
     Scattergood in this work.
12. Marie Francois Xavier Bichat (1771-1802), a French anatomist and pathologist who is
     regarded as one of the pioneers of modern histology and pathology.

A medical witness may have not only formally to dissect a body by legal order but, by having been called in on first alarm may be compelled to act as a witness to other extrinsic circumstances. Here it is of the most importance that all the minute circumstances should be noted. The medical man in this position is often the most or only intelligent or self possessed person present…He has the opportunity & ability of knowing many more circumstances that others cannot…His training ought to have fitted him for minute observation, and it is quite certain that he will be severely taken to task if he does not exercise this faculty.

So he encouraged his students to note "for one reason or another", the place of a dead body. In other words, was it "on [the] floor — bed — chair; relation to door — window — fireplace; attitude or position — expression of anger or resistance on face". Was the victim "clenching a handkerchief", or did the victim have "weapons in hands or near — exact position; bottles near — exact position, whether within reach & smell if no contents". Scattergood suggested that his students should also note the clothing of the victim — its "arrangement or disarrangement" — and whether there were spots of blood on the clothing, or on any part of the body, and to observe the direction in which the blood had flowed.

So too in relation to a suspected rape, Scattergood again reveals his own experience of dealing with such cases, and suggested that:

> The trousers & linen should be examined in search of blood or seminal stains. If
> no stains are found on the clothes he has on, the policeman should be directed
> to obtain more of the accused's clothes amongst which a stained garment may
> be found. Of course the absence of stains on clothing does not prove that the
> man is innocent, nor their presence that he is guilty.[13]

Scattergood also knew a great deal about murder. However, he reminded his students that "for every case of homicide in England and Wales, there are probably 3 or 4 cases of suicide and 40 accidental deaths", and thus

---

13. This latter comment was added into his notes in pencil, which suggests that Scattergood
     revised his lectures—perhaps based on cases that he himself had consulted upon, or which
     had been reported in the press.

they would have to decide if the body that they were examining had died as a result of an accident, the person had taken their own life, or had been murdered. To that extent, Scattergood advised his students that they should examine any wounds on the body very carefully, in relation to "nature — extent — situation — shape & direction — number and presence of foreign bodies". In his notes he then felt that he should clarify what he had meant by his advice about the "nature of wound", and wrote that "contused wounds" — where the skin is unbroken — "are rarely suicidal". He also warned his students to remember that "it is important to remember that a murderer may inflict slight wounds on himself to avert suspicions" and that "the existence of a number of wounds is generally considered to afford a presumption of homicide".

Of course, wounds which were visible were relatively easy to examine, but death by poisoning was by its very nature invisible — there was no blood letting, no wound to diagnose, and often no witnesses to question either. Worse still, the cause of death could often be confused with other Victorian illnesses, and so it was here that Scattergood's background and training as a chemist and toxicologist came into its own. Not only could he suggest to the court a cause of death, but he could also identify the poison that had been used. For example, while his notes refer only occasionally to the Marsh test and the Reinsch's test[14] — which suggests that they were by this time so commonplace as not to be worth mentioning in any detail — his notebooks of the cases that he worked on are filled with poisons and poisonings. Of the 300 cases recorded in his three volumes of notebooks, 20 were homicides and eleven involved poisons. He also records working on 19 cases of suicide, all of which had come about as a result of the victim taking poison.

In other words, Scattergood was well placed to make an informed opinion about cases of suspected poisonings, and therefore to act as an expert witness on this matter at court. As an expert witness Scattergood could give evidence of both fact and opinion, and thus help the judge and the jury come to an appropriate verdict as to whether or not the victim died as a result of poisoning. He would make visible that which had been

---

14. See *Chapter 3* under the sub-heading "Arsenic"

unseen, but he had to do this in such a way that the complicated chemical tests that he had conducted, and the conclusions that could be drawn from them could be easily understood by a lay jury. Above all, as an expert witness—most likely on behalf of the prosecution—he would have to be confident enough in his own skills and abilities to withstand rigorous cross-examination from any defence barrister. For, as Scattergood put it to his students, the medical expert should:

> On the question at hand… be prepared to give a distinct opinion as to whether death was or was not the result of injury… The Law will admit one cause of death only, and to this if it be possible we should make up our own minds… Other predisposing circumstances may be stated, and proper weight given to them as reasons why such and such injuries were more likely to be fatal or more quickly fatal than under other circumstances they should have been, but we should be distinct in our opinion as to the actual cause [of death].

Scattergood and the West Auckland Arsenic Cases

Scattergood only once directly named Mary Ann Cotton in the first of the three volumes of his notebooks—she appears as "M A Cotton"—and instead he refers throughout to the "West Auckland Arsenic Cases". The fact that Mary Ann is only mentioned once may have contributed to the fact that this source has not previously been used about Cotton, as some prior knowledge that the "West Auckland Arsenic Cases" and Cotton were one and the same thing would needed to have been known.[15] Scattergood seems not to have named Cotton for professional reasons—he wanted his notebooks to be seen as neutral, impartial and unbiased. He was a scientist, and these notebooks were the fruits of his labours. As such, what concerned him was not the personality of the accused, or indeed of the victim, but rather what science would reveal about how that victim had died. We should also note that Scattergood refers to the "West Auckland

---

15. Indeed, it is interesting that I had to point out the significance of the notebook in relation to this case to the librarians who work in the special collections department at the Brotherton Library. They had never previously heard of Mary Ann Cotton. Nor is his association with Cotton mentioned by either Green or Watson, both of whom have written about Scattergood—see footnote 11 above. In all of this we have yet another example of how Cotton has been able to disappear.

Arsenic Cases" — he is using the plural — because he had been asked to analyse not just the remains of Charles Edward Cotton, but also those of Frederick Cotton Jnr, Joseph Nattrass and Robert Robson Cotton.

His notes about these cases cover 17 pages of his notebook — from page 179 to page 206, and they begin with a simple statement that:

> Received from Supt. Henderson of Bishop Auckland, through Sgt. Hutchinson Friday 20th July 1872 — 6 glass jars and 2 parcels wrapped in paper: all duly sealed, secured & labelled. The seals perfectly intact. All related to Charles Edward Cotton.

What Scattergood is trying to show through this first entry is not only how he came to be in possession of the evidence, but also that this evidence had not been tampered with — "the seals perfectly intact". In line with the advice that he would give to his students, he was carefully noting down everything that might later be questioned in court by a prosecution barrister, or more likely by the defence.

We might also note that poor Charles Edward was by this stage reduced to the contents of six glass jars and two parcels wrapped in paper, and ever the professional, Scattergood carefully records what these parcels and glass jars contained. In the first jar was a portion of the contents of Charles Edward's stomach; the second contained his intestines; the third a portion of his liver; the fourth housed his heart and lungs; the fifth his spleen and some further parts of his lungs; and the final jar contained his stomach and more portions of his intestines. Scattergood reveals that in one of the parcels was a "napkin containing last evacuation from the bowels of C E Cotton", and in the other were powders that might be relevant to the case and which had been "found in the prisoner's house by the police".

Scattergood then carefully noted what he did with these remains, and this analysis would become the basis for the evidence that he would later give at court. So, in relation to "Jar No. 2", Scattergood notes:

> Contained apparently all remainder of small intestine attached to [word illegible]. It was all cut up, washed and examined. Contents yellow and fecal below — mucous above. It was in a good state of preservation; lower portion

carefully ex[amined] for fever appearances, but there were none…one fourth taken for Reinsch. The one fourth was treated by Reinsch's process and coated copper freely with characteristic steel grey coating.

In other words, he had found clear evidence of arsenic, and was later to estimate the amount of arsenic in Charles Edward's stomach's contents as being .2592 grains. He went through similar processes with the contents of the other jars and also found arsenic present in the bowels, liver, heart, lungs and kidneys, although not in the spleen. He would later give evidence at Durham Assizes that this suggested to him that:

> In my opinion, they point rather to repeated doses [of arsenic] over several days. The presence of the arsenic in the stomach implies recent administration. The quantity found is no indication of the quantity administered.[16]

Similar tests were also employed to analyse the other samples that had been sent to him, and so, for example, having received "a hamper containing viscera of Joseph Nattrass" he was able to conclude that there were 17.71 grains of arsenic in Joseph's remains. Here we should remember that 4-5 grains of arsenic were likely to have been fatal, and so Joseph had almost four times the lethal dose of the poison in his body. No wonder he was in such agony on his death bed. Scattergood also found evidence of arsenic in the remains of Frederick Cotton Jnr and in the kidneys, liver and spleen of the baby Robert Robson Cotton, whose dead body had been left in the same room as Joseph Nattrass. Scattergood noted that the baby's "rectum was quite firm and fresh and at its lower part [was] a distinct red patch occupying about 1/8th of its surface. There was nothing to indicate fever." This latter point is of interest because if symptoms of fever had been present, it might reasonably be concluded that the baby had died of natural causes. Indeed, the cause of death listed on the baby's death certificate was "convulsions from teething". This was of course completely inaccurate, and Scattergood was going to say so at court—if he was allowed to—but there was a problem.

---

16. A great many local and regional newspapers covered Cotton's trial, although I used the *Northern Echo*, 7th and 8th March 1873 to build up a picture of Scattergood's cross-examination. Appleton's account is also useful.

Durham Spring Assizes

Mary Ann's trial lasted for three days, beginning on Wednesday 5th March and ending on Friday 7th March 1873. The trial was presided over by the Canadian-born judge Sir Thomas Dickson Archibald, who had been knighted only a month previously, and Charles Russell was appointed to lead for the prosecution. This was a controversial appointment, given that County Durham was a county palatine and therefore had its own Attorney General in the shape of John Aspinall QC, the Recorder of Liverpool. Even so, Aspinall was passed over and the Crown was represented by Russell, who would himself become Attorney General under Gladstone, and then later Lord Chief Justice. Given all the problems that she had had with her lawyer George Smith, Cotton had to have counsel appointed to represent her in the shape of the Leeds QC — Thomas Campbell Foster. And, despite the fact that he had had very little time to develop his case, he mounted a spirited and clever, if ultimately unsuccessful, defence.

Mary Ann didn't have far to travel for her trial, as the court and prison are located next to each other. As she arrived on the first day there was a large crowd eager to catch a glimpse of the "West Auckland Poisoner", and so great was public interest in the case that tickets had to be issued to enter the court building. Hundreds were disappointed, but they remained out-side the court watching all the comings and goings. Newspaper accounts suggested that Mary Ann looked depressed, pale and that she seemed much older than when she had appeared before the Bishop Auckland magistrates, although this is hardly surprising given that she was facing a capital charge.

The case against Cotton was in many respects straightforward — she had poisoned her stepson Charles Edward Cotton by administering arsenic to him — but there were at least two major issues which would come to dominate the trial. The first related to whether evidence about the other deaths that had occurred in Mary Ann's household would be admissible, and the second revolved around the issue of whether or not the arsenic that Scattergood had found in Charles Edward's body might have been the result of innocent and accidental ingestion. After all, arsenic in the Victorian era was everywhere, although curiously none had been found in Mary Ann's house when it had been searched by the police. This simple fact would give Campbell Foster his opening, and the idea that Charles

Edward had died accidentally would become the main narrative of his defence for Mary Ann. Ironically, this put pressure on the prosecution to be allowed to introduce Scattergood's evidence of what he had found in his analysis of the remains of Joseph Nattrass, Robert Robson Cotton and Frederick Cotton Jnr.

As for the first of these issues, a formal ruling on whether what we now know as "similar fact evidence" could be admitted at court would not come for another 40 years, and that too came in a trial of a serial killer. George Joseph Smith, aka Oliver George Love, Charles Oliver James, Henry Williams and John Lloyd, was found guilty of the murders of Bessie Mundy, who was found dead in her bath in 1912, Alice Burnham, who died in similar circumstances in Blackpool the following year, and Margaret Lofty, who was also found dead in her bath in Highgate in December 1914. All three women had gone through a form of marriage with Smith (who was in fact already married), and had then made a will in favour of their "husband" before tragically drowning in their baths—a result, claimed Smith, of each woman suffering from an epileptic fit. Smith, who never confessed to any of the murders, was nonetheless found guilty at his trial—despite the absence of actual physical evidence to convict him—but the jury was asked simply to come to a conclusion about the awful, tragic pattern of what happened to Smith's "wives". He was duly convicted.

At his appeal in front of the Lord Chief Justice, Smith's counsel, Marshall Hall, claimed that evidence about the deaths of all three women should not have been introduced into the original trial and that therefore Smith should have been found not guilty. Hall suggested that "It would be difficult to believe that the same number could come up at a roulette table five times in succession, but if it happened you would not be entitled to convict the croupier as a dishonest man". The Lord Chief Justice was incredulous and suggested that if the same number came up at a roulette table five times in succession he at least would be "suspicious". In other words this would be unusual and outside the boundaries of chance, and not simply a remarkable coincidence. The Lord Chief Justice could not help but see a pattern in the deaths of three new brides, all of whom seemed to have drowned in their baths shortly after they were married, and having made wills that favoured their husband. As a result he dismissed Smith's appeal—who was later hanged—and to this day *Rex v. Smith* (1915) is still used to allow evidence of similar crimes—or a pattern of crimes—to be introduced as evidence in court.[17]

Mr Justice Archibald did not have this precedent to help him, and even as Russell opened the prosecution and outlined the case against Cotton, he had to be reminded by the judge that "You have done enough: leave the details". It was only when Scattergood gave his evidence on the second day of the trial that the issue of admissible evidence once again came to dominate. After all, Scattergood had examined not just Charles Edward's remains, but also the remains of three others. Russell asked Scattergood about these other examinations of members of Cotton's household, but said that the prosecution would not press for evidence of this kind to be presented if the judge thought it unwise. This was a key moment, perhaps the key moment of the trial, and Campbell Foster immediately got to his feet and objected, and then asked that the jury should retire so that the issue could be clarified privately. However, Mr Justice Archibald, who had clearly been thinking about this, ruled that the evidence that Russell wanted to be introduced was the same as had been presented before the magistrates at Bishop Auckland, and that there was no precedent to send the jury out. He then retired to take further advice, and concluded that the evidence that Russell wanted to be introduced could be admitted.[18] Campbell Foster tried once more to object, but the judge, Mr Justice Archibald, was not to be moved.

Archibald's ruling dealt with the first of the two issues that came to dominate Cotton's trial, but what about Campbell Foster's argument that the arsenic that Scattergood had discovered in Charles Edward's body had

---

17. For an account of Smith's crimes and his trial see Wilson (2009), *op cit*, in the *Introduction*, pps. 55-83

18. Mr Justice Archibald seems to have relied on the precedents of *Regina v. Garner* (1848) and particularly *Regina v. Geering* (1849) as authorities. In this latter case—held at Lewes Assizes in the summer of 1849—Mary Ann Geering was charged with poisoning her husband in September 1848, and so as to demonstrate that his death had not been accidental, evidence was allowed to be presented by the prosecution that she later administered arsenic to her three sons some months after her husband had died. Two of these sons had also subsequently died. Crucially this evidence was not ruled inadmissible by reason of its tendency to create suspicion of other crimes that may have been committed. It was also noted that Geering lived in the same house as the four victims and that she prepared all of their meals.

been accidentally ingested by the boy? Campbell Foster had been particularly strong on this point during his cross-examination of Dr Kilburn. He suggested to the doctor that the green wallpaper in the room where Charles Edward had slept was "arsenical—you have seen them. They are bright green are they not?" Kilburn agreed that they were and that arsenic could throw off fumes with heat. There had been a fire in Charles Edward's room, although Kilburn did not think that the temperature generated by the fire would be strong enough to throw off poisonous fumes. Poor Dr Kilburn was getting out of his depth, and Campbell Foster persisted.

Campbell Foster: Do you know that people have been attacked by chronic arsenical poisoning and some killed by living rooms covered with paper in which arsenic has been employed?

Kilburn: I have heard so; but I should not think it very likely in these cases. It may cause suffusion of the eyes; irritation of the nostrils, and colic pain about the stomach, but I don't think it would produce death from a wallpaper.

In the end Mr Justice Archibald was forced to come to Kilburn's assistance and point out to Campbell Foster that his cross-examination was of a "very speculative character". There was to be more speculation with Scattergood.

Campbell Foster asked Scattergood whether it was easy to separate arsenic and soft soap, and also whether he agreed that the green pigment in wallpaper contained a great deal of arsenic and was therefore dangerous. Scattergood agreed that it was for the following reason:

Scattergood: Because a portion of this green substance wears off, or falls off, as the paper becomes dry, and it gets diffused with the air. Still more of it might be removed if the walls were swept or brushed in cleaning.

Campbell Foster: That is exactly the answer I anticipated you would give. A sunbeam shining through the window, doctor, would show the atoms or particles floating in the air.

Scattergood: Yes.

Campbell Foster: Is that not the danger of these green papers that those in the room inhale these floating particles which may be the poison of arsenic?

Scattergood: It is said that persons have suffered in their health from that cause.

Judge: Have you ever known of death from that cause?

Scattergood: No, my lord, nor have I read of one.

What Campbell Foster was attempting to do was suggest to the jury that Charles Edward had been accidentally poisoned—either through dried particles of arsenic that floated around the room after having flaked off from the wallpaper, or through the soft soap that had been used to kill bugs on his bed, but had then fallen to the floor. In other words, he was trying to establish some doubt in the prosecution's case that Mary Ann had deliberately poisoned Charles Edward. He wasn't questioning the fact that arsenic had been found by Scattergood, but rather suggesting that he had not given due consideration to other more innocent possibilities. As Campbell Foster put it with some flourish—"When the boy was spinning his top, tossing his ball, playing at marbles, might he not have picked up two or three grains of arsenic?" Scattergood did not think so, and probably going beyond what he had actually observed, replied that Charles Edward couldn't have spun his top (even if he possessed one) as "there was a carpet on the floor".

This produced laughter in the courtroom, but we might also note that there is no evidence to suggest that Scattergood had ever actually been into Mary Ann's house in Front Street, and so this exchange might also reveal that he was somewhat rattled by this line of questioning. There is some support for this conclusion from his notebook. On page 188, and dated March 14th 1873, it is clear from the notes that he made that Scattergood had attempted to scientifically test Campbell Foster's suggestions.

On my return from Durham I examined the soft soap and arsenic with a view to test Mr Campbell Foster's hypothesis of its dangers by exposure. The mixture [was] originally contained in a chip box, had been removed (what remained of it) in September last into a test tube & left in [a] closet in my room uncorked in a tube sack. In preparation for the examination at B[isho]p Auckland it had been placed after the broken top had been broken off, in a wide mouthed bottle with [a] wooden cap. The examination at B[isho]p Auckland was on Feb 21 & the tube was placed in the bottle 2 or perhaps 3 days before i.e. between 17th & 20th. On examining it now it was quite soft & pasty and seemed to have dried only so much as to render[?] it flowing down the tube at once when inverted, as it would have done at first. It could not possibly have been powdered any more than butter could have been powdered.

So here we have Scattergood trying to establish for himself the likelihood of soft soap drying to the extent that flakes could break off and then be innocently ingested. He observed no such drying taking place, but rather the soft soap remained soft and pasty so that it ran down the test tube when turned upside down. And, with a finality that suggests some emotion — it is certainly an observation which is out of character with the remainder of his entries — "It could not possibly have been powdered any more than butter could have been powdered".

As for Campbell Foster's second suggestion that arsenic may have flaked off from the wallpaper in the room and then been inhaled, Scattergood also made notes about whether or not this might have been possible.

With regard to another point in Mr Foster's defence namely that AS [arsenic] derived from a green paper on the wall might have been inhaled: this would not account for the presence of solid ASO_3 in the stomach. Again as to the ASO_3 in the stomach being derived from the soft soap I have shown that it would not form dust: at the trial I ventured to say that inhalation would not account for ASO_3 in the stomach in a solid form: this has been challenged: but on no solid ground of fact. We have no instance on record that I can find, where after death from inhalation — if that has can [sic] taken place — the presence of solid ASO_3 has been demonstrated in the stomach at all, still less to the amount in Nattrass of 4 to 4½ grains in the stomach & bowels (besides 13 to 14 grains dissolved).

Again this entry is uncharacteristic of Scattergood and he comes across as a scientist who has been irritated by someone who does not understand science. His views have been challenged—but "on no solid ground of fact"—and that must have been especially annoying. We should also note the underlining. He is giving emphasis to the point that he is making that he can find no record of anyone dying from inhaling particles of arsenic from dust in the air, and above all even if this was possible it would still not account for the solid arsenic that he had found in Joseph's stomach. No, for Scattergood, all of this led to one inescapable conclusion—the victims had been murdered.

That, of course, was for the court to decide and on Friday 7th Russell and Campbell Foster gave their closing addresses, and the judge made his final summing up. Russell in particular emphasised the evidence that had been presented by Scattergood, and his view that Charles Edward had been murdered through repeated doses of arsenic that had been administered to him by Cotton over some seven days. On the other hand, Campbell Foster continued to bemoan the fact that evidence from other cases had been admitted into the trial and, ironically, given what he had just complained about, asked the jury to consider how it would be possible for a mother to have killed her own 14-month-old child, Robert Robson Cotton:

A mother poisoning her own child! A mother nursing it, calling in the doctor, dancing it upon her knee, looking fondly at it, listening to it prattle, seeing its pretty smiles, while she knew she had given it arsenic, making its limbs writhe as it looked into her face wanting support and protection!

At this point in his address Mary Ann is reported to have started to cry, and when Campbell Foster finished his address—which lasted for two hours—a member of the public stood up and applauded him, only to be rebuked by the judge. Clearly this type of emotional appeal influenced some members of the public, and no doubt some were also sympathetic to Mary Ann. Campbell Foster also reminded the jury that Cotton had called in Dr Kilburn to attend to Charles Edward—and to the others who had been referred to—and that as a nurse she was kind to the sick. Finally, he complained that much of the evidence that had been presented against her was the work of "the gossip of old women who were called one after another and who tried to make three black crows out of one."

Mr Justice Archibald summed up the evidence that had been presented as he saw it, and explained that the crime of murder consisted of killing with "malice aforethought".[19] He stated that the law did not need the jury to consider motive, and that they should only be concerned with intention. He further explained that they had to arrive at a decision which was beyond reasonable doubt, and that they should decide the case on the evidence that had been presented—not on the suggestions of counsel. In his summing up, Archibald referred to the evidence presented by Scattergood repeatedly, and was at pains to remind the jury of what he had said that was at odds with the idea that this had been an accidental poisoning. "No fewer than four people [dying] in succession in some accidental manner," said the judge, was "a series of accidents going beyond the bounds of probability". His conclusion here might be seen as foreshadowing the "suspicions" of the Lord Chief Justice in 1915 about the same number coming up five times in a row at a game of roulette in the appeal of George Smith. Archibald finally asked the jury to consider that if the arsenic had been administered wilfully who had done so, and if they considered that the poison had been administered by Cotton then they were duty bound to find her guilty.

The jury left to consider their judgement at ten minutes to four, and returned almost an hour later. It was an unanimous decision—they found Mary Ann Cotton guilty of the murder of Charles Edward Cotton.

Mr Justice Archibald donned a black cap, and with Mary Ann still

---

19. The classic definition of murder has been attributed to Sir Edward Coke and is embedded in the Offences Against the Persons Act 1861, and so would have been the authority that Mr Justice Archibald was citing. This stated that "murder is when a man of sound memory, and of the age of discretion, unlawfully killest within any county of the realm any creature *in rerum natura* under the King's peace, with malice aforethought, either expressed by the party or implied by law, so as the party wounded or hurt etc. die of the wound or hurt etc. within a year and a day after the same". This definition remains more or less as it did in 1861, although the "year and a day" provision has now been ended.

maintaining her innocence, said:

> Mary Ann Cotton, you have been convicted, after a patient and careful trial, of the awful crime of murder. You have had the benefit of the assistance of counsel for your defence, and everything that could possibly be urged on your behalf has been said, but the jury have been led to the only conclusion to which they could come — that you are guilty. You have been found guilty of the murder, by means of poisoning, of your step son, whom it was your duty to cherish and take care of.
>
> You seem to have given way to that most awful of all delusions, which sometimes takes possession of persons wanting in moral and religious sense, that you could carry out your wicked designs without detection. But, whilst murder by poison is the most detestable of all crimes, and one at which human nature shudders, it is one the nature of which, in the order of God's providence, always leaves behind it complete and incontestable traces of guilt. Poisoning, as it were, in the very act of crime, writes an indelible record of guilt.
>
> In these last words I shall address to you, I would earnestly urge you to seek for your soul that only refuge which is left for you, in the mercy of God through the atonement of our Lord, Jesus Christ.
>
> It only remains for me to pass upon you the sentence of the law, which is that you will be taken from hence to the place from whence you came, and from thence to a place of execution, and there to be hanged by the neck until you are dead, and your body to be afterwards buried within the precincts of the gaol. And may the Lord have mercy upon your soul.

Mary Ann's execution was scheduled for the morning of Monday 24th March 1873.

Chapter Five

An Execution

"I'm ashamed to say I saw her hanged. My only excuse being that I was but a youth, and had to be in town for other reasons. I remember what a fine figure she showed against the sky as she hung in the misty rain, and how the tight black silk gown set off her shape as she wheeled half-round and back":

> Thomas Hardy writing about his attendance at the execution of Martha Browne in Dorchester in August 1856.

There were a number of noteworthy features about Mary Ann's execution. First, the state hangman, William Calcraft who was by 1873 a rather elderly man (he was in his seventies) and whose methods were often the subject of controversy—given that he had a number of botched executions to his name—was hired to carry out the execution; the scaffold on which Cotton was to be "launched into eternity" was still in the open air, if at least hidden behind the prison's walls; and, of course, Mary Ann was a woman, who was nursing a baby until five days before her execution. Women, by and large, did not get executed, and it was much more normal for those who had received guilty verdicts to be reprieved by the Home Secretary.[1] Indeed, the last hanging of a woman in the county of Durham had been of Mary Nicholson in 1799, after she had been found guilty the previous year of poisoning her mistress Elizabeth Atkinson.

The Victorians held rather peculiar attitudes about the execution of a woman, seemingly finding it both unpleasant, but also intriguing. Thomas Hardy captures perfectly this ambiguity when he described watching the "fine figure" of the unfortunate Martha Browne, twisting and turning in

---

1. The website www.capitalpunishment.org records that between 1900 and 1958 92 men were executed at Durham and only three women—including Mary Ann Cotton.

the air, dressed in her "tight black silk gown" which the novelist remembered "set off her shape". There are clear erotic overtones here, and Hardy would return to this theme when he wrote about another condemned woman — Edith Thompson — who was executed at HMP Holloway in January 1923, in his poem *On the Portrait of a Woman About to be Hanged*, written in the days after Edith had died. Thompson's execution was controversial, for she did not participate in the stabbing of her husband Percy — who was murdered by Edith's lover Frederick Bywaters. However, Hardy's poem is not at all interested in how this might have been a miscarriage of justice, but is much more concerned with how Edith's sexuality was the cause of the situation that she found herself in.

Comely and Capable one of our race
Posing there in your gown of grace,
Plain yet becoming;
Could subtlest breast
Ever have guessed
What was behind that innocent face,
Drumming, Drumming!

Would that your Causer, ere knoll your knell
For this riot of passion, might deign to tell
Why, since it made you
Sound in the germ
It sent a worm
To madden Its handiwork, when It might well
Not have assayed you.

Not have implanted, to your deep rue,
The Clytemnestra spirit in you,
And with purblind vision
Sowed a tare
On a field so fair,

And a thing of symmetry to the view,
Brought to derision![2]

Hardy is clearly imagining an execution that he did not personally witness, so he uses various descriptive techniques to take the reader with him behind the prison's walls to capture the moments before Edith was killed. His reference to "drumming, drumming" for example, suggests the beat of a drum being played at the build-up to an execution; Edith's "gown of grace", alludes to the prison uniform that she would have been wearing; and his phrase about her "posing there" suggests the actual moment on the scaffold before she was to die. Yet each of these words, lines or motifs can have other meanings too. "Posing", for example, suggests on first reading that Edith has chosen this particular situation. However, like an artist's model who poses, she is acting out a scene, not only for the artist, but also for the viewer of the artist's work. The fact that she is therefore "posing" is not her choice, but the choice of another who has asked her to act in this way, and which therefore diminishes her personal responsibility. Why should her prison uniform be a "gown"? This description also clearly evokes the "tight black silk gown" that had been worn by Martha Browne, which had "set off her shape" as she was hanged. Finally, drums and drumming also suggest passions racing and pulses quickening—as they might do between lovers–and it is tempting to see the ambiguity that Hardy expressed on witnessing Martha Browne's execution re-emerging in how he describes Edith's death.[3]

There are other issues to consider in how Hardy portrays Edith in this poem, which not only develops more fully the sexual tension that he seems to be describing, but also throws some further light onto how Mary Ann must have been viewed by her contemporaries. "Comely", for example, suggests a little about what Edith looked like. It implies that she was not

---

2. Hardy's poem is reproduced in C M Bowra (1946), *The Lyrical Poetry of Thomas Hardy*, published in 2009 by The Byron Centre for the Study of Literature and Social Change, University of Nottingham.

3. See Frances Gray (2003), *Women, Crime and Language*, Basingstoke: Palgrave Macmillan. For a good biography of Hardy—and one which takes a different view from my reading of Hardy's memories of Martha Browne's execution, see Claire Tomalin (2006), *Thomas Hardy: The Time-Torn Man*, London: Penguin.

a great beauty, but pleasant, and so too the description "capable" alludes to a skill in getting things done. In short Edith, as the third line makes clear, was "plain, yet becoming", although—and this seems to have been Hardy's main point in the poem—this appearance was deceiving. "Could subtlest breast," he argues "ever have guessed, what was behind that innocent face"? Hardy is describing a temptress, or a *femme fatale*, who is going to seduce those that she encounters, and which is why he employs the ancient Greek myth to suggest that Edith had the "Clytemnestra spirit" in her. Again, the fact that this "spirit" was in Edith might imply that Hardy did not view her as personally responsible for her actions, but even so nothing in the poem challenges the awful fate that awaited her, or implies that Hardy found the sentence that she had received wrong, or indeed the type of punishment that awaited her repugnant.

Mary Ann could be seen in these terms too: she was comely rather than beautiful; capable—as a nurse would have had to have been; she was successful in attracting husbands and lovers; and, of course, she was skilled at getting things done. Above all Mary Ann was, in a phrase still used in our own day, "capable of murder", and so, like Edith, her appearance was deceiving.

Public Spectacles and Private Rituals

What Hardy is also doing in *On the Portrait of a Woman About to be Hanged* is imaging a scene for his readers; conjuring up a picture of what was about to happen, and attempting to convey something of the drama that was unfolding in the moments before the execution took place. Until 1868 this type of imagining would have been unnecessary because capital punishment was administered in public, and so people could have chosen to view an execution for themselves, and therefore would have had no need to turn to poetry. And they did view hangings—in their thousands. When the valet Francois Benjamin Courvoisier was executed in 1840 for the murder of his master Lord William Russell, for example, 40,000 people attended his execution at Newgate, and over one and half million handbills about the murder were sold at a penny a copy. Indeed London was known as "The City of the Gallows", and it has been calculated that a Londoner born in the 1780s could have by the 1840s attended some 400 execution days outside of Newgate, and in doing so watched 1,200 people die. In other words there were lots of executions to attend. Some 35,000 people were condemned to death in England and Wales between 1770 and 1830, and of these 7,000 were executed as opposed to being pardoned or transported abroad to America or Australia.[4] However, by 1837 capital punishment was reserved for those who had been found guilty of murder, attempted murder, high treason, rape, piracy and arson.

Of course public hangings weren't just a feature of the landscape of early Victorian London, but were fully embedded into the life of most major provincial cities. A crowd of 50,000 people, for example, came to watch William Palmer executed at Stafford in 1856—he had been convicted of the murder (by poison) of his gambling associate John Parsons Cook,[5] and over the years public executions became an excuse for a holiday. These were occasions which one historian has characterised as "popular festivals, orgiastic carnivals, and melodramas of bad taste".[6] The ambiguity of large crowds of people behaving badly—often stealing and fighting—getting drunk, but at the same time watching someone about to hang, perhaps for offences less severe than those being committed within the crowd who had gathered to watch the execution, was not lost on contemporary commentators. Dickens—who attended at least four public executions, including that of Courvoisier in 1840—was never a supporter of executions being held in public and questioned whether such occasions "prevent crime in those who attend?" He clearly felt that they did not, and wrote that:

...The spectators include two large classes of thieves—one class who go there as they would go to a dog-fight, or any other brutal sport, for the attraction and excitement of the spectacle; the other who make it a dry matter of business, and mix with the crowd solely to pick pockets. Add to these, the dissolute, the drunken, the most idle, profligate, and abandoned of both sexes—some

4.   These calculations and figures appear in V A C Gatrell (1994), *The Hanging Tree: Execution and the English People, 1770-1868*, Oxford: OUP. The description of London as "The City of the Gallows" is in Harry Potter (1993), *Hanging in Judgement: Religion and the Death Penalty in England*, London: SCM Press, p.8

5.   See Ian Burney (2006), *Poison, Detection and the Victorian Imagination*, Manchester: Manchester University Press.

6.   Potter, *op cit*, p. 69.

moody ill-conditioned minds, drawn thither by a fearful interest—and some impelled by curiosity; of whom the greater part are of an age and temperament rendering the gratification of that curiosity highly dangerous to themselves and to society—and the great elements of the concourse are stated.[7]

Of course holding these views did not stop him from attending other public executions. In a curious foretaste to how Hardy would later recount Martha Browne's execution in 1856, Dickens remembered the execution of Maria Manning who had, with her husband George, been convicted of murdering their lodger Patrick O'Conner in 1849, and he vividly described how Maria had a "fine shape, so elaborately corseted and artfully dressed, that it [i.e. her body] is quite unchanged in its appearance as it slowly swings from side to side".[8] However, he wrote to *The Times* about how he was appalled by the behaviour of the 30,000 crowd:

I believe that a sight so inconceivably awful as the wickedness and levity of the immense crowd collected at the execution this morning could be imagined by no man, and could be presented in no heathen land under the sun...When the sun rose brightly...it gilded thousands upon thousands of upturned faces so inexpressibly odious in their brutal mirth or callousness that man had cause to feel ashamed of the shape he wore, and to shrink from himself as fashioned in the image of the Devil.[9]

Leaving to one side the hypocrisy of Dickens criticising others for their participation in an event that he too chose to witness, it was increasingly clear that the public spectacle of execution was no longer having the effect that those with power desired. After all, public hangings were meant to be part of a wider moral, judicial and religious drama, all played out on a peculiar stage to demonstrate the power of the state. The judge delivering

---

7.   Quote taken from Miscellaneous Papers, www.dickens-online.info
8.   The Manning case is described in some detail by Flanders *op cit*, in the *Introduction*, pps. 157-182.
9.   See Slater, *op cit*, in *Chapter 3*, p.298. Of note the American novelist Herman Melville "paid half a crown" to also be present at the execution, and he described how the "mob was brutish. All in all, a most wonderful, horrible & unspeakable scene"—quoted in Flanders, *op cit*, p. 169.

his decision, the cleric on the scaffold "reclaiming" the soul of the about-to-be-executed, and the hangman himself were all state functionaries; civil servants playing a role in what amounted to a visible display of government. The unruliness and insubordination of the crowd—and sometimes even the behaviour of the condemned themselves, who might refuse to accept their fate either in the past, or what might be waiting for them in the future—were increasingly seen as undermining the "Majesty of the Law", the "Glory of God" and the supposed unlimited power of the state to deliver justice and control. Above all, this spectacle no longer appeared to be civilised.

So in a surprisingly few short years public executions were no longer seen to imply the power of the state, but rather its weakness and contradictions. The problem was not so much the nature of the punishment—execution—or as it was put to Mary Ann "being hanged by the neck until you are dead". Nor was the issue the mechanism by which that punishment was delivered—hanging—although it was clear that some of those who were executed were slowly strangled to death, rather than died quickly and efficiently (see later in the chapter). Rather the problem was the reality that the public process of the ceremony for administering this punishment had fallen into disrepute, at least as far as those with power were concerned. The solution was therefore to render private what had once been public, and so to make capital punishment invisible by hiding it behind the prison's walls. Journalists would still be allowed to attend executions and report upon what they saw—at least until 1934[10]—but the noisy, disrespectful,

---

10. The last execution which a journalist attended was on 4th May 1934 at HM Prison Wandsworth when Albert Probert (26) and Frederick Parker (21) were hanged. Parker and Probert had murdered an elderly shopkeeper called Joseph Bedford at Portslade in Sussex. The executioner was Thomas Pierrepoint, assisted by his nephew Albert Pierrepoint. The journalist who attended the execution was W G Finch of the Press Association. All details taken from S McLaughlin (2004), *Execution Suite: A History of the Gallows at Wandsworth Prison, 1878-1993*, London: HMP Wandsworth. Of note, McLaughlin—who is a senior officer at HMP Wandsworth (at least until 2011)—maintains the Wandsworth Prison Museum, which opened in 2008 in a disused shed beside the prison and many of its artefacts are concerned with capital punishment. Anyone wishing to visit the museum simply phones up McLaughlin at the prison and arranges an appointment. I interviewed McLaughlin as part of the research for this book and had him explain to me his thinking behind setting up the museum. This is an extract of what he said to me, and which reveals the precarious nature of what becomes collected and remembered: "I'd always been

rude, crude and unpredictable public were to be excluded. The state still wanted the power to kill, and so too the church still retained for itself the right to re-claim the souls of the sinful for God, but all of this was now to become imprisoned behind the foreboding walls of the Victorian gaol.

So the move to put the scaffold out of the public's view was not so much about humanity, but rather about civility. And, as such, the state could sanitise and hide the suffering of those who were to be executed, without necessarily diminishing that suffering, or the horrors that attached themselves to the scaffold. In one sense late Victorian social order rested on this increasingly hidden state violence, although perhaps it is also fair to reflect that by the middle of the century the state no longer needed this violence to be public; exhibiting its power publicly was no longer as important as it had once been. After all, the state had become bureaucratically and professionally competent, and so exercised power that did not require the population to be impressed by visible displays of its might and majesty through public executions. So, for an increasingly polite nation, the barbarity of executions had to be camouflaged; hidden not only behind walls, but within rituals that appeared professional, practiced, competent, speedy and routine.

The last public execution was of Irishman Michael Barrett on 26th May 1868, and the first that took place behind the prison's walls was of 18-year-old Thomas Wells at Maidstone Gaol on 13th August 1868. The execution of Barrett was controversial and his case caused considerable disquiet, given

---

interested in local history, and had read some books about Wandsworth, but there was no single book about the history of the prison. I asked about the prison for any old documents that we might have. Most were held by the Works Department. Around that time the Prison Service Museum at Newbold Revel was being formed, and I was walking around the prison with a contractor and just thought that not enough of the prison's history was being preserved. I arranged to get things sent up to the Prison Service Museum—things like the corporal punishment frame. I then started collecting things about the prison, and I tracked down old staff that used to work here and talk to them about their memories of the place. A new Governor arrived in 2001—when Wandsworth was 150-years-old and so we put on a display which was opened by the Princess Royal. After that I needed to find a place to house the materials that we had gathered, and in 2004 another new Governor allowed me to remove the filing cabinets that were filling up this garage and put on a permanent display. I set up an account based on monies gathered from TV companies filming in the gaol as a start-up fund to support the museum. It took two years to get the place decorated—I did much of it myself in my own time. Prince Michael of Kent opened the museum officially in 2008".

that his involvement in an attempt to free Irish prisoners from Clerkenwell House of Detention — which had caused considerable loss of life — was at best peripheral. However, feelings against Irish Catholics were running high and Barrett's execution was probably seen as a way of responding to this popular anxiety.[11] So, on the morning of 26th May, the state hangman William Calcraft entered Barrett's cell, pinioned his arms, placed a hood over his head, then the noose, and opened the trap door. Seemingly, he died without mishap, but Calcraft — who would also hang Mary Ann — was not always so competent and professional.

William Calcraft

The next, and even future generations of state hangmen, were particularly hostile to William Calcraft. Albert Pierrepoint, for example, liked to claim that while Calcraft "strangled" his victims, he "executed them", and William Marwood and James Berry — the latter who regarded his work as a science — were keen to describe the "Table of Drops" that they had developed, so as to more efficiently execute their victims and thus distance themselves from Calcraft and his methods.[12] This table calculated the distance of the "drop" that the prisoner would have to fall, based on the weight of the person who was about to be executed, so that his neck would break — making death almost instantaneous — and thus avoid the spectacle of someone slowly strangling to death at the end of a noose. Berry, for example, calculated that a man of 14 stones would need a drop of eight feet, while someone half a stone lighter would require a two inches longer drop, and so on depending on the weight of the person to be executed. A man or woman weighing eight stones would therefore require a drop of ten feet.[13]

This overall approach was known as the "long drop", and was the exact

11. For an account of Barrett's execution see Potter, *op cit*, p.94.
12. On Berry and Marwood's Table of Drops, see Stewart Evans (2004), *Executioner: The Chronicles of a Victorian Hangman*, Stroud: Sutton Publishing. Quote by Pierrepoint taken from Whitehead, *op cit*, in the *Introduction*, p. 50.
13. Berry wrote two autobiographies in which he explains his approach to execution and describes his table of drops. James Berry (1892), *My Experiences as an Executioner*, London: Percy Lund and Co., and James Berry (1905), *The Hangman's Thoughts Above the Gallows*, Bradford: Parker Bros, and Co.

opposite of the method employed by Calcraft, which was known as the "short drop". When Calcraft pulled the lever to open up the trap-door of the scaffold, the person being executed never fell further than about three feet, which was rarely sufficient enough to break the person's neck and who would therefore often twist and turn, struggling for breath before dying slowly as a result of strangulation. On many occasions Calcraft was reduced to swinging on the victim's legs, or pushing down on their shoulders to speed the process of execution along, and unsurprisingly he developed a reputation for being surly and sinister looking. Even so, he was employed to hang Courvoisier, the Mannings, Michael Barrett and Thomas Wells—all of whom we have encountered in this chapter—and in the course of a 45-year career it has been calculated that he participated in 450 executions.

Inevitably, given the length of his career and his use of the "short drop", Calcraft was also associated with some notoriously bungled executions. For example, in March 1856 he was engaged to hang William Bousfield at Newgate, who had murdered his wife and three children in London. Bousfield was clearly suffering from some form of mental illness, and would refuse to speak for long periods of time, but then when he did speak he would claim that everything that had happened had been a dream. Before his execution he threw himself into the fire in his cell, and was very badly burned. Bousfield was actually already more dead than alive on the day of his execution, and so had to be carried to the scaffold on a chair. *The Observer* described the scene:

> It is almost impossible to imagine a more hideous and revolting spectacle than the death like and swollen appearance of the face, and the utter helplessness of the limbs as they hung downwards, and nothing can be compared to it than a bloated and swollen mummy.[14]

However, no matter how grotesque Bousfield's appearance might have been, nothing could have prepared the crowd of onlookers for what was about to happen next. Calcraft put the noose around Bousfield's neck as

14. *The Observer*, 6th May 1856.

he remained sitting in his chair — seemingly already dead — but when the drop fell he sprang to life and managed to get his legs onto the platform of the scaffold, and so prevented himself from falling. The prison staff helping Calcraft pushed Bousfield's legs off the platform, but on two further occasions he managed to get a footing so as to prevent his execution, and only died after Calcraft — who had hurriedly left the execution through fear that he might be shot — returned to the scaffold and pulled on Bousfield's legs and strangled him.[15]

Of course the generation of hangmen that followed Calcraft liked to dwell on stories of this kind, for they served to suggest the distance that they themselves had travelled in developing a more scientific, rational, quick and therefore more humane way of killing people. Not for them the ghastly and uncivilised prospect of hanging onto the legs of their victims, but rather a quick, speedy, seemly and seemingly technically proficient method of dispatching the guilty to their maker. Of course, that was the theory, but the practice could also go terribly wrong. In particular the "long drop" — if badly calculated — might also result in the head of the person being executed being completely severed from the body, as it did in the case of Robert Goodale who was hanged by Berry at Norwich Castle in November 1885. This execution became known as the "Goodale mess".[16] While this event was witnessed and described by a number of journalists, it did not have the same impact as the horrors attached to a bungled public execution. Increasingly, not only was an execution hidden behind the prison's walls, but also further camouflaged within the prison by being confined within specially designed execution chambers — effectively isolating the condemned prisoner with a few specially selected staff and the chaplain, and screening him from the view of even his fellow inmates.[17]

---

15. For an account of Bousfield's execution see Gray (2011) *op cit*, p. 13-14 and Judith Rowbottom (2010), "Execution as Punishment in England, 1750-200," in A-M Kilday and D Ash (eds), *Histories of Crime: Britain, 1600-2000*, Basingstoke: Palgrave Macmillan. A good history of Newgate is by Kelly Grovier (2008), *The Gaol: The Story of Newgate: London's Most Notorious Prison*, London: John Murray.

16. Evans (2004), *op cit*, pps.100-110.

17. This isolation within the prison was still a feature of executions in the 1960s. For example, Robert Douglas (2008), *At Her Majesty's Pleasure*, London: Hodder & Staughton, remembered working at HM Prison Winson Green in Birmingham when Oswald Augustus Grey was executed on November 20th, 1962. He describes how: "The condemned cell is on C2

Viewing an execution became the preserve of a very small group of people, each performing an increasingly specialised role, and all the public would see of this process was a black flag hoisted on the gate of the prison after the execution had been completed. This was viewed as progress.

Cotton was not to be executed in public, but reflecting the slowly developing practice of Victorian executions, nor was she to be executed within a specially designed execution suite. Instead she was hanged in the open air behind the prison's walls, because at this time the prison had yet to organize a gallows within the gaol itself. And, linking her to the past, she was to be executed by Calcraft by means of the "short drop". Her execution was therefore almost at the half way point in the development of the culture of executions—looking both backwards to the barbarism of the past but also towards the future, where civility through speed and efficiency would be the order of the day—although this could hardly have given Mary Ann any comfort.

Mary Ann's Last Few Days

Mary Ann was sentenced on Friday 7th March and it was the custom that there should be three Sundays between sentence and execution. As far as Cotton was concerned, this meant that she had 17 days left to live. During this time she would write letters—many encouraging friends, family and acquaintances to petition the Home Secretary asking for a reprieve; receive a number of visitors; re-discover (or at least renew) her faith; have her baby adopted; and then finally prepare for death. However, neither in her letters, nor in what she is reported to have said to her visitors, did she admit to her guilt in relation to Charles Edward's death.

---

landing. The jail is always locked up when a condemned man is on the move; no prisoners ever get to see him... even though we officers rarely see the condemned man, and the cons don't see him at all, everyone is conscious he is THERE", pps 62-63. This process of making execution invisible—started in 1868—has continued to this day. For example it is impossible to see the Victorian execution suite at HM Prison Durham, and I noted the following in my own reflexive diaries about my visit to HM Prison Wandsworth—which had a working gallows well into the 1990s: "There's nothing to see; some brick discolouration which implies that a wall—a building—might have had some previous use, but unless you knew, no one would ever guess that the cleaning store now being used once housed a gallows, or that the staff rest room had functioned as the condemned cell. The gallows has disappeared not just in law, but in the solid fact of bricks and mortar, and which means that it is also in danger of disappearing from history".

We have already encountered some of the letters that she wrote at this time—most notably to Henry Holdforth, bemoaning the fact that she was a "frendless [sic] woman", and remembering her childhood as "days of joy". She also wrote to her former husband James Robinson on 12th March, begging him to bring his three children—one of whom, George Robinson, was also her son—to come and visit her. This is a quite extraordinary letter, and worth quoting in full.

My dear friend

I so pose you Will mor then I can tell you conserning my Afull faite i have come I Wish to know if you will Let me see the 3 Childer as soune as you possible you can I should Like to see you Bring them if you can Aske sum Won Eals to Bring them i have been told today you say you onley had Won Letter from me since i left you if you have not got Enny mor they have been detaining from you ie hope you Will get this And i thinke if you have Won sarke of kindness in you Will Try to get my Life spared you know your sealfe there has been A moast dredfull to hear tell of the Lyies that has been told A Bout me ie must tell you you Art h Cause of All my trouble fore if you had not Left th house And So As i could hav got in to my house When i came the dor i Was to Wandr the steets With my Baby in my Armes no home fore me no place to Lay my head you Know if you call your mind Backe i should not solde my things in susickle street to come to you then i had mother to call on then But When you closed the dore i had no Won for you Knowe your sealfe i Am Knot guilty of the Lyies that have been tolde Consirnig me if you speake the nothing But the trouth i can not draw my mind on the past for it is mor than nature can bare Won thing i hope Will try to get my Life spared for ie Am not guilty of the crime ie have to dyie fore considr things And do What you Can fore me so ie must Conclude At this time i hope to hear from you By return of post

Yor K W   M A R

                                             M A Cotton

By any estimation this is a bizarre letter—even allowing for the fact that its author was awaiting execution, and so in a presumably heightened emotional state. For example, did she really expect Robinson to bring the three children to see her? Presumably she had forgotten the other children that she had killed while living in Robinson's house, and the fact that she had actually abandoned baby George with a neighbour in Sunderland. Perhaps she was simply trying to present herself as a dutiful mother—as she had in court—and so not asking to see the children prior to her execution might have been interpreted as odd. Of course, by doing so, she was also re-connecting with Robinson, as the children—especially George—maintained a bridge between her and her former husband. We should also note that she signed her letter "M A R", which we can safely presume was meant to be "Mary Ann Robinson", as well as M A Cotton, although it is difficult to decipher what she meant by the initials " K W".

Her intention in all of this was a conscious attempt to blackmail Robinson for one specific purpose—"you Will Try to get my Life spared". Indeed, if this moral blackmail did not work on the basis of appealing to their children, Cotton even went as far as blaming Robinson as "th Cause of All my trouble". This is of course self-serving nonsense that conveniently ignores the money that she stole from him and the murders that she had committed in their house, as well as everything that had happened previously in her life. Even so, perhaps reflecting the emotional significance that she placed on her return to their house in Pallion, Cotton locates and reduces the cause of what was subsequently to happen to her as "you closed the dore". In other words, the fault for all the problems that then befell her were not rooted in her own appalling behaviour, both before and after her move to Pallion, but in the behaviour of Robinson as a father, and especially in his behaviour as a husband who would lock his wife out in the street.

We should also consider whether Cotton thought that Robinson would make this letter public. Perhaps not, for it certainly allows us to peer behind her mask and to see something of the real woman, rather than the carefully constructed public image of the breast-feeding mother at court, quietly sobbing at the mention of Charles Edward's name, or of the former Sunday School teacher writing to friends and remembering her childhood.

Her letter to Robinson provides for us a quite different insight into Mary Ann's personality, for it is aggressive and ill-judged, and comes across as short-tempered and petulant. Can we also detect in her final sentence—"i hope to hear from you By of post"—a glimpse into the domineering, as opposed to the "capable" side of her personality?

In any event, Robinson did not visit Mary Ann—which prompted her to write to him again—although he did get as far as the prison gate before he changed his mind. He made the journey with his brother-in-law—a man called Burns—who did go into the prison and who visited Cotton in her cell.[18] Burns implored Mary Ann to make her peace with God, and to confess to her murder of Charles Edward—which she again refused to do. Burns also provided some detail about Mary Ann's cell, which he thought surprisingly large and comfortable, if rather sparsely furnished. There were religious books on a table, and two female warders—whom we would now call prison officers—sat on a bed, while a third nursed baby Edith.

Apart from Burns, Mary Ann was visited by several other members of her extended family, although we should note that none of them petitioned for her reprieve. Her first visitors were Margaret Stott, the wife of Mary Ann's step-father's brother, and Jane Stubbs—whom Mrs Stott had brought along as a companion. Seemingly Mrs Stott asked Cotton why she had murdered Charles Edward, but Mary Ann denied any involvement and, in a theme which she would later develop in her letters, suggested that James Robinson was the real culprit by leaving her locked out of their home in Sunderland. Her final visitor was her step-father George Stott, although this does not seem to have brought her any comfort—Stott impressed upon Cotton the gravity of her situation, and chastised her for the poor spelling she displayed in her letters. Even so, it is reported that on seeing her step-father, she jumped up from the stool that she had been sitting on, and threw her arms around his neck, saying "Oh, father, father. I knew you would come and see me". She is then reported to have "burst into a paroxysm of weeping". George asked her if she had anything to confess, but once again Mary Ann denied any involvement in the murder of Charles Edward. Instead she said:

18. See account in Appleton, *op cit*, in the *Introduction*, pps. 110-112.

Father, I have not led a good life, but I am innocent of the crimes laid to my
charge. I know the public are against me, but I am going to die for a crime
I am as innocent of as the child unborn. I never intentionally gave that boy
anything to destroy him. It was in the arrowroot that I bought for him from
a grocer at West Auckland.

However, George believed none of this, although the arrowroot theory
took on a life of its own. As he was leaving Mary Ann asked him if he
would go and see Robinson on her behalf, and after her step-father had
gone Mary Ann had to be consoled by her female guards.[19]

Between Margaret and then George Stott visiting, Mary Ann had baby
Edith adopted by Sarah and William Edwards, who had been her former
neighbours in Johnson Terrace in West Auckland. There had been about
50 applications to adopt Edith, some of the prospective adopters being
"in a good position in society", and the *Northern Echo* thought that it was
"rather singular that [Edith] should have been transferred by the culprit to
a person in humble circumstances."[20] The couple came to pick up Edith on
Wednesday 19th March, and were accompanied by Mary Ann's last lodger,
William Lowrey. Lowrey wrote about this visit in a letter published in the
Northern Echo on 21st March, although he must have written to the paper
on the evening of his visit to the prison. The letter confirmed that Cotton
wanted the Edwards to have baby Edith, and that Lowrey had found her
cell to be "fifty times better that I expected". He continued:

Everything was as clean as a new pin. The first thing I saw was Mrs Cotton
sitting on a stool close to a good fire, giving the breast to her infant. She was
dressed in a skirt, a loose jacket, but no shoes on, and nothing on her head.
Looking round the cell I saw three chairs, one table, one bed and some good
books. The walls had pretty paper on…God forbid, Mr. Editor, that I should
ever see such a sight again. Just imagine a little child on its mother's knee,
looking up at its mother's face and laughing, and her on the brink of another

19. There is an account of this last visit in Appleton, *op cit*, pps. 125-126, which is taken from
The *Durham County Advertiser*, 22 March 1873. There is a further account in the *Newcastle
Courant*, 28th March 1873.

20. *Northern Echo*, 20th March 1873.

world, and her heart as hard as a stone. These are the words that she said: "I wish I may never have any power to rise off this seat. I never gave that boy Charles Edward any poison wilfully. It was in the arrowroot, and all got it. I am going to die for a crime I am not guilty of". But nevertheless we got the child home all right. It has a kind father and mother: may God bless them. I may just say the female warders are very kind to her.[21]

It is perhaps fair to suggest that Mary Ann encouraged Lowrey to write this letter to the press, for there are clear attempts to engage the sympathy of the newspaper's readers. For example, Mary Ann is inevitably breast feeding in Lowrey's account, and baby Edith is described as looking up into her mother's face and laughing. There is also the suggestion that the cause of Charles Edward's death was arrowroot, rather than arsenic, and as we have seen, Mary Ann would also later repeat this to her step-father when he visited her in her cell. However, what are we to make of Lowrey's observation that Cotton's heart was "as hard as a stone", and the fact that she described Charles Edward as "that boy" — a phrase that she would also use when talking to her step-father? Does this description of Charles Edward not imply some callousness, or at the very least distance, and so counterbalances the description of the intimacy of Mary Ann breast feeding Edith. Perhaps Lowrey's suggestion that Cotton's heart was as hard as a stone's indicates that he was not in fact convinced of her innocence at all. However, we shouldn't underestimate the broader impact of melodramatic letters such as Lowrey's and how this may ultimately have influenced public opinion about Mary Ann.

Cotton was also visited on several occasions by the Reverend W Stevenson, a Wesleyan minister, whom Mary Ann obviously found more conducive than the prison chaplain, the Reverend J C Lowe. In due course Stevenson would also be accompanied by two other Wesleyan ministers on the Durham circuit — the Reverend J M Mountford and the Reverend J Bennett. Stevenson must have reminded Mary Ann of her youth, and he left her a bible from which she would quote passages aloud to her guards. However, even though he visited her on a number of occasions she did not

21. *Northern Echo*, 21 March 1873.

confess her guilt to him, and over time Stevenson came to believe that she might be innocent.[22] The Reverend Mountford, who would address the press after her execution, was more certain of her guilt, although even at the very end Mary Ann stuck to her story of her innocence — or at least not intentionally poisoning Charles Edward. In any event, both Mountford and Stevenson attended to her at her execution, and accompanied her on her walk to the gallows.

Hanged by the Neck Until Dead

The morning of Monday 24th March 1873 was misty and damp, but that hadn't stopped a small crowd of about 200 people from gathering outside the door of the gaol by half past seven.[23] What were they hoping to see? Obviously they could no longer view the execution itself, but perhaps they simply hoped to catch a glimpse of the executioner Calcraft and his Welsh assistant Robert Evens. A group of about 20 reporters were also waiting to gain entry to the prison, and it is reported that when the executioners pushed past the journalists and entered the gaol some angry words — in a "crabbed tone of voice" — were directed at them by Calcraft. The *Northern Echo* suggested somewhat incredulously that Calcraft "was made nervous by reporters".

At the time that Calcraft was entering the gaol, Mary Ann had already been awake for some four hours. She had retired to her bed on Sunday evening at about half past 10, and the *Northern Echo* commented that she had "passed on the whole a comfortable night", although this can hardly be accurate. Indeed, the *Newcastle Courant* is probably closer to the truth when it suggested that her sleep had been "troubled; she tossed about from side to side and occasionally moaned." At half past five in the morning she had been served with a cup of tea, and some 30 minutes later several ministers — including the Reverend Mountford and the Reverend Stevenson — entered her cell, and started to pray with her. It is reported that they

---

22. See account in Appleton, *op cit*, pps. 120-123.
23. This account of Mary Ann's execution is taken from two different sources — the *Newcastle Courant*, 28th March 1873 and the *Northern Echo*, 25th March 1873. They each provide slightly different and significant details about what took place, even if they are agreed about the broader conduct of the execution.

were trying to "produce in her a solemnity of mind and a corresponding calmness of demeanour befitting her awful situation". Seemingly, their efforts proved successful, and the *Northern Echo* suggested that Mary Ann "was evidently deeply impressed with the terrible nature of her position, and prayed most fervently for the welfare of her husband Robinson and her little child".

It is interesting to note that Robinson is yet again a focus of Cotton's attention at this time, which further indicates, just moments before her death, the significance that he must have held for her in her lifetime. However, who is "her little child" that she is praying for? Perhaps this would have been Edith—given that she had only recently been taken away from Mary Ann—but it might equally have been any number of the other children that she bore and killed. It does not seem to have been Charles Edward. After they had prayed, the Reverend Mountford questioned her about her guilt in the murder of Charles Edward, and it was reported in the *Newcastle Courant* that she did admit that she had "administered poison to all the deceased persons, but she still asserted that she had not done so intentionally, as the arsenic had been mixed amongst the arrowroot she gave to the deceased at the time she purchased it". Mary Ann also prayed with the three female guards who had been with her in the condemned cell, and is reported to have "wept bitterly" that Robinson had not visited her. Her tears notwithstanding, the *Northern Echo* thought that throughout the past few weeks Cotton had been "reserved and indifferent", and that her manner had been "peculiar and determined".

Just after seven thirty, the various reporters were allowed into the prison, and were taken to the site of the scaffold, while Calcraft, Evens and the under sheriff of the County were ushered into the Governor's office. The Governor—Colonel Armstrong—was actually in London giving evidence to a parliamentary committee on the day of the execution, and so events were being managed by the deputy governor, James Young. The reporters were annoyed that they were not allowed to view the "pinioning"—when Mary Ann's arms would have been bound to her sides by being attached to a leather belt—and the *Northern Echo* was particularly put out by this being done in private. "Doubtless the Governor of the gaol had some special reason for this alteration", the paper suggested, or perhaps Calcraft had simply insisted that he didn't want the reporters to be present. No doubt this also indicates how the process of the conduct of an execution was still being formalised and standardised, after having been moved behind the prison's walls. However, the *Northern Echo* explained that its keenness to view this particular moment was because it believed that it was at this stage "when a resolute culprit, faced by the immediate preliminaries of death, will make a confession".

This also suggests something of what the *Northern Echo* thought that it was important to report to its readers; in other words, it viewed a confession as "news". The paper also provided other details, such as the fact that Mary Ann was "dressed in a black stuff gown, which hung loosely on her now slender form; the half of her black and white check shawl was thrown over her shoulders, and so fastened in front to hide the pinioning straps". There had been some fears that Cotton would be unable to walk to the scaffold, and a chair—to which she would have been tied—was ready if this was the case. In any event, Mary Ann decided that she would walk, and as she left her cell at ten minutes to eight, she is reported to have stated, "Heaven is my home".

Richard Bowser, the under sheriff of the county, and his deputy, demanded that Young hand over the body of Mary Ann Cotton for execution. After this formality had been completed, there was then a mini procession from Cotton's cell to the site of the execution, with two male warders holding Mary Ann by the elbows so as to push her along; Calcraft and Evens behind the warders; then the deputy governor; followed by various ministers—including Mountford and Stevenson. A number of other warders were also present, and two of Mary Ann's female guards also walked a little way towards the scaffold, but Miss Robinson and Miss Jellis took fright at the last moment and hurried from view and were unable to watch the final act of Cotton's drama.[24]

As the clock struck eight, the execution procession left the main confines of the prison and walked to the scaffold, which was in the eastern quadrangle of the prison in a large open space between the south and east wings. The scaffold itself was a fairly rudimentary affair, consisting of two

24. Appleton, *op cit*, p. 130.

upright posts about eight feet high, with a cross beam at the top to hold the black painted rope and noose. There were no steps to climb, as the trapdoor was at ground level, but above an eight foot pit into which Mary Ann would drop—although Calcraft would use only the "short drop" and not the full eight feet.

Mary Ann would not have been able to see the scaffold from her quarters, and the walk to her death took at least four minutes. The first that the journalists knew of her approach was when they heard the sounds of the ministers praying and Cotton sobbing. The *Newcastle Courant* described her as looking like a "doomed wretch" who "appeared much agitated as she as she was led out to die; her hands were clasped, her eyes brimming over with tears, and the prayers to which she attempted to give utterance were half choked by hysterical sobbing". Even the reporter from the *Northern Echo* was moved by the occasion—if less so than his Newcastle peer—and described how:

> When she reached the yard where the reporters were stationed she glanced hastily and wildly at the little crowd, opened her hands as if in mute amazement, and then knit them tightly together again, uttering an exclamation like "Lord have mercy". Steadily pursuing her course to the south eastern quadrangle, she never diverted her attention from the prayers. She murmured the whole of the way; and when she reached the drop Calcraft immediately stood before her, and covered her face with the white cap. She trembled perceptibly, but never ceased her devotions. Calcraft's assistant then put the rope around her neck, and worked it round to the proper place, at which the prisoner visibly shuddered. Calcraft then strapped her legs together, and when he had finished this, saw that the rope was duly adjusted, and withdrew to the place where the handle of the bolt was raised above the ground, while the two male warders retained their position on the planks on each side of the prisoner. She clasped her hands close to her breast, murmured in an earnest tone, "Lord, have mercy on my soul", and in a moment the bolt was drawn from behind by Calcraft's assistant.

Mary Ann fell some three feet into the eight foot pit, and was then slowly strangled to death. Her chest was reported to have heaved and her hands twitched up and down, and so Calcraft was forced to put his hands on her shoulders to steady her—perhaps also to add his own pressure to her neck. When he moved his hands away again Mary Ann continued to sway from side to side, and so awful was the scene that Browser—the under sheriff—nearly fainted, and had to be supported by some of the warders. Eventually, after some three minutes, she died.

In the minutes after her death, and possibly in reply to some questions from the reporters, the Reverend Mountford addressed the crowd, and stated that he had impressed upon Mary Ann the great importance of making a full confession. This she had not done, but according to Mountford she had stated:

> That she believed that she had been the agent (she did not use the word agent but she meant it) and that she had been the poisoner of this child, but not intentionally. She made that statement this morning, a little after six o'clock.

And that was as much as Cotton ever admitted.

After an hour or so Mary Ann's body was cut down, and the prison surgeon confirmed that she was indeed dead. The cause of her death was given as asphyxia by hanging. Her body was then laid in a coffin, painted black on the outside and was taken to the prison chapel. A formal inquest—attended by a grieving Mrs Stott—was held at 11 am in a classroom in the prison, and Mary Ann's body was formally identified by two female warders. There was some debate about whether the rope should be allowed to be taken away by Calcraft, or whether it could be buried with Mary Ann, although in the end the coroner—John Favell—ruled that he knew of no law that allowed for the rope to be buried with the deceased, and so Calcraft got his trophy. A cast of Mary Ann's head was made by the West Hartlepool Phrenological Society—so as to allow for further academic study—and then finally, at two o'clock she was buried near to the west wall, within the confines of the prison.

Chapter Six

Disappearing from View and Becoming Unseen

"The hanging has led to a mixture of facts, myth and legend that tries to give an account of why the woman was hanged":

A Potted History of West Auckland, p.14.

Within days of her execution photographs of Mary Ann in her black and white checked shawl were being sold in Durham, and as late as 1973 Appleton remembered that there were still some that could be bought of her locally even then.[1] A little over a week after she had been hanged, "a great moral drama" called "The Life and Death of Mary Ann Cotton" opened at West Hartlepool Theatre, and various children's nursery rhymes could be heard being half-sung, half-recited around the playgrounds of the north east. The most famous of these was:

> Mary Ann Cotton,
> She's dead and she's rotten,
> She lies in her bed,
> With her eyes wide open.
> Sing, sing, oh, what can I sing,
> Mary Ann Cotton is tied up with string.
> Where, where? Up in the air,
> Sellin' black puddens a penny a pair.

There were many local variations to this basic rhyme, and on a visit to West Auckland in 2011 one woman told me that the verse that she had

---

1.   Appleton, *op cit*, in the *Introduction*, p. 134.

sung was "Mary Ann Cotton, she's dead and she's rotten, lying in her bed with her finger up her bottom" (See *Appendix 1*).

This hardly amounts to a great deal, especially when compared to the infamy and interest in other Victorian and contemporary serial killers. In a very short space of time all that was left of Mary Ann and of her story were some souvenir photographs of Cotton herself, a play—that did not run past the summer—and a few children's nursery rhymes. Even the cast of her head that had been made by the West Hartlepool Phrenological Society was lost, and over the years Mary Ann Cotton has slowly faded from history. The teapot at Beamish Museum that she was supposed to have served tea from is in all likelihood not Cotton's at all, and nor does Mary Ann seem to have ever sat upon the stool that the museum holds. She has become, at best, a half-remembered, and essentially a local curiosity, where facts are scarce and opinions many, with the author of *A Potted History of West Auckland* even suggesting that "The guilt or innocence of Mary Ann Cotton is, today, a subject of debate in some quarters. Those living today can never truly know. You can only read and make up your own mind."[2]

In short, History has been kind—far too kind—to Mary Ann; she has either been totally forgotten in a national context, or when she is remembered in the north east, she is given the benefit of the doubt as to her hand in the murder of Charles Edward, and her other likely victims. How are we to account for this extraordinary state of affairs?

Mary Ann's disappearance from History is all the more difficult to explain given that it is now generally accepted that women who murder are seen to disrupt and confuse wider cultural views about who women are, and how they should behave.[3] As a consequence when women kill their murders are often used to generate meanings about the particular time and society in which these murders took place, so that their murders become a metaphoric "window" into a culture.[4] So too, while agreeing

2.   Martin Connolly (2009), "A Potted History of West Auckland", np. This booklet is available from West Auckland Post Office, West Auckland, DL14 9HJ.

3.   See, for example, W Chan (2001) *Women, Murder and Justice*, Basingstoke: Palgrave and B Morrissey (2003) *When Women Kill: Questions of Agency and Subjectivity*, London: Routledge.

4.   For a discussion on this subject see E Seal (2010), *Women, Murder and Femininity: Gender Representations of Women Who Kill*, New York: Palgrave.

with these general conclusions, father and daughter American academics, Elizabeth and Harold Schechter, have recently questioned in relation to serial murder, whether "light can be shed on the controversial issue of gender differences by considering the phenomenon of female serial murder vis-à-vis the analogous atrocities perpetrated by men."[5] They also suggest that because female serial killers undermine the conception of women as the "gentler sex", they are often not judged as morally wicked as male serial killers, perhaps because their preferred methods of murder—such as poisoning—can sometimes be interpreted as "mercy killing". All of this is in dramatic contrast to the serial murders committed by men—who rip and slash, deface and torture—and so it is usually male serial murderers who catch the eye and in doing so become iconic.

Did Mary Ann disappear as a result of her gender? There must be something in this for, until relatively recently, serial killing has been almost exclusively dominated by theorising that considered the biography of the individual serial killer and *his* background, or by questions of definition as to what we mean when we describe someone as a "serial killer", as opposed to say a "spree" or a "mass" murderer. In short, serial killing has tended to be viewed as an overwhelmingly male phenomenon, although over a decade ago Kelleher and Kelleher were developing a typology of female serial killers that included the "black widow", "angel of death", "sexual predator", "revenge" and "profit or crime".[6]

This male bias notwithstanding, it is also fair to reflect that there have been a number of true crime accounts of individual British female serial killers, with Myra Hindley in particular becoming iconic of the genre. Even so, this does not explain why, for example, Rose West and Hindley have gained notoriety while the cases of Beverly Allitt[7] or Mary Ann

---

5.   E Schechter and H Schechter (2010), "Killing with Kindness: Nature, Nurture, and the Female Serial Killer", in S Waller (ed.) *Serial Killers: Philosophy for Everyone*, pp.117-128, Oxford: Wiley-Blackwell, p. 119.

6.   For a discussion about female serial killer types see Gurian, E (2011), "Female Serial Murderers: Directions for Future Research on a Hidden Population", *International Journal of Offender Therapy and Comparative Criminology*, 55(1): 27-42. Also of use is Holmes, S T, Hickey, E and Holmes, R M (1991), "Female Serial Murderesses: Constructing Differentiating Types", *Journal of Contemporary Criminal Justice* Vol 7 No. 4: 245-256.

7.   For example, there has only been one biography of Allitt, written by Nick Davies (1993) *Murder on Ward Four: The Story of Bev Allitt, and the Most Terrifying Crime Since the Moors*

Cotton remain relatively obscure. Cotton has to all intents and purposes disappeared from public view, or to use the more academic description that I have employed earlier, she has become "unseen".

This idea of the "unseen" serial killer comes from my co-authored work about a male serial killer called Trevor Joseph Hardy. Hardy murdered three young women in Manchester, England between 1974 and 1976, and is now one of Britain's longest serving prisoners. However, he was largely ignored by the national media at the time of these murders and has since become almost forgotten. Was it this initial lack of interest in his case that resulted in Hardy's subsequent disappearance — becoming "unseen" — in popular and academic writing which is concerned with the phenomenon of serial killing?[8] Might all of this have something to do with what is known as "newsworthiness" — in other words what it is that is thought to grab the reading public's attention? What is it that makes a good "mass media" story? Perhaps the relationship between serial killing and the role of the mass media within that relationship is much more complex than had previously been described, and is dependent on a range of case-specific variables that might — or might not — engender the circumstances which would allow any particular serial killer to have "newsworthiness" and emerge into public consciousness and become "seen".

Let's re-examine Mary Ann's case in light of these issues, and see if we can come to some more definitive conclusions about why she disappeared from view, assess her more generally as a serial killer, and then try to establish how many people she actually killed. But so as to throw greater light onto this analysis, let's also compare Mary Ann with the activities of that more iconic Victorian serial killer — Jack the Ripper–and by doing so better test Schechter and Schechter's argument, and question whether the difference in our interest in Jack the Ripper and Cotton perhaps stems from who it

---

Murders, London: Chatto & Windus. It is interesting that Davies uses the Moors Murders in his title as a way of allowing his readers to measure the severity of Allitt's crimes. Apart from this one book, there was also an official inquiry into the Allitt case — C Clothier (1994), *Allitt Inquiry: Independent Inquiry Relating to Deaths and Injuries on the Children's Ward at Grantham and Kesteven General Hospital during the Period February to April 1991,* London: The Stationery Office. Davies and Clothier disagree with each other on almost every aspect of the case.

8. Wilson, D, Tolputt, H, Howe, N and Kemp, D (2010) "When Serial Killers Go Unseen: The Case of Trevor Joseph Hardy", *Crime Media Culture,* Volume 6 Number 2: 153-167.

is that they targeted and how they killed, and whether these differences in method and victim selection can also tell us something more generally about gender differences within serial murder. Let's start by considering how many people Cotton might have murdered.

Body Count

In the days after her execution various newspapers speculated about how many people Mary Ann might have killed. The usual estimate was "about twenty", but the *Newcastle Courant*—a paper that was never particularly supportive of Cotton—went as high as thinking that she had "hurried to the grave the large number of 25 human beings."[9] Her biographer Appleton thought that she might have been responsible for and that "perhaps 14 or 15 is about the truth"[10] and, as we have seen, based on his analysis of death and burial certificates, Whitehead believed that she was only guilty of four murders, with her responsibility for ten others "not proven".[11]

There is clearly a very wide gap between four and 25—a gap which is difficult to narrow for a number of reasons. First, Mary Ann was only charged and convicted of one count of murder, and the other charges that would have been brought forward to court were left to lie on file. This was actually not that unusual, and even today serial killers are suspected of having murdered many more victims than those that they get convicted of having killed. Even after a public inquiry to look into the deaths for which he was responsible, Harold Shipman, for example, is suspected of perhaps having killed another 45 of his patients. So too Dennis Nilsen, Robert Black, Steve Wright, and Peter Tobin are all also suspected of having killed many more people than they have been convicted of having murdered. Second, Cotton never confessed to any murders at all. This is again not unusual behaviour for serial killers, but of course her reticence frustrates the desire to be precise about her hand in other deaths. Finally, as we have seen, arsenic poisoning did mimic the symptoms of other Victorian ailments, and it is therefore difficult to be definitive about the cause of death of people within her household without every one of those

9. *Newcastle Courant*, 28th March 1873.
10. Appleton, *op cit*, p. 135.
11. Whitehead, *op cit*, in the Introduction, p. 55.

suspected of having been murdered being exhumed, and their bodies subjected to chemical analysis. This is of course impossible.

Yet if we were today doing a "cold case review" what might we conclude about Mary Ann and the number of people that she might have been responsible for killing? Even accepting that we cannot do a chemical analysis on the remains of each potential victim, we can note that there were other chemical tests done by Scattergood on the remains of Frederick Cotton Jnr., Robert Robson Cotton and Joseph Nattrass. He found significant quantities of arsenic in all three, and without doubt he would have given evidence to that effect if these charges had been brought to court. Of course, the police had also tried to have Frederick Cotton Snr. exhumed, but his body could not be found in the graveyard. Do we really imagine that if his body had been located and then handed over to Scattergood for analysis, that it would have been free of arsenic? It is surely quite clear that Mary Ann was guilty of this sequence of deaths—for at the time she was trying to cement her relationship with Quick-Manning, and therefore clearing her house of anyone who might stand in her way. Added to this sequence we should also include Margaret Cotton, although her body was never exhumed at Walbottle. Margaret left a considerable sum of money to her brother, which Mary Ann inherited on Frederick's death.

Mary Ann also claimed that she had had four children with her first husband when she was living in Cornwall between 1852 and 1856. She suggested that all four of these children had died. However, there is no proof whatsoever that these children ever lived—there are no birth, christening or death certificates about them—and nor were any of these children insured. In short, it is difficult to claim that Cotton killed these children when we are not actually certain that they ever existed.

And what of the other eleven potential victims? There is no way of being definitive, but it is hard to escape the simple reality that Mary Ann benefited from all of their deaths. These benefits were social and personal, as much as they were financial—an issue discussed later in this chapter—for it was a recurring criminological pattern in her history that when Mary Ann entered a household as a wife, partner, daughter, friend or housekeeper that the other occupants of that household started to die. This is more than a simple co-incidence, because these deaths usually occurred at a point in time when Mary Ann might have wanted to reduce the work that she would have had to do to maintain that household, or more usually when she was eager to move on with a new relationship. The illness of her mother Margaret Stott, for example, came at a time when Mary Ann had moved in as James Robinson's housekeeper in Sunderland, and at the very least travelling to New Seaham to look after her mother was likely to disrupt what she was planning and hoping for in Sunderland. It took only nine days for Mrs Stott to die after Mary Ann had arrived to nurse her, and no matter what underlying health problems her mother may have had, it is difficult to escape the conclusion that Cotton helped her on her way.

So, taking all of these factors into consideration, it seems likely that Mary Ann murdered 17 people—including her mother, various children and step-children, several husbands, a lover and a friend. She killed more people than John Haigh, Reg Christie, Peter Manuel, The Moors Murderers, Dennis Nilsen, Peter Sutcliffe, the Wests, Robert Black, Steve Wright and Peter Tobin. Indeed if we were looking at the most prolific serial killers in British history starting in 1850, Cotton would rank third in order, after Harold Shipman and Peter Dinsdale.[12] This makes it all the more remarkable that she has disappeared from History. However what was it that might have prompted and then maintained her murderous behaviour?

Cotton as a Serial Killer

Cotton most obviously conforms to the modern typology of female serial killers known as "black widows". In other words, "black widows" are women who kill husbands and lovers, or anyone else that they perceive to be problematic to their own happiness, such as children and step-children. This is especially apparent in the three weeks between 10th March and the beginning of April 1872 when Mary Ann murdered three victims because she wanted to quickly cement her relationship with Quick-Manning. She was clearing her household of unwanted people—people who no longer fitted into the world that she wanted to make for herself. However, we could also see in Cotton's behaviour aspects of another female serial

---

12. See table produced by Wilson (2009), *op cit*, in his Introduction, pps. 8-9. Peter Dinsdale
     suffered from mental health problems and was convicted of murdering 26 people in 1981 by
     setting fire to their flats.

killer typology—the "angel of death"—in that her nursing background allowed her sufficient medical knowledge to take the lives of her unsuspecting and trusting patients, and also provided her with enough cover to be above suspicion. Indeed, she may have first gained her knowledge of arsenic from her work as a nurse in the Sunderland Infirmary, where medicines—including arsenic—were left in the operating theatre for the nurses to collect and administer.

This nursing background also seems to have given her confidence when dealing with doctors and death. Mary Ann had absolutely no qualms about asking various local doctors to come in and attend to her ailing family members, even as she was slowly poisoning and killing them. Her murders were clearly committed in private, but she had no hesitation about subjecting this murderous activity to public scrutiny. She clearly felt that she could outwit these local medical men, and for a long time that is exactly what Mary Ann did. Even at the very end, had it not been for the perseverance of Thomas Riley insisting that there was something suspicious about Charles Edward's sudden demise, and crucially in his ability to influence Dr Kilburn—who in turn would involve Dr Scattergood—Mary Ann might have got away with murder yet again. Where did this type of confidence come from? Partly it was the confidence that came from her abilities as a killer. She knew that arsenic poisoning mimicked the symptoms of other kinds of equally deadly Victorian ailments, and that a busy local doctor was therefore unlikely to become too suspicious—and it also reflected the fact that having got away with one murder, it became much easier for Mary Ann to kill again and again.

In all of this we might reflect that attempting to place female serial killers into one distinct typology is problematic, and that the lines between such typologies are often blurred, as they are with male, serial killer typologies.[13] We might also reflect on the general poverty of the circumstances in which Cotton—a working class woman—and the circumstances of her various families existed within and which saw, for example, her wanting to have Charles Edward sent to the workhouse. A few shillings per week

---

13. For a discussion of the overlaps between male serial killer typologies see Fox, A J and Levin, J (2005) *Extreme Killing: Understanding Serial and Mass Murder.* Thousand Oaks, Ca: Sage.

were often the dividing line for the working classes between a tolerable existence and abject poverty.

All of this suggests that we need to place serial killers such as Mary Ann, and the phenomenon of serial killing more generally, into a broader framework that accommodates social and economic factors. This aspect of serial murder has been almost totally neglected, although some scholars who have been inspired by the work of Elliott Leyton[14] have begun to argue, for example in the case of post war Britain, that "the responsibility for serial killing does not lie so much with the individual serial killer, but can be better found within the social and economic structure of Britain since the 1960s, which does not reward the efforts of all and in particular marginalised large sections of society."[15] Clearly Cotton was marginalised by her class and her economic circumstances, which I will discuss more fully later in the chapter, but what does her case tell us about gender?

Cotton as a Woman and as a Serial Killer

The Schechters have argued that American female serial killers "radically violate some sweeping stereotypes about women in our culture", and they then go on to compare the murders committed by John Wayne Gacy with those committed by Jane Toppan, whom they describe as "our country's most prolific multiple murderer". In doing so, they argue that female serial killers constitute what philosophers call a "natural kind" in that:

> Female serial killers tend to kill in certain kinds of ways (either indirectly, through their partners, or covertly, via poisoning or smothering); they tend to choose similar victims (their own children, their unsuspecting husbands,

14. See in particular Leyton, E. (1986) *Hunting Humans: The Rise of the Modern Multiple Murderer,* Toronto: McClelland and Stewart.

15. Wilson, D (2007), *Serial Killers: Hunting Britons and Their Victims, 1960–2006,* Winchester: Waterside Press, p.17. See also Grover, C and Soothill, K (1999) "British Serial Killing: Towards a Structural Explanation", The British Criminology Conferences: Selected Proceedings Volume 2, URL (consulted October, 2009) http://wwwlboro.ac.uk/departments/ss/bccsp/vol02/08GROVEHTM; Soothill, K (2001) "The Harold Shipman Case: A Sociological Perspective", *Journal of Forensic Psychiatry* 12(2): 260–2; Soothill, K and Wilson, D (2005) "Theorising the Puzzle that is Harold Shipman", *Journal of Forensic Psychiatry and Psychology 16*(4): 658–98; and Wilson, D. (2009) *A History of British Serial Killing,* 1888–2008. London: Sphere.

their elderly charges, their ailing patients), and victims with whom they have a certain kind of personal relationship.[16]

There is much in this analysis which fits with Cotton. The Schechters also argue that, as far as gender is concerned, female serial killers simultaneously undermine and reinforce gender stereotypes. In other words, their very presence undermines the conception of women as the "gentler sex".

Several of these current ideas about female serial killers can be seen in contemporary reporting of Cotton's case at the time of her trial and execution. The *Newcastle Journal*, for example, believed that "the most astounding thought of all is that a woman could act thus without becoming terrible and repulsive"; *The Times* described Cotton as "a comely-looking, gentle-eyed woman"; the *Northern Echo* reminded its readers that Cotton was "a woman and a mother", and compared her fate to that of a drowning kitten; and the *Durham County Advertiser* thought that "perhaps the greatest wonder is that a woman could successfully practise for so many years a system of poisoning without betraying her secret".[17] In other words, these Victorian journalists were finding it hard to make sense of Cotton as both what we would now call a "serial killer", and as a woman. She was "comely-looking and gentle-eyed", not "terrible and repulsive" (although newspaper pictures of Cotton were subsequently deliberately coarsened to make her appear more frightening and which was clearly more in keeping with their notions of what a murderer would look like); and the "greatest wonder" was that a "woman" could keep the murders a secret for as long as Cotton had done, and which thus also alludes to another contemporary gender stereotype.

The *Newcastle Courant* in particular tried to make sense of how a woman could have committed such awful crimes. In its editorial of the 28th March 1873, for example, while recognising that "Mary Ann Cotton …will henceforth be remembered as one of the most hardened criminals and worst poisoners", the paper also noted "some considerations of the case were calculated to awaken the sympathy of the public on her behalf". Specifically,

16. Schechter and Schechter, *op cit*, quotes taken from p. 121, p. 117 and p.123.
17. Quotes taken from *Newcastle Journal* 11th March 1873; *The Times* 21st March 1873; *Northern Echo*, 24th March 1873; *Durham County Advertiser* 28th March 1873.

these circumstances were that she was a "woman and a mother", and "humanity shudders at the very thought of a woman having thus to end her days".[18] In an earlier editorial it tried to reconcile Cotton's gender with her crimes by describing her as "having long acted" as

> an adept can only do, the part of a fox in deception and cunning. She surely must have had something particularly winning about her, seeing that she could with ease one wooer and husband after another in rapid and exciting succession. It was in keeping with her usual tactics, we fear, to call in the doctors and make a great ado about her victims, as if she had been their best and truest friend. But her real character has at last come out; the evidence against her leaves no loophole for her escape or hope; and, taking all the circumstances of her crimes into account, the West Auckland poisoner deserves to be spoken of in the same breath as the blackest murderers that have ever disgraced humanity.[19]

So increasingly, contemporary newspapers tried to make sense of what Mary Ann — the "fox" — had done by looking at her nature and character, and found evidence to support this individual and psychological interpretation of how she had, for example, conducted herself after conviction and while awaiting execution. Again the *Newcastle Courant* led the way, describing her at her execution as displaying the "coolness and hardness of heart which she displayed on the stage of life" and then suggesting that she had "died as she had lived — a taciturn, fair-faced, clever hypocrite". Other newspapers were far more charitable about Mary Ann at the time of her death, but then increasingly simply ignored her. However, in a surprisingly modern interpretation of her life and career, the *Newcastle Courant* thought that Cotton was a "different type of murderer", because her crimes had not been committed whilst drunk, or on the spur of the moment. Instead, it suggested:

> She perpetrated her fearful crimes at a time, when, so far as appears in the evidence, she was perfectly sober, and with a purpose, perseverance, and absence

---

18. The *Newcastle Courant*, 28th March 1873.
19. The *Newcastle Courant*, 14th March 1873 — and therefore editorial written prior to her execution, but after her conviction.

of provocation, which stamp her as one of the most systematic, cold-blooded and shameless murderers that either Durham or any other county has produced. Long continued habits of intemperance, combined with strong passions naturally lead many persons to commit deeds under special circumstances from the very idea of which they would otherwise revolt in utter horror. With criminals of the Mrs Cotton type however, it is different; and we apprehend that, although the evidence against her was entirely of a circumstantial character, less effort will be made to spare her life ...[20]

This is a very interesting analysis, coming as it does over a hundred years before the term "serial killer" was in common usage, and before any real understanding had been developed about this type of murderer. Yet, even so, the *Newcastle Courant* is describing how Cotton's murders had been committed when she was sober and without provocation, but with purpose, perseverance and systematically in cold blood. It is, in other words, perfectly describing what we would now call a serial killer—an issue that I discuss more fully below.

However, the *Newcastle Courant* was unusual in this type of thinking, and very quickly most of the local and regional newspapers simply stopped talking about Cotton, the crimes that she had committed, and what might have prompted her behaviour. There seemed to develop an unspoken consensus that she should simply be ignored and forgotten. It was almost as if there had been a collective decision that Mary Ann was so unusual and unique that nothing further could be gained from considering her case.

This is an early example of the "conceptual impossibility" about female serial killers that Schechter and Schechter describe, and which as we have seen is clearly present in how Cotton was being described at the time of her trial and execution. In the process Mary Ann was being "commonly denied or merely ignored", or as I have put it in relation to Hardy, she was becoming "unseen".

The Schechters illustrate their argument with a comparison of the 31 murders committed by Jane Toppan, a nurse who killed family members and friends by poisoning them, and those murders perpetrated by John

---

20. The *Newcastle Courant*, 14th March 1873.

Wayne Gacy, who would eventually confess to having killed 33 young men whom he would overpower, handcuff, torture and rape prior to murdering them. In short, Gacy's style of murder was promiscuous, rapacious and penetrative, while Toppan's "conforms to the standard picture of female serial murder, which often seems like a grotesque, sadistic travesty of intimacy, nurturing, and love; not the savage violation of a stranger's body but the tender administration of a lethal potion to a loved one".[21] How might all we know about Cotton's murders be compared with her near-contemporary male serial killer known as Jack the Ripper?

Jack the Ripper

The first victim that is usually attributed to Jack the Ripper is Mary Ann Nichols on 31st August 1888, and then, in order: Annie Chapman on 8th September, Elizabeth Stride and Catherine Eddowes on the night of 30th September, and finally Mary Jane Kelly on 9th November.[22] All of his victims were alcoholics and worked as prostitutes. Mary Ann had a bruise on the right side of her face, and another on the left. There were two cuts to her throat — one four inches long, and the other eight inches in length — and these reached through to the vertebrae. In short, her throat was cut open. There was also bruising on her abdomen, and, on the right side, three or four cuts running downwards, and a contemporary account describes that the "lower part of the person was completely ripped open". All of the wounds had been inflicted using a sharp knife, and while not commented upon by the coroner at the time, there were several newspaper reports that Mary Ann might have been wearing a ring which had been removed by the killer.

It would seem fair to conclude that Mary Ann turned her back to her murderer — possibly as a way to have intercourse — and that this also afforded him the opportunity to cut her throat. So too cutting his victim's throat would mean that she would not be able to scream and that

---

21. Schechter and Schechter (2010), *op cit*, pps. 118-119.
22. All details taken from Evans, S and Skinner, K (2000) *The Ultimate Jack the Ripper Sourcebook*. London: Robinson. Two good general introductions to the Whitechapel killings are Rumbelow, D (1988) *Jack the Ripper: The Complete Casebook*, London: Penguin Books and Begg, P (2004), *Jack the Ripper: The Facts*. London: Robson Books.

the killer could therefore have more time to do other things to his dying victim. This suggests that Jack the Ripper was "act focused"—he wanted to kill his victims quickly—and that he was not interested in prolonging the process by which they died. What he sought was a dead victim, so that he could thereafter feed his fantasies with an inert body. All of the murders (with the exception of Elizabeth Stride, when the murderer was disturbed) were characterised by cuttings and slashings and mutilation, and the womb was often the specific focus of Jack's attacks. So much so that Dr Llewellyn—who conducted a full *post mortem* examination on Mary Ann—thought that the killer must have had some crude anatomical knowledge. This opinion has become part of the folklore of Jack the Ripper with anyone who has, or who claims to have had, a medical background or training considered to be particularly noteworthy as a suspect. However as the novelist Patricia Cornwell notes—perhaps using her novelist's imagination to good effect: "This isn't surgery; it is expediency, or grab and cut".

The Ripper's second victim was born Annie Smith in either September 1840 or 1841. Her father, George, was a soldier in the Life Guards. Annie's first job seems to have been as a domestic servant, and in May 1869 she married a coachman named John Chapman. Together they had three children, but Annie was often drinking very heavily and her "dissolute habits" eventually led to their separation in 1882. She was given an allowance of 10s a week by her ex-husband, but when John died in 1886 the allowance came to an abrupt end. As a result Annie drifted into one relationship after another, and at one stage she had tried to support herself by selling matches and flowers that she had bought at the Stratford Market. Her friends described her at the time of her murder as "addicted to drink". However, it was the death of her ex-husband, and the fact that she no longer received a regular allowance that led her into prostitution, which reveals the precarious nature of life in late Victorian England for working class women.

On the night of her murder Annie had been drinking in the Britannia public house on the corner of Dorset Street, near where she had been staying at a lodging house. She seems to have returned to her lodgings, and like Mary Ann Nichols, was asked for money to pay for her bed. She didn't have the money, but assured the warden—Tim Donovan—that he should not let out the bed for she would return soon enough with the cash. Donovan remembers that she was drunk, but walked straight, and there were also some unsubstantiated reports that she may have then gone on to the Ten Bells pub on the corner of Fournier Street. In any event Annie was found dead, lying on her back, in the rear yard of 29 Hanbury Street. Her throat had been cut through to the spine, and a portion of her small intestines and her abdomen was lying on the ground over her right shoulder, but still attached to her body. Begg describes the remainder of her injuries as: "from the pelvis the uterus and its appendages, with the upper portion of the vagina and the posterior two-thirds of the bladder, had been entirely removed".

Elizabeth Stride and Catherine Eddowes were both killed on the same night, and this is therefore often described in the true crime literature as the "double event", given that this is how their murders were described in a postcard purportedly written by Jack the Ripper on 1st October 1888. Elizabeth was murdered first, and then shortly after, Catherine, and their murders are of particular significance given that both seem to have been witnessed.

Elizabeth Gustafsdotter was born in Sweden in November 1843, and had a variety of nicknames—Long Liz, Hippy Lip Annie and Mother Gum. She emigrated to London in February 1867, after inheriting some 65 Swedish krona from her mother's estate and this seems to have been a chance to put her past behind her, given that she had already been arrested by the police in Sweden for working as a prostitute. She married a carpenter named John Stride in March 1869, and at first they ran a coffee shop together. However, John does not appear to have been a well man, and in January 1879 Elizabeth asked the Swedish Church in London for financial assistance due to her husband's illness. He was eventually admitted to Poplar Workhouse in August 1884, and then sent to the Poplar and Stepney Sick Asylum where he died of heart disease two months later in October.

By this stage Elizabeth was no longer living with her husband, and their marriage seems to have collapsed by 1881, with Elizabeth's heavy drinking reportedly the predominating cause. She spent time in the Whitechapel Workhouse Infirmary, and would eventually be sentenced to seven days hard labour for being drunk and disorderly and soliciting on 13 November

1884. Elizabeth used to like to tell people that her husband and two of her children died in a shipping accident in 1878, and Cornwell notes that Elizabeth had: "led a life of lies, most of them pitiful attempts to weave a brighter, more dramatic tale than the truth of her depressing, desperate life". Begg suggests that Elizabeth might also have been masquerading as another woman by the name of Elizabeth Watts.

Until her murder Elizabeth lived on and off with a man named Michael Kidney. It was by all accounts a stormy relationship, with Elizabeth disappearing for days and weeks at a time. "It was the drink that made her go away", claimed Kidney after Elizabeth's death, and some support for this statement comes in the form of the numerous appearances that his partner made before the magistrates throughout 1887 and 1888. She was charged, for example, in February and October 1887 and again in February 1888 with being drunk and disorderly and using obscene language, and again as late as 3rd September 1888 on the same charges. Kidney and Elizabeth parted company for the last time on 25 September—just five days before her death—and as a result he was, at one time, suspected of her murder. Elizabeth was seen drinking in the Bricklayer's Arms in Settles Street on the might of her death, and may also have been sold a bunch of grapes by Matthew Packer between 11 pm and midnight, although no grapes were found in her stomach at her post mortem.

Elizabeth's body was discovered in a passageway beside 40 Berner Street, which had been converted into the International Working Men's Educational Club. On the night of her murder about 100 people had turned up at the club to debate "Why Jews Should Be Socialists", with most not leaving before 11.30 pm, and several others staying on to drink until well after midnight. This makes clear there were many people still walking about Berner Street at the time that Stride was being accompanied by a client—whom she may have been drinking with in the Bricklayer's Arms. In particular, Israel Schwartz followed a man into Berner Street from Commercial Road, and when this first man reached Elizabeth—who was standing outside the gates of the club—he stopped, exchanged a few words with her and then assaulted her. Schwartz thought that this was a domestic dispute, and crossed the road to avoid becoming involved. He then saw a second man leave a pub on the corner, who stopped to light his pipe, and then he heard someone shout "Lipski"—a reference to a notorious Jewish murderer who had been hanged the previous year—and which might have been intended to scare off Schwartz. Schwartz did run away—as did the man who was seen lighting his pipe—but he reported all that he had witnessed the following day at Leman Street Police Station. If Schwartz is to be believed, he without doubt saw the man who murdered Elizabeth Stride, and provided the police with a description of Jack the Ripper. Schwartz stated that the man that he saw was aged about 30, with broad shoulders but only five feet and five inches tall, fair complexion, dark hair, a full face with a small moustache, and who was wearing a dark jacket and trousers and a black cap which had a peak.

Whether as a result of Schwartz, or the man lighting his pipe, or both, or the arrival several minutes later at the club of Louis Diemshutz, who worked there as a steward, the killer did not have much time to linger with Elizabeth's body. Her throat had been cut, but her body had not been mutilated in any way. This would suggest that the killer had unfinished business, business which seems to have been fulfilled by the murder of Catherine Eddowes.

Catherine Eddowes—who was also known as Kate Kelly–had been born in Wolverhampton on 14 April 1842. Her father was a tinplate worker and her mother a cook, and the family moved to London in 1843. Nonetheless, Catherine spent some of her childhood back in Wolverhampton, and would eventually find work there as a tin plate stamper. She was fired from this job and so ran off to Birmingham, where she stayed with an uncle who made boots and shoes. Again this did not work out, and she returned to Wolverhampton in 1861 where she met and set up home with a former soldier called Thomas Quinn. This relationship produced a son. Soon they moved to London and three further children were born. However, Catherine's heavy drinking, and her fiery temperament ensured that her relationship with Quinn did not last, and by 1880 it had collapsed completely and she turned to prostitution. Catherine moved into a lodging house called Cooney's in Flower and Dean Street and there she met John Kelly. Kelly denied that Catherine was involved in prostitution, but did admit that she sometimes drank to excess—we know that she was charged with being drunk and disorderly in September 1881.

On the day of her death Catherine had been drinking heavily enough to be arrested by PC Louis Robinson at 8.30 pm, and taken to Bishopsgate Police Station to "sleep it off". Just before one o'clock the following morning the station sergeant asked police constable George Hutt to check if anyone could be released. Catherine was by this time sober, and was let out of the station by PC Hutt who asked her to shut the door of the station as she left. "All right. Good night, old cock," she is reported to have said as she walked out into the early hours of the morning, just as Elizabeth Stride's body was being found.

Catherine seems to have gone in the opposite direction to Flower and Dean Street where she was lodging, and eventually must have wandered into Mitre Square where her body was found. By all accounts the square was poorly lit, but a patrolling constable PC Watkins reported nothing unusual at 1.30 am when he was on his rounds. However, five minutes later a commercial traveller in the cigarette business named Joseph Lawende, noticed a couple standing at the entrance of a passage leading to the Square. Lawende had little doubt that the woman that he saw was wearing clothes that were similar to the clothes being worn by Catherine, and while he was rather mysteriously excused from giving a description of the man that he saw with her at the inquest, *The Times* provided a brief pen picture, and the Home Office files contain a full description that must have come from Lawende. It would seem that the police were trying to keep Lawende from putting too much information into the public domain, and perhaps—as Begg suggests—this might imply that the intelligence that he had provided was being used to target a suspect.

In any event, Catherine's body was discovered by PC Watkins when he returned to Mitre Square on his beat at 0145 hours and, as he was later to tell *The Star* newspaper, Catherine had been: "ripped up like a pig in the market...I have been in the force a long while, but I never saw such a sight". In short the attack on Catherine had been ferocious. Her throat had been cut; after death her killer had mutilated her face and her abdomen, her intestines had been removed and placed over her right shoulder, and her left kidney and uterus had also been taken away. The damage to Catherine's face—the tip of her nose and her ear lobes had been cut off, as well as her cheeks cut—was clearly deliberate, and as Cornwell observes:

"the face is the person. To mutilate it is personal".

A search was made of the area around where Catherine's body had been discovered and some graffiti was found which has again become part of Jack the Ripper folklore. This graffiti—depending on which account is believed—is reported to have said 'The Jews are the men that will not be blamed for nothing', although there is no way of knowing if this graffiti was recent and connected to the murders, or had been in existence for some time.

As awful as all of these injuries were, they were merely a foretaste of those inflicted on Mary Jane Kelly—Jack the Ripper's final victim—who, unlike all of his previous victims who had been murdered in the open, was killed in a room in Miller's Court in Whitechapel. Perhaps because he had longer to be alone with Mary Jane and also less chance of being disturbed by a passer-by, Jack the Ripper almost completely obliterated Mary Jane's face, with her ears, nose, cheeks and eyebrows partly removed. Both her breasts had been cut off, with one found beneath her head, and the other beside her right foot. Dr Thomas Bond—who conducted Mary Jane's initial *post mortem* at Miller's Court—described the state of her body:

> The legs were wide apart, the left thigh at right angles to the trunk & the right forming an obtuse angle with the pubes. The whole surface of the abdomen & thighs was removed & the abdominal cavity emptied of its viscera. The breasts were cut off, the arms mutilated by several jagged wounds & the face hacked beyond recognition of the features...the viscera were found in various parts viz; the uterus & kidneys with one breast under the head, the other breast by the right foot, the liver between the feet, the intestines by the right side & the spleen by the left side of the body. The flaps removed from the abdomen & thighs were on a table...the Pericardium was open below & the Heart absent.[23]

Their Differing Styles — Their Differing Infamy?

It is obvious even from these brief descriptions of how Jack the Ripper killed his victims that they are in marked contrast to how Cotton's victims died. As the American cultural commentator Camille Paglia has put it more

---

23. Quote taken from Wilson, D (2009) *A History of British Serial Killing, 1888–2008*. London: Sphere, pps. 43-44.

generally about women who murder, "there is no female Jack the Ripper".[24] However, this does not mean to imply that women cannot be aggressive or violent and that some women will commit violent crimes, even if their violence and aggression is often different to that shown by men. Anne Campbell suggests that women's violence, for example, is "expressive" and that displayed by men "instrumental", so that men use violence to gain "power over another person, a power that can be used to boost self-esteem or to gain social and material benefits...aggression feels good to men but not to women".[25] She further suggests that men are violent more often when there are onlookers — their violence is public — whereas there is the opposite effect on women, as "same-sex spectators...seem to remind her of the norms about restraint shared by the community of women".[26]

So too the American scholar Dana Jack emphasises that women's aggression develops within a different social reality and that as a consequence their aggression is often worn behind a "mask" that serves to both protect and hide. As such, this mask "configures a woman's appearance to accord with a moral norm that is required of her gender more than of men. From the inside, the mask obscures the wearer's vision of the inequities and myths that stop her from taking action in the world". Thus the mask is "fashioned from a cloth of stereotypical feminine behaviour such as sweetness, silence and passivity. This strategic performance of femininity disguises women's intent to hurt, control, or oppose others".[27]

As the evidence given in relation to how Joseph Nattrass died should remind us, just because Cotton did not stab, or mutilate like Jack the Ripper does not imply that her victims died in any less pain. Indeed, we might also note that Cotton was always present when her victims died, which would have prevented them from perhaps sharing their fears with any friends or neighbours who came to visit them. Nor were their deaths quick, something which we might infer in relation to the victims of Jack the Ripper, as Cotton's victims died over a period of days — sometimes

---

24. Paglia, C (1991) *Sexual Personae: Art and Decadence from Nefertiti to Emily Dickinson,* New Haven: Yale University Press, p. 247.

25. Campbell, A. (1993) *Men, Women and Aggression.* New York: Basic Books, pps. 7-8.

26. *Ibid,* p. 78.

27. Jack, D C (2001). *Behind the Mask: Destruction and Creativity in Women's Aggression,* Cambridge, MA: Harvard University Press, quotes taken from p. 115 and pps. 236-237.

weeks. So too how should we interpret the fact that Cotton held down Joseph Nattrass when he was having a fit? We now know that this was not being done as a result of her caring for Joseph and was thus merely a physical manifestation of the power that she held over him. This was also a power that she was also prepared to flaunt in front of a number of male and female neighbours and male doctors and can therefore be interpreted as a public display of that power, and which may have further fuelled her sense of worth.

We should also consider the popularity of Jack the Ripper as an historical subject — a popularity that is not shared by Cotton, even acknowledging the Victorian nursery rhymes about Mary Ann and her exploits. Entering "Jack the Ripper" into Google, for example, produces 2,840,000 mentions devoted to the serial killer, with the most comprehensive site being www. casebook.org This claims to be the "world's largest public repository of Ripper-related information" and new subscribers are encouraged to read the site's Frequently Asked Questions (FAQs), and look at the Chat Room and new Photo Archive before considering whether to join the site's mailing list. On the other hand, Cotton produces just over 700,000 hits. Paul Begg also comments that 85 books have been published about Jack the Ripper since the centenary of the murders in 1988, and that "the iconic Ripper is an inspiration for stories, novels, musicals — even an opera".[28] The contrast with Cotton cannot be more extreme and it would be difficult to claim that she has become "iconic" of serial killing generally, or even of female serial killing specifically.

How are we to account for these differences? Are they the result of the "conceptual impossibility" claimed by the Schechters in relation to American female serial killers, or are there other factors at work? As with any analysis based on one case it is, of course, difficult to generalise more broadly from the findings of a particular example and thus to be confident as to the reasons why Cotton has disappeared from public and academic consciousness, while her near-contemporary Jack the Ripper has become iconic. We should also remember that more recent and male serial killers have also gone "unseen" and perhaps — like Hardy, who murdered

---

28. Begg (2004), *op cit*, p. ix.

in Manchester, also in the north of England—the geographic region in which these murders took place has played a part in Cotton's disappearance. Indeed, in an American context, Fox and Levin suggest that no one outside of Wisconsin had ever heard of the serial killer Edward Gein and that he and his crimes were not "important, at least to the national media, as what occurs in a large city like Chicago or Washington DC… [Gein is] hardly a household name or a box office attraction, he might have been immortalized like Charles Manson in the film *Helter Skelter* (1976) had he killed in Los Angeles". [29]

In covering Cotton's case newspapers of the time were also reporting on events that had happened in the past, whereas with Jack the Ripper new murders were being reported, often almost as soon as they had happened, with all the added excitement that a "whodunnit?" brings. One Sunday newspaper—*Lloyd's Weekly*—for example, was able to put together an extra special edition in under two hours to capitalise on the news of the murder of Catherine Eddowes on 30th September 1888.[30] Jack the Ripper's murders were thus also quite deliberately used as part of a Victorian circulation war between the popular and "respectable press".[31]

Perhaps it is the legacy of these factors that has been the basis for maintaining our interest in Jack the Ripper. As recently as 2009 it was noted that Jack the Ripper was by far the most "popular" subject of the 100 best-selling books in Amazon's criminology list and, as well as books, Amazon also listed 34 DVDs, 20 Music CDs, a video game, and an assortment of toys and games. In the latter category, for example, it was possible to purchase a Jack the Ripper "action figure", with the promise that "this faceless villain comes alive with MEZCO TOYZ 9-inch Jack the Ripper roto-cast figure. Jack is fully articulated and comes complete with appropriate accessories including five knives, satchel, hat, and cloth cloak".[32] Amazon also directed buyers to a Jack the Ripper walking tour where you could join a guide to retrace the steps of the "Ripper" visiting the murder sites on

29. Fox, A J and Levin, J (2005) *Extreme Killing: Understanding Serial and Mass Murder*, Thousand Oaks, CA: Sage, pps. 4-5.
30. For a discussion of how Victorian newspapers covered the Jack the Ripper case see L Perry Curtis (2001) *Jack the Ripper and the London Press*. Stroud: Sutton.
31. See, Fido, M (2001) *A History of British Serial Killing*, London: Carlton Books, p. 22.
32. Wilson (2009), *op cit*, p. 29.

the haunts that were frequented, such as the famous pub the Ten Bells in Whitechapel. And, as if to confirm all of this interest, Jack the Ripper was voted the "worst Briton over the last 1,000 years" in a poll conducted for BBC *History Magazine's* February 2006 issue, beating historical figures such as Thomas Becket, Titus Oates, King John, Eadric Streona and, from more recent times, Oswald Mosley, for the title. Cotton can hardly complete with these "bad boys".

Undoubtedly gender has been a factor in Cotton being "unseen" by a national and more recent audiences, although this has perhaps worked in ways that are more complex than those suggested by Schechter and Schechter. As has been described they suggest that female serial killers are either denied or ignored as a conceptual impossibility. Cotton was certainly not ignored at the time of her trial — even if she has been subsequently — when her actions were seen by contemporary newspapers to have been "hideous" and she herself was described as a "monster". This latter description surely reflects that her awful behaviour was neither denied, nor seen as being acceptable. Her violence was also, to use Campbell's description, "instrumental", rather than "expressive" in that it was used to gain social and material benefits, and thus more closely corresponds to why men behave violently.

However, in the time between her trial and her execution, which also generated considerable sympathy for her in some quarters, she seems to have been able to sufficiently re-present and re-create herself — often through the letters that were written by her visitors — within contemporary gender conventions to the public which, in turn allowed Victorian culture to reclaim Cotton as a woman. It was almost as if her life and circumstances became a melodrama; a Victorian soap-opera that kept the readers hooked, until their attention inevitably moved elsewhere. In the process Mary Ann's audience seemed to forgive her, and she in turn accepted another stereotype of the wronged and doomed woman which has been handed down in local history. In short, she returned to wearing a "mask" that allowed her to strategically perform femininity. In all of this the public's knowledge that Cotton was pregnant at the time of her arrest — and that her daughter was only removed from her five days before her execution — seems to have laid the foundations of the circumstances that have became the catalyst for Cotton becoming quietly forgotten nationally and only of passing interest regionally. Indeed, it is interesting to note that this re-presenting of herself as a woman has not been something that any of the other and more recent female British serial killers have been able to do and, of course, neither Allitt, West nor Hindley were executed.

Antisocial Personality Disorder and the Psychopath

Can we try to understand, and then make sense of Mary Ann's behaviour from a psychological perspective? And while it is always difficult to telescope backwards into History and diagnose the past from the present, perhaps Mary Ann has left us clues to understanding her behaviour in the incidents involving both Nattrass and Robinson. We might also gain some further insight into her behaviour by how she was described at the time of her conviction. The *Newcastle Courant*, for example, described her "coolness" and "hardness of heart"; as a "taciturn, fair-faced, clever hypocrite"; and, of course, we also know that she repeatedly murdered to achieve her objectives.

If faced today with someone who had behaved as Mary Ann had done, and had committed similar crimes we would not hesitate to suggest that she was suffering from an antisocial personality disorder (APD), and perhaps also label her as a "psychopath".[33] The label APD is often used in preference to the description "psychopath", and while there are differences between these two concepts, there is also considerable overlap between APD and psychopathy. According to the Diagnostic and Statistical Manual if someone is to be diagnosed as having APD they would have to show a consistent disregard for the rights of others, which would be indicated by at least three of the following: repeated illegal behaviour; repeated lying, or cheating of others for profit or pleasure; impulsivity; aggressiveness; disregard for their own safety or the safety of others; irresponsibility—such as poor work performance, or failure to meet debts; a lack of remorse which

---

33. A good introduction to these concepts can be found in Peter Ainsworth (2000), *Psychology and Crime: Myths and Reality*, Harlow: Longman, pps. 84-101. The most commonly used instrument to measure psychopathy is the Hare Psychopathy Checklist-Revised (PCL-R)—see Robert Hare (1991), *The Hare Psychopathy Checklist-Revised*, Toronto: Multi Health Systems. See also *Appendix 2*, 'Was Mary Ann Cotton a Psychopath?'.

would be shown by being indifferent to the hurt or pain of other people, or stealing from them. Thus there are two dimensions to APD — the anti-social behaviour itself, and the lack of anxiety, remorse or guilt that would normally flow from the commission of these acts.

Often people with APD are self-centred and pleasure seeking — even if to achieve that pleasure their actions might harm other people. For those labelled as a psychopath, this pleasure seeking behaviour might lead to promiscuous sexual behaviour, with the result that they will have many short-term marital relationships, and therefore engage in what is described as a "parasitic lifestyle". And, because they seek pleasure they are often impulsive and irresponsible. However, their true nature is often masked because they are invariably of above average intelligence, and possess good social skills which will allow then to charm those who surround them. If challenged they can lie convincingly, and will be able to offer what seems like a plausible explanation for their behaviour. In other words, they are conning and manipulative, and fail to accept responsibility for their actions.

In all of this Mary Ann was an expert.[34] Read again her letter to Henry Holdforth, in which she said "der frend I hope you Will not juge me rong As I have been", and consider how this letter allows us to glimpse the lying, conning and manipulation that had become part of Cotton's life, and which she no doubt used to convince others to take her on as a housekeeper, to befriend her, and to marry her.

Leaving to one side her many husbands, lovers and partners — which suggests her promiscuous sexual behaviour — it is clearly possible to inter-pret various key incidents in Mary Ann's life as indicative of her underlying antisocial personality disorder: cheating Robinson out of his money (which also suggests the "criminal versatility" that would characterise the psycho-path), and then lying about this when she was caught out; impulsively leaving Robinson's home in Pallion, and then later irresponsibly aban-doning their baby with a neighbour; her murder of Charles Edward after

----

34. With a colleague — Dr Elizabeth Yardley of Birmingham City University — we inde-pendently scored Mary Ann on Hare's Psychopathy Checklist-Revised. Our scores, and the reasons that we assigned a particular score can be followed in the table below. Mary Ann's total score was 25 which would have meant that had she been alive today she would have been labelled as a psychopath.

she had been frustrated by Riley in having him placed in the local work-house—which in itself indicates her lack of empathy towards her stepson; her extraordinary callous behaviour—which might be seen as "coolness" and "hardness of heart"—towards Nattrass; her ability to attract people to her; and, of course, her repeated inability to accept responsibility for her actions by, for example, failing to confess to what she had done, and instead blaming Charles Edward's death on "arrowroot".

Finally, one other item on Robert Hare's psychopathy checklist is also helpful in explaining Cotton's behaviour over her lifetime—"lack of realistic, long-term goals". After all, what was it that she actually wanted? There were a number of times in Mary Ann's life when she seemed as if she had "landed on her feet"—most obviously when she established her relationship with Robinson and when, we might have presumed, that she would have been satisfied with what she had achieved. So too, after at last being able to form a relationship with Nattrass—a man she had followed to Seaham Harbour and then to West Auckland—she murders him so as to be able to establish a new relationship with Quick-Manning. On one level these behaviours simply indicate impulsivity and poor behavioural controls, but the fact that Mary Ann was prepared to give up two relationships which she had fought hard to establish is also telling us something more profound about who she was as a person. These behaviours seem to suggest that Mary Ann put no limit on what she thought that she was capable of achieving, and so when she had—by most people's standards—got what she had aspired to, that simply encouraged her to aspire for even more, no matter how unrealistic this might be. We can see other glimpses of this grandiosity and exaggerated self-worth in, for example, hiring neighbours to help her clean her home and have them fetch errands for her, and in her willingness to have doctors come into her home to attend to those whom she was secretly murdering. However, one question which I am not able to answer is where would all of this have stopped? Would she have been happy with Quick-Manning, or would he too have ended up poisoned when someone even more desirable came along?

A Summing Up

But is that it? Should we just accept that Cotton disappeared partly as a result of her gender, partly as an accident of the area where she committed her crimes, and largely because of the means by which she dispatched her victims—all of which worked together and spectacularly failed to capture the public's imagination in any long-term way? Is it enough to simply look at her personality and character as explanations for the murders that she committed, and be satisfied that she had an antisocial personality disorder? Or is it enough to simply explain what happened by labelling her a psychopath? Surely the answers for what motivated her to commit her crimes have to also be based on macro sociological issues, as much as it is tempting to dwell on the micro of the individual and the psychological? For as we have come to realise over the last 20 years, serial killers like Mary Ann are not aberrations within our culture—monsters from another time and place—but are the very embodiment of the time and space they occupy. Consider this observation of the Canadian scholar Elliot Leyton:

> [Serial killers] are not mere freaks: rather, they can only be fully understood as representing the logical extension of many of the central themes in their culture—of worldly ambition, of success and failure, and of manly avenging violence. Although they take several forms...they can only be accurately and objectively perceived as the prime embodiment of their civilisation, not twisted derangement.[35]

It is Leyton who has more than anyone else championed a social analysis of serial murder, rather than one that relentlessly focuses on the individual, psychological motivation of the serial killer. As such he does not see serial killers as odd or unusual—"freaks"– but rather as the inevitable outcome of the dominant values of the culture in which that serial killer operates. What Leyton wants us to do is to consider the social, as much as the psychological. This becomes all the more obvious when we consider the phenomenon of serial killing from the perspective of those who fall victim to these killers, rather than looking at the killers themselves, and

35. Leyton (1986), *op cit*, p. 10.

develop an analysis of the phenomenon of serial killing over an extended period of time.

In relation to our own recent history, for example, the high-point of British serial killing was 1986 — when four serial killers were active in our country.[36] It is difficult to ignore that this year was also the high-point of "Thatcherism". Here I am not implying some crude economic determinism, but it is surely more than co-incidence that the most recent high-point of British serial killing coincided with the high point of "Thatcherism". By "Thatcherism" I do not just mean the coming to power of Mrs Thatcher in 1979, but also a "new right" ideology — based on ideas popularised by Friedrich von Hayek, Milton Friedman and Robert Nozick — which gained ascendancy under her leadership.[37] This "new right" ideology emphasised that the British state had become involved in too many areas of civil society, and specifically that too many national resources were being spent on welfare. In turn the demands on government were increasing, and as a consequence taxes on business had become too high, limiting the private sector's profit-making and wealth-creating potential. As a result, it was argued, there should be less government regulation and intervention in the economy, and far less provision for those who were poor and unemployed, from fear that this would create "welfare dependency".

While this broad outline seems fair enough, I am not trying to push this analysis too far, and it also has to be remembered that, for example, much of the welfare state did survive Thatcherism. Nonetheless, it is scarcely controversial to suggest that Britain did change after 1979, and that those changes are related to policy directions influenced by "new right" thinking. But what has this got to do with serial killing?

In our own time the economist Will Hutton has suggested that, as a consequence of this type of thinking dominating the policy agenda of

36. Wilson (2009), *op cit*, pps. 273-281. The four serial killers who murdered in 1986 were John Duffy (in 2001 his accomplice David Mulcahy would also be convicted of these murders); Kenneth Erskine; Robert Black and Harold Shipman. There was also an Italian-born serial killer called Michele De Marco Lupo active in London during 1986 although given that he is Italian born and raised I have not included him in my calculation. The four British-born serial killers murdered 19 people between them during the year.

37. F von Hayek (1944), *The Road to Serfdom*, London: Routledge & Sons Ltd.; M Friedman (1953), *The Methodology of Positive Economics*, Chicago: University of Chicago Press; R Nozick (1974), *Anarchy, State and Utopia*, Oxford: Blackwell.

government, Britain became a "40/30/30" society, or a society of "us and them", where the rich have got richer, and the poor got left behind. By "40/30/30" Hutton is suggesting that only 40 per cent of the workforce is in full-time, secure employment; 30 per cent are insecurely self-employed, or working casually; and the remaining 30 percent — the "marginalised"— are unemployed, or working for "poverty" wages. Hutton has gone further and argues that since 1979 "capitalism has been left to its own devices".[38] By this he means that Britain has become a low-cost, deregulated producer, with correspondingly low social overheads, and a minimalist welfare state. Thus, for example, supplementary benefit for the unemployed as a proportion of full time earnings dropped from 26 per cent in 1979 to 19 per cent in 1993; union membership was discouraged and fell dramatically from 13.3 million to 9 million over the same period; and Hutton argues that the state was also trying to wash its hands of future generations of old people. So too by 1993 there were three million people who were unemployed, and between 1966 and 1977 wages of all men in all social classes grew at the same rate. However, from 1979 they started to diverge, and between 1979 and 1992 those already on the highest wages saw their income grow by 50 per cent, whilst those on the lowest wages were actually worse off than they had been in 1975.

Of course Hutton was writing before New Labour's victory in 1997, but their coming to power does not seem to have particularly altered the course that was being pursued by their Tory predecessors. In particular there would seem to have been a continuation of the social and economic policies of the outgoing Conservative government, albeit that these have been characterised as being a "Third Way" — bringing together social justice and a dynamic economy. Nonetheless, New Labour has drawn directly from neo-liberal discourses in its analysis of the global economy. Indeed "globalization" became a favourite justification of the New Labour "project", and thus the British economy, it is argued has to continue to make itself as attractive to investors as possible by maintaining a deregulated economic approach, and limiting any social interventionist strategies. And now of course we have "the Big Society" of David Cameron's coalition government.

38. W Hutton (1995), *The State We're In*, London: Jonathan Cape Ltd.

The result, as far as serial murder is concerned in our own time, is that those groups who get repeatedly targeted by serial killers are the elderly, young people, babies and infants, prostitutes and — the only group of men to regularly fall victim to British serial killers — gay men. Is it any surprise that the poor and the vulnerable fall victim to serial killers, and that those without power are more likely to be killed? What emerges from the history of serial killing in Britain is that we need to learn that serial killers exploit fractured communities, in which some lives are seen as more valuable than others and where increasingly people have to struggle simply to survive. So too we must learn that serial killers exploit police — or in Mary Ann's case medical — incompetence, at least until Scattergood arrived on the scene, and public indifference to the young, vulnerable women who sell sexual services, or gay men who have a lifestyle that is seen to be challenging to the status quo; that they exploit the isolation, loneliness and powerlessness of the elderly; and that they exploit the public policies of successive governments which no longer sees value in the young or the old, and which prioritise the rich over the poor.

In this dreadful way serial killing tells us something about our culture, our values and our civic society. It emerges as the elephant in the sitting room of public policies that create a culture of "them" and "us" and a society where there is a widening gap between the "haves" and the "have nots". In such societies it is presumed that some people simply don't have value for the development of that society, and can therefore be cast adrift as challenging the status quo and unrepresentative, or as a burden on the state's resources.

Mary Ann — a woman in a different time but, all the same, a time which had similar economic values to our own — was perhaps one of the first people to see all of this clearly. Born into an age which we would now characterise as the "industrial revolution", she was one of the first generation of Britons who made their way not by renting a farm and thereafter surviving on subsistence agriculture, but by selling her labour. Of course the labour that she had to sell was constrained by her gender, but Mary Ann knew that if she wanted to prosper she could do so by application, hard work, drive and determination, and then by moving on to where there were fresh opportunities for a "capable woman". She had first watched her father and mother do this, and then also a number of her husbands who worked in the mines. Was this not capitalism in action — seeing an opportunity and then pursuing it with dogged determination? And what if that opportunity did not quite come up to scratch? Even if it did, what if there were richer pickings to be had elsewhere? No worries. Leave everything behind, and start again; clear the decks and make a fresh start.

Of course for Mary Ann this involved murder, but in an economic game that had few winners and many losers, Cotton chose the side that she wanted to be on because that was the side that Victorian England valued above all else. Casting her family adrift was what she knew she had to do if she was to be a good Victorian entrepreneur, and achieve the economic and social success that Victorian society had elevated almost to a religion.

So as a serial killer Cotton was organized, persistent and showed a degree of calculation and cunning so as to achieve the ends that she wanted, no matter who stood in her way. In this respect she was the equal of any celebrated — or as they are usually described "eminent" Victorian banker, industrialist, or factory owner, although these worlds were, of course, closed to her. Mary Ann's world was the hospital and above all the home, but like any good entrepreneur she could move from one to another, and also sell her nursing skills to the highest bidder — or at least the bidder that she thought she could best exploit. And while we might take comfort from simply seeing her as a psychopath, that label would fail to acknowledge that Mary Ann was in reality just like many other Victorians.

That Cotton should be better known is without doubt. However, what emerges from an analysis of her case is that the relationship between which serial killers emerge into public consciousness, and those who do not is complex and dependent on a range of case-specific variables, one of which is gender — a variable which might in turn operate in a number of ways to either push the serial killer into the public's consciousness, or alternatively, like Mary Ann, leave them "unseen". Bringing Cotton back into public view — making her "seen" — has not been easy, and rarely has it been a pleasant experience. However, until we begin to acknowledge that Mary Ann was as much a product of the world that has made us, and try to do something to change that world, then we will continue to be dogged by those who, like her, will want to kill, and kill again.

A Guide to Further Reading and Primary Sources

For specific references to those secondary sources that I have used within the text, readers should consult the various footnotes. However, this guide is for those who might be interested in beginning to pursue the themes at the heart of the book more fully. Obviously my focus has been about a serial killer—a specific female serial killer. However, while there is really only Arthur Appleton's (1973) *Mary Ann Cotton* (London: Michael Joseph) earlier biography of the particular serial killer we have been on the trail of (as well as a few other sources which are referenced within the footnotes), there is a wide range of academic books about serial killing more generally, and about female serial killing more specifically that can be recommended.

For serial killing more generally in a British context, my own (2007) *Serial Killers: Hunting Britons and their Victims, 1960-2006* (Winchester: Waterside Press) and (2009) *A History of British Serial Killing* (London: Sphere) can provide the background for much of what has appeared within this book, and can also help the interested reader pursue their studies further. For general books that look at the phenomenon of serial murder in North America, Stephen Holmes and James de Burger (1988) *Serial Murder* (Newbury Park, Ca: Sage) and Ronald Holmes and Stephen Holmes (1994) *Profiling Violent Crimes* (Thousand Oaks, Ca: Sage) are standard introductions to the subject. Also of use is James Fox and Jack Levin (2005) *Extreme Killing: Understanding Serial and Mass Murder* (Thousand Oaks, Ca: Sage). It is also important to be aware of the interesting analysis made by Elliott Leyton (1986) *Hunting Humans: The Rise of the Modern Multiple Murderer* (Toronto: McClelland and Stewart), which I discuss in the concluding chapter and which takes the focus of inquiry away from the psychology and motivation of the serial killer and instead tries to understand the social structure that produces serial killers.

The academic literature related to female serial killers is less extensive than the literature devoted to male serial killers. However, a good starting point is S T Holmes, E Hickey, and R M Holmes (1991) "Female Serial

Murderesses: Constructing Differentiating Types", *Journal of Contemporary Criminal Justice* Vol. 7 No. 4: 245-256, and more recently Elizabeth Gurian (2011) "Female Serial Murderers: Directions for Future Research on a Hidden Population", *International Journal of Offender Therapy and Comparative Criminology*, 55(1): 27-42. The monograph by E Seal (2010) *Women, Murder and Femininity: Gender Representations of Women Who Kill*, New York: Palgrave is also a very useful introduction for the reader new to theories related to how women who kill are perceived in terms of their gender. Seal's book is concerned with murders committed by women that are considered to be particularly unusual, and while she does not include Mary Ann Cotton's case, she does discuss Myra Hindley, Rose West, Lizzie Borden and Aileen Wournos.

If we think about the process which brought Cotton to justice, clearly Victorian forensic science and Victorian forensic scientists were important. In relation to the former, Katherine Watson (2011) *Forensic Medicine in Western Society: A History* (London: Routledge) is a very useful introduction to the subject. However, Watson does not mention Dr Thomas Scattergood in this monograph, although she does cover his career extensively in "Medical and Chemical Expertise in English Trials for Criminal Poisoning, 1750-1914", *Medical History*, 2006, Vol.50: 373-90, as does M A Green (1973) "Dr Scattergood's Case Books: A 19th Century Medical-Legal Record", *The Practitioner*, Vol. 211: 679-684.

Of course, what Scattergood was trying to detect in his chemical analysis—at least in Mary Ann's case—was arsenic, and both John Emsley (2005) *The Elements of Murder: A History of Poison* (Oxford: Oxford University Press) and James C Wharton (2010) *The Arsenic Century: How Victorian Britain was Poisoned at Home, Work & Play* (Oxford: Oxford University Press) are excellent ways of developing an understanding of the role that arsenic played in Mary Ann's culture. Both books are written in a lively and accessible style—which does not demand too much scientific knowledge—and have the added advantages of also discussing the Marsh test and Reinsch Test. A more theoretical account of a Victorian murder involving poison is Ian Burney (2006) *Poison, Detection, and the Victorian Imagination* (Manchester: Manchester University Press). Burney's book is concerned with the 1856 case of William Palmer—a rogue doctor, gambler, forger, adulterer and murderer—and while the poison that Palmer used would appear to have been strychnine, the developing role of the medical expert at court is usefully outlined.

Burney also discusses Palmer's execution, but for a more general introduction Harry Potter (1993) *Hanging in Judgement: Religion and the Death Penalty in England* (London: SCM Press Ltd), while dated, is still a very accessible and scholarly account of how the Church of England gradually moved from being a supporter of capital punishment to advocating for its abolition. V A C Gatrell (1994) *The Hanging Tree: Execution and the English People, 1770-1868* (Oxford: Clarendon Press) remains the standard introduction to this particular subject, but there is also much to be learned from Judith Rowbotham (2010) "Execution as a Punishment in England, 1750-2000", in Anne-Marie Kilday and David Nash (eds.), *Histories of Crime: Britain 1600-2000* (Basingstoke: Palgrave Macmillan), pps.180-202.

For how Victorian newspapers covered murder cases more generally, I found Judith Flanders (2011), *The Invention of Murder: How the Victorians Revelled in Death and Detection and Created Modern Crime* (London: HarperCollins) particularly helpful, although she devotes only a few pages to Cotton's case, and as a general introduction to Charles Dickens and his work—which I refer to throughout the text—Michael Slater (2009) *Charles Dickens* (New Haven: Yale University Press) is invaluable. Finally, I was able to build up a picture of Northumberland mining communities in the Victorian era through reading Alan Metcalfe's (2006) *Leisure and Recreation in a Victorian Mining Community: The Social Economy of Leisure in North-East England, 1820-1914* (London: Routledge). For other issues related to other historical themes, offenders, the hangman William Calcraft, characters mentioned within the text, the organization of Victorian prisons, coroner's and magistrate's courts and so forth, readers should consult the relevant footnote identified within the text.

A wide number of primary sources were consulted and used, and various libraries and organizations visited to inform my understanding of Mary Ann Cotton, her life and crimes, and how she was brought to justice. Chief amongst these were the National Archives at Kew, where records related to Mary Ann's trial and her incarceration at Durham are held. The Brotherton Special Collections within Leeds University Library houses

Dr Thomas Scattergood's Notebooks of Medical Case Histories, with press cuttings of inquests, litigation and other medico-legal matters, as well as his Notes for Lectures on Forensic Medicine. He refers to his work in relation to the "West Auckland Poisoning Case" in his Notebooks, and here I should acknowledge that I have taken the liberty of imagining some of the issues that he might have been concerned with, rather than simply reporting directly what he recorded. I believe that I am justified in doing so because his Notes for [his] lectures on Forensic Medicine—which are littered with half-thought out sentences and numerous scorings out and so forth, allow the researcher a glimpse of what Scattergood thought about certain ideas and issues and how his opinions were developed and formed. However where I am quoting directly from either his notebooks or notes I use inverted commas or indents, and he did actually attend the execution at Armley Gaol, Leeds, which ends the book.

Two million pages of 19th Century British newspapers are available to read online at www.newspapers.bl.uk and I especially used *The Newcastle Courant, The Newcastle Journal, The Northern Echo, Illustrated Police News, Leeds Mercury* and *Durham County Advertiser*. These papers—as I discuss in the text—also reproduced letters from Mary Ann that she had written to her friends from her condemned cell. However, while reading these newspapers is obviously eased by their online accessibility, I cannot help but reflect that I still find it useful to read a newspaper in its original format. There is nothing to beat the smell of a musty newspaper to invoke a sense of the period in time that is being researched, and unsurprisingly—at least for someone of my generation—the eye naturally picks up details within a newspaper that might other otherwise be lost when scanning electronically. I benefited from being able to read the relevant newspapers housed in Newcastle City Library and at Cambridge University Library. While mentioning libraries, I would also like to thank the staff of the University Library of Birmingham City University, and the Radzinowich Library in the Institute of Criminology at Cambridge University who were both very supportive of my research.

Taking this theme of direct experience further, I visited Beamish Museum—the "Living Museum of the North"—on several occasions, and was generously allowed easy access to their various regional resource collections, which of course house the teapot and stool that are reputed to have belonged to Mary Ann Cotton. I also visited the villages and towns that were once important to Mary Ann, walked the boundary of HMP Durham (which I had previously visited), and interviewed various locals about what they remembered of Cotton's story. Aspects of this research trip were written up for a *Mail on Sunday Magazine* article which is reproduced as *Appendix 1* to this book.

Of course I have also had direct experience of working with serial killers, and on cases of serial murder, and I used this background to inform the text. I have written about these particular experiences before in (2008) *Hunting Evil: Inside the Ipswich Serial Murders* (London: Sphere), and (2010) *The Lost British Serial Killer: Closing the Case on Peter Tobin and Bible John* (London: Sphere), both of which I co-authored with Paul Harrison and which attempt deal with the murders committed by Steve Wright in 2006, and Peter Tobin over a number of years.

Appendix 1

Article written for *Mail on Sunday Magazine*, 5 February 2012
Murder Grew With Her — On the Trail of Mary Ann Cotton[1]

"And you really think that this address will still work?" asked Brian, as he tapped away at his Sat Nav before shooting me a look as if to say, it will never work and what have I let myself in for?

"A Victorian serial killer?" he queried, more as ridicule than for clarification, *"and you think we'll be able to track her down from this?"*

A few seconds later we were driving to West Auckland, and four hours after that I found myself knocking on the door of 13 Front Street, where Mary Ann Cotton killed her final victim, and from where she was arrested before being imprisoned in, and then executed at HMP Durham in March 1873.

Actually, it's no longer number 13, but has morphed into number 14, perhaps from fear that evil could be passed down across successive generations of home owners. And Mary Ann Cotton was certainly evil, given that she may have killed up to 21 people, and can rightly claim to be the first of that most modern of British icons — a serial killer. Almost two decades before Jack the Ripper would start to terrorise the streets of Whitechapel in London, Mary Ann Cotton had already become a killing machine.

But even if you're familiar with the names of Harold Shipman, Dennis Nilsen, Fred and Rose West, Peter Sutcliffe, Myra Hindley and Ian Brady, chances are that you've never heard of Mary Ann, who has almost disappeared from history, and has at best become a half-remembered, local curiosity.

Unlike Jack the Ripper who has remained a source of inspiration for film makers, authors and academics alike–there is even a walking tour that retraces his steps across modern-day Whitechapel—Cotton has generated little scholarly or popular interest as our first female serial killer. There has only ever been one professional biography written about her–which was published on the centenary of her execution in 1973, and there is certainly no walking tour that re-traces her murderous rampage through the mining villages of the north east, nor any sad monuments erected to honour the memories of her victims. And, when she is remembered, it is often difficult to separate fact from fantasy.

So Brian and I are on her trail, trying to re-discover her story and, using a few precious clues, answering some questions, so as to re-create the life and crimes of our first serial killer.

Like all investigations, sometimes things don't go to plan.

No one answers the door of number 13/14 Front Street, and so we were both immediately a little bit crestfallen. However, it didn't take long before we met some women sitting outside the local nursing home, and enjoying the summer sunshine.

"Ooh, don't put our names in your book," pleaded my first interviewee, who was anxious to speak, but not to be identified.

"Yes, I've known all about Mary Ann Cotton as I grew up in West Auckland. We used to have a nursery rhyme — 'Mary Ann Cotton, lying in her coffin, with her finger up her bottom'—but it's all about Jack the Ripper isn't it? She's buried in the churchyard, but we're not proud of her — given what she did, there's nothing to be proud of."

But what did Mary Ann Cotton do?

Most of the people that we spoke to in the places where she once lived and killed — West Auckland, Walbottle, Murton and Seaham Harbour weren't too certain.

Ryan Beattie, a barman at the Seaham Harbour View Hotel, situated right next door to where Mary Ann moved to in 1865, and who was once a prison officer at HMP Durham, suggested to us that *"she was a lovely person and wrongly hanged — wasn't it a conspiracy against her?"*

Even Brian looked shocked at this suggestion, and so Ryan quickly changed his view and added *"maybe she wasn't so nice!"*

Ryan can be forgiven, for as time has gone on it has become difficult to get at the truth. Beamish Museum — the "living museum of the north" — for example, states that it holds a tea pot, and a stool that are reputed to have once belonged to Cotton, although reading the provenance letter that came with the teapot it is obviously not Cotton's at all, and nor does the stool appear to have ever been used by her. As Kate Reeder, the Keeper of Social History and Collections Administration told me *"it's wonderful to have objects that have stories attached to them"* and, even if Mary Ann's teapot isn't really her teapot, *"it's the best kept teapot at Beamish."*

So it has only been through delving into the Home Office archives, reading scores of local newspapers, and bits and pieces of collected papers in regional resource centres that I've been able to put together a reasonably accurate account of what Mary Ann actually did, and what she didn't do.

Born Mary Ann Robinson in 1832, Cotton was originally brought up at Low Moorsley, County Durham, and while it is not possible to know exactly how many people she murdered by poisoning them, starting in 1852, her victims probably included eight of her children, seven step-children, her mother, three husbands, a lover, and a friend — a total of 21. That's an average of one victim a year, although when the need arose — as when she moved into the home of James Robinson at Pallion in December 1866 — she could be equally adept at ridding a household much more quickly, sometimes dispatching unwanted children on a monthly basis. She was eventually tried for the murder of her seven-year-old step son Charles Edward Cotton in January 1873 — whom she had poisoned the previous summer, in the hope of clearing the way for another new relationship with a man called Quick-Manning (his first name remains a bit of a mystery), who also lived in West Auckland, and with whom she had a child that was born in the prison while she was awaiting execution. Her trial at Durham Crown Court lasted for three days, and after being found guilty she was executed in Durham Gaol on 24th March by William Calcraft — the state hangman.

At the time of her execution — in a reporting fashion that would become common many years later – *The Newcastle Journal* described her as a *"monster in human shape"* and noted that *"murder grew with her"*.

Mary Ann's choice of poison was arsenic, which has been used as a means of murder for hundreds of years – its fatal success built on the reality that those being administered arsenic — which dissolves in hot liquids like soups or tea – have the all too common symptoms of vomiting, diarrhoea and dehydration. A busy and unsuspecting doctor — especially if his patients were poor and under-nourished – was always more likely to diagnose this cluster of symptoms as gastroenteritis, which, in any event in the past could prove to be equally fatal, rather than attribute the illness to poisoning and murder.

Mary Ann used all of this to her advantage, and so death and burial certificates were of little use, and it was only through reading the accounts of her neighbours who witnessed the slow death of her lover Joseph Nattrass—whom she had followed to Seaham Harbour and then later also to West Auckland—that I was able to gain some sense of just how sadistic and deadly Mary Ann actually was.

Jane Hedley's testimony, for example, is the most moving, given that she was present when Joseph actually died, and it is worth quoting in full so as to glimpse Mary Ann as a killer. Under oath Jane stated that:

> I lived at West Auckland and was very friendly with the Prisoner. I assisted ... during the time of the illness of Joseph Nattrass. I saw him several times during his illness. The Prisoner waited on him and was constantly about him. I saw no one else wait on him. The Prisoner gave him anything he required. Nattrass was several times sick and purged. This [sic] was occasionally he complained of pain at the bottom of his Bowels. I saw him have fits, he was very twisted up and seemed in great agony. He twisted his toes & his hands & worked them all ways. He drew his legs quite up. He was throwing himself about a good deal & the Prisoner held him & had to use great force. He was unconscious when in the fits. After the fits were over he sometimes said it was a very strong one and sometimes said it was not. Robert Robson Cotton died on the Thursday before Easter & was laid out in the same room where Nattrass was.
>
> On the Friday before Nattrass died I was in the Prisoner's house with Dr Richardson, Nattrass & the Prisoner. Dr Richardson asked him if the pain had left him. He said no. Dr Richardson then said if he could stop the purging he thought he would get better. Nattrass said it is no fever I have. The doctor said if he knew better than him it was no use his coming. He then asked Nattrass if he had taken the medicine & he said no. I was present just at the time of Nattrass's death. He died in a fit, which was similar to the previous ones. The Prisoner was holding him down. I did not say anything about Nattrass having proper support. I have seen her several times give him a drink.

On the Thursday before Nattrass died the Prisoner told me that Nattrass had said she, the Prisoner , was to have his watch and Club money, as she had been his best friend. On the same day the Prisoner asked me to get a letter written for the Burial money from the Club of the deceased. I lived about half a dozen houses from Prisoner at this time. Shortly after Nattrass's death, namely about a week, the Prisoner was in my house assisting to clean. She sent me to her house for a pot that stood of the pantry shelf. She said there was soft soap & arsenic in this pot. I went for and got this pot and showed it to the Prisoner. She said it was the right one & what she got to clean beds with…I got the pot from the top shelf in the pantry of Prisoner's House and which was the place where Prisoner told me it was.

So Nattrass was in so much pain that he was "twisted up", "throwing himself about", having "fits", and was in such agony that he drew his legs up beneath him, and so had to be held down by Cotton. In other words, she was physically restraining him as he died. Worse still, the body of her previous victim—a baby called Robert Robson Cotton—had been left in the same room as Joseph, almost as an awful foretaste of the fate that awaited him, and which at a more practical level clearly saved on the costs of two funerals.

Jane's account also let's us see a little of how Mary Ann—who had some nursing experience in Sunderland—was able to perform these murders in front of the local doctors, whom she would willingly call in to attend to her victims. What better way to deflect blame away from herself, especially if every doctor was as peevish as Dr Richardson, who reacted badly when Joseph had the temerity to question his diagnosis. Mary Ann could appear to be the dutiful and attentive partner, wife and mother— *"[she] waited on him and was constantly about him"* —whereas in fact her attentions masked her true intention.

We also capture in Jane's account some suggestion of motive. Cotton was to have Joseph's watch and club money, and which would imply that Mary Ann was that type of serial murderer that we now describe as "black widows"—women who kill their partners to inherit their savings or estate–but this only begins to scrape the surface of what was driving our first ever serial killer. After all, in killing Joseph she was killing the man that for years she had followed from one village to another, and for whom she had absolutely obliterated two families — the Mowbrays and the Cottons — so that she could cement their relationship. So, given that she had at last got the man that she wanted, why kill him? It could hardly be for the paltry sums that she received from the Prudential.

No, for Mary Ann there was always a bigger goal in mind; a much larger canvas on which to paint and which could hardly be achieved with the small amounts of cash that the deaths of her victims generated.

Cotton dispatched Joseph because by then she had her eye on Quick-Manning, and he, in turn, would have been killed when she next spotted someone more suited to her needs and tastes — needs and tastes which would appear to have been boundless and without limit. And so, had she not been arrested, I have no doubt that she would not have stopped at 21 victims, and might even eventually have surpassed Shipman's total of 215.

Mary Ann's murders were always motivated by her own personal goals, and these were in turn shaped by the culture that created her. So for me when and who she killed she tells us something about who she was as an individual, the type of values that she came to hold, and to which she was encouraged to aspire.

Cotton was one of the first children born into an age that would increasingly become dominated by industrial capitalism — the first generation that would see their lives dominated not by agriculture but by industry; not by the countryside but by towns and cities; not by the rhythms of the seasons but by the awful possibilities that could come from selling your labour, taking on credit and then speculating. Like much more obviously and traditionally successful capitalists, who might experience the ups and downs of the financial markets, and perhaps even an occasional bankruptcy along the way, Mary Ann simply tried to put her 'mistakes' behind her by killing those that she no longer needed or wanted, and having done so, start again in pastures new, always with the hope that something better would emerge.

But why isn't Mary Ann better known? Why has her story never really emerged from the North East and like that of Jack the Ripper defined an area, a period in time and a type of killer? Even Seaham Harbour — where Mary Ann lived for over a year — has named their new shopping centre

"Byron Place" in honour of Lord Byron, who as Yvette Adamson, the owner of the Seaham Harbour View Hotel, put it *"hated the place and in any event only stayed here for six weeks"*. Why is it that some historical figures become iconic and others, like Cotton, disappear?

There are some obvious answers—gender and geography most immediately—but also method. Mary Ann didn't leave ripped or broken bodies on the streets, and like most serial killers she maintained her innocence until the last, which has also served to confuse the reality of the awfulness of her crimes. However, what has emerged from my search for Mary Ann is the picture of a dreadful, female serial killer who was organized, persistent and who showed a degree of calculation and cunning so as to achieve the ends that she wanted, no matter who stood in her way.

That Cotton should be better known is without doubt—she was, after all, the first of a dreadful kind—but what I've discovered from an analysis of her case is that the relationship between which serial killers emerge into public consciousness, and those who do not is complex, and dependent on a range of case-specific variables, and which might in turn operate in a number of different ways to either push that serial killer into the public's consciousness, or leave them, like Mary Ann Cotton, forgotten or half-remembered.

My search ended in Durham, with Brian and me standing outside the new, modern Gate of HMP Durham—its flags flying in the wind, its Mission Statement proudly on display and all conspiring to hide the Victorian buildings within. We started to chat with some Prison Officers, and asked them where we might see the original, Victorian Gate that Mary Ann would have entered through, prior to her appointment with the hangman. One of the officers kindly showed us some of the original brickwork near the Crown Court, and I started to take a few photographs. A couple of minutes later, we spotted him running furiously back towards us, re-tracing his steps and heading once more into the prison.

"Left the doors open?" asked Brian.

"Don't worry," he replied, *"no one ever escapes from here."*

Nor did Mary Ann, and she remains—despite what they believe in West Auckland—buried in the prison's grounds.

Note

1. The sense that no one had heard of Mary Ann was the basis for this article although it
    was heavily revised before publication. In the article I do not really go into depth about
    Scattergood, so as to keep something "up my sleeve" for the book. However, what was
    of immediate interest to me is that the publication of the article resulted in a flurry of
    comments, letters and emails to me at the university, with many people claiming that they
    had all indeed heard of Mary Ann. Many suggested that my argument that she was largely
    unknown was simply evidence of either Southern academic bias, or my need to "generate
    a story". However, my correspondents would then often go on to reveal through their
    comments that their recollection of the story was somewhat unreliable — often confusing
    fact with fiction — and there was a fundamental divide in opinion about whether she was
    in fact guilty of murder, or the victim of an awful miscarriage of justice.

    Some of my correspondents also wanted to share with me their understanding that it
    had been their own ancestors that had brought Mary Ann to justice — clearly something
    that had been handed down from one generation in their family to the next. However,
    although I will not name these correspondents, they were often mistaken about the role
    that their ancestor may or may not have played. I was equally rather amazed that another
    of my email correspondents was Beamish Museum (see footnote 6 in *Chapter 1*), who wrote
    to me to suggest that I should come to view Mary Ann's teapot!

    One particular set of emails was particularly interesting and also rather troubling.
    Someone — I am actually uncertain if this correspondent is one or a number of people,
    but will presume that it is one person — calling himself "Robson Cotton", but signing
    his emails Robson Cotton and Ian Smyth Herdman (although the content of these e
    mails was written in the singular) and who maintains a website — www.maryanncotton.
    co.uk — wrote to my literary agent to advise that "I am in confidential contact with Mary
    Ann Cottons [sic] living relations, the only author who has such paramount access. On
    reading Mr Wilsons [sic] comments presumably taken from his manuscript, and indeed
    assumptions stated by Mr Wilson, can be categorically refuted by written statements and
    documentations [sic] available from Mary Ann Cotton's family themselves!" The author
    (Cotton or Herdman? I still do not know which) was concerned that "a further genera-
    tion of inaccuracies and hearsay's [sic] appear to be proposed." The gist of what was being
    complained about was that Mary Ann was innocent — which could be proved through her
    family's correspondence, or correspondence that her family held–and that my contention
    that she was a serial killer was inaccurate.

    I replied to this e mail — largely about a statement which I had made in my article
    concerning evidence given at court which revealed that Mary Ann had been holding down
    Joseph Nattrass while he died — and again on one further occasion about other matters.
    It is clear that my correspondent does not view my analysis of what happened in West
    Auckland as being accurate — even when I am quoting from official documents, but would
    prefer to take the views of those whom he describes as Mary Ann's surviving family mem-
    bers as more reliable. However, he does not reveal what these views might be, although
    presumably they must be supportive of Mary Ann. No new correspondence was produced
    to refute what I had argued in the *Mail on Sunday* article, although it is perfectly possible
    that there may be letters that I have been unable to gain access to. For my part, all I can
    state is that I have been careful to balance what appears in the text with that which is avail-
    able within the public record. For what it was worth I did also consult the above mentioned
    website — where I would have presumed that an alternative version of events bolstered by

the "written statements and documentations" held by Mary Ann's family would have been revealed. However, after having consulted this website I did not want to change my text, although I accept that some of what I argue is based on my interpretation of events.

Perhaps what the reaction to the article revealed most of all was the continuing sense that Mary Ann's story is everywhere but nowhere; a story that has become so ingrained in the telling that trying to get to the truth is not only difficult, but will also upset how the word-of-mouth of oral history has allowed that story to be shaped and perpetuated — both in support and in opposition to Mary Ann. After all, for all the anxieties of "Robson Cotton" that a "further generation" would be introduced to "inaccuracies and hearsay's" many correspondents actively presumed that Mary Ann had indeed been unfairly convicted and executed — a view with which "Robson Cotton" would surely concur.

Appendix 2

Was Mary Ann Cotton a Psychopath?

The 20 items on Robert Hare's Psychopathy Checklist-Revised (see *Chapter 6* under the heading 'Antisocial Personality Disorder and the Psychopath') are:

glibness/superficial charm; grandiose sense of self-worth; need for stimulation/proneness to boredom; pathological lying; conning/manipulative; lack of remorse or guilt; shallow affect; callous/lack of empathy; parasitic lifestyle; poor behavioural controls; promiscuous sexual behaviour; early behavioural problems; lack of realistic long-term goals; impulsivity; irresponsibility; failure to accept responsibility for actions; many short-term marital relationships; juvenile delinquency; revocation of conditional release; criminal versatility.

The PCL-R is a standardised instrument which yields a quantitative score concerning the degree of psychopathy of an individual. Normally to be used only by a trained professional, the instrument is scored on a 20 item 40 point scale, where the individual is scored zero if the item does not fit; one for a partial fit; and two if there is a reasonable fit. The validated research cut off for determination of a psychopathic personality is a score of 25 in Britain (30 in the USA). Mary Ann Cotton scored 25 in the blind trial below.

Clinical Examples and Consensus Scores for the 20 PCL-R Items for Mary Ann Cotton—as scored by the author in a blind trial with a colleague, Dr Elizabeth Yardley (which by its historical research-based nature had to be conducted in an academic rather than real setting) and were:

1. *Glibness/Superficial Charm:* (2)—MAC frequently and quickly established herself in different communities, making friends easily and gaining employment in a number of households. See Jane Hedley's account and note that she was "very friendly" with

201

Cotton, even though Mary Ann had just moved into the village.

2. *Grandiose Sense of Self-Worth:* (2)—MAC often employed women to clean for her and predicted the deaths of her mother and her step son. She was happy to challenge the medical competency of doctors.

3. *Proneness to Boredom/Need for Stimulation:* (0)—There is no documentary evidence to support this.

4. *Pathological Lying:* (2)—She was happy to pretend that the ailments of her family members were not the result of arsenic poisoning; she maintained her innocence in the face of overwhelming evidence to the contrary.

5. *Conning/Manipulative:* (2)—She had a history of multiple, concurrent relationships—note that she established a relationship with Quick-Manning almost as soon as she started to nurse him, all the while maintaining a relationship with Nattrass. She fraudulently withdrew the money of James Robinson.

6. *Lack of Remorse or Guilt:* (2)—She maintained her innocence until her execution, and while the fact that she was on a capital charge may have affected her ability to show remorse/guilt there is nothing in the public record to imply that she cared about what had happened to her victims.

7. *Shallow Affect:* (1)—During interviews she was mostly dramatic e.g. demanding to see James Robinson and the child that she abandoned with a friend.

8. *Callous/Lack of Empathy:* (2)—Evidenced by her crimes.

9. *Parasitic Lifestyle:* (1)—She worked as a housekeeper and this seems to have given her access to men (and others) that she

could then use to her own ends. However, she also worked as a dressmaker and as a nurse.

10. *Poor Behavioral Controls:* (0)—There is no documentary evidence to support this within the historical record, although choosing to abandon Robinson when she appeared to have achieved a comfortable lifestyle is perhaps suggestive of poor behavioural control.

11. *Promiscuous Sexual Behavior:* (2)—She used her ability to establish relationships with men as a means to gain access to them and their households. There was some reporting after her execution that she was a "prostitute". She probably killed her stepson Charles because she had established a new relationship with Quick-Manning in West Auckland.

12. *Early Behavior Problems:* (0)—There is no evidence to support this in the historical record.

13. *Lack of Realistic Long Term Goals:* (2)—She lived a somewhat nomadic, day-to-day existence, and her abandoning of her baby in Sunderland—which she then demanded to see when she was in Durham Gaol—indicates that she had no clear view of what she actually wanted.

14. *Impulsivity:* (2)—There are numerous examples of poor impulse control in her adult life.

15. *Irresponsibility:* (0)—This item does not seem to apply—in fact she wanted responsibility, as evidenced by the fact that she became first a Sunday School teacher and then a nurse.

16. *Failure to Accept Responsibility for Own Actions:* (2)—She maintained her innocence throughout her trial and brief imprisonment.

17. *Many Short-Term Marital Relationships:* (2)—Based on the definition of "marriage" as any live-in relationship that involved some degree of commitment she had at least four "marriages".

18. *Juvenile Delinquency:* (0)—No evidence of this in the historical record.

19. *Revocation of Conditional Release:* (0)—No evidence of this in the historical record.

20. *Criminal Versatility:* (1)—Fraud in relation to James Robinson.

Index

Ingram Content Group UK Ltd.
Milton Keynes UK
UKHW041357290623
424256UK00002B/17

9 781909 976191